GONDOLAS AND GROWLERS

THE HISTORY OF THE LONDON HORSE CAB

Trevor May

ALAN SUTTON PUBLISHING LIMITED

To the memory of my grandfather, Henry Holdham, coachbuilder,
and for my daughter, Susannah, horsewoman.

First published in the United Kingdom in 1995
Alan Sutton Publishing Ltd · Phoenix Mill · Far Thrupp · Stroud · Gloucestershire

British Library Cataloguing-in-Publication Data

May, Trevor
Gondolas and Growlers:
History of the London Horse Cab
I. Title
688.609421

ISBN 0–7509–0697–9

Typeset in 10/14pt Times.
Typesetting and origination by
Alan Sutton Publishing Limited.
Printed in Great Britain by
Hartnolls, Bodmin, Cornwall.

CONTENTS

Preface   v

Picture Credits   viii

I   The Hackney Coach Monopoly   1

II   The Introduction of the Horse Cab   13

III   The Trade is Thrown Open   25

IV   'Hansom Cab' or 'Chapman Cab'?   36

V   The Cab Business   48

VI   Improved Cabs and Lordly Cabmen   63

VII   The Police and the Cab Trade   76

VIII   The Cab Driver   95

IX   Cabs and the Railways   115

X   From Horse to Motor   129

Postscript Suburban and Provincial Cabs   153

Appendices   163

Notes   168

Bibliography   178

Index   181

'A London Type': the hansom cab driver. From George R. Sims, *Living London*, 1906

PREFACE

L ondon's last horse cabs were licensed in 1943, and they disappeared from the streets four years later. By that time they were a curiosity, adding a little colour to a drab, post-war metropolis, but contributing nothing to its transport needs. Horse cabs had been at their peak half a century earlier when, in 1898, there had been 11,547. Already the first signs of change had come, for in the previous year eighteen experimental electric cabs had been introduced. Their trial proved unsuccessful, but the licensing of the first motor cabs in 1903 witnessed the start of a continuous and rapid decline of the horse-drawn vehicle. By 1910 the number of motor cabs had overtaken that of horse cabs, and in the decade 1905–14 the percentage of London's cabs drawn by the horse fell from 99.82 to 16.07. When the First World War broke out there were fewer than 1,400 left. In 1923, the centenary of the London cab, only 347 horse-drawn vehicles plied the streets. By 1930 there were only 69.[1]

The horse-drawn London cabs thus had an effective life of about one hundred years, during which period they made a major contribution to the internal transportation of the capital, and constituted a considerable part of the street traffic. At no time in the nineteenth century were there even half as many buses and trams as there were cabs. In the 1870s the number of these vehicles on the streets constituted less than 18 per cent of the number of cabs, rising to just over 46 per cent in 1900. Even allowing for the greater passenger capacity of the bus and tram, the significant contribution of the cab to London's urban transport network remains clear.

Most people, when they think of the London cab, think of the hansom, a vehicle that immediately summons up images of Sherlock Holmes and pea-soupers. 'The Gondola of London' Disraeli called it in his 1870 novel, *Lothair*, and its grace and elegance made it worthy of that title. There was nothing elegant, however, about that four-wheeled workhorse, the London 'growler', a poor relation of the more aristocratic brougham. Growlers did important work, but throughout the nineteenth century there were never as many of them on the streets as there were hansoms. Only in 1910, when Edwardian England gave way to a new Georgian Age, did the growlers overtake the gondolas in point of numbers, and they had the final laugh for they tended to be the last of the horse cabs to survive, in both London and the provinces.

London and provincial cabs were different, particularly in respect of their administration, for what was a local authority function in the provinces was under the

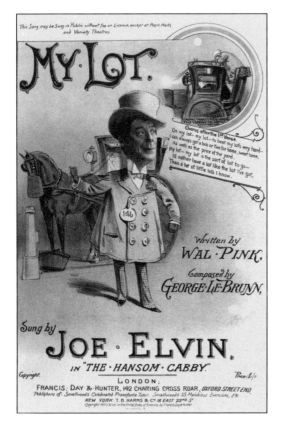

A turn of the century music hall song. The dapper hansom cabby takes a swipe not only at the growler, but also at motor cars, which 'rattle like a cattle truck, and smell like some oil van./ They puff like mad, and smoke as bad as any baked "tater" can.'

direct control of the Home Secretary in London. Part of the explanation lies in the problem of creating an appropriate metropolitan authority for the rapidly expanding capital, but even after the London County Council was formed in 1888, cabs continued to be administered by the Home Office and the Metropolitan Police, to whose revenues they made an important contribution.

But the story of the London horse cab is not just the story of vehicles and their control; it is about people. The cab trade was a major employer. By 1851, when the Census listed 5,111 railway workers in London, there were 6,039 licensed cab drivers. That number had swelled to 15,219 in 1891, and was still greater than the number working on the railways or in the London docks. Admittedly, as cab-driving tended to be a casual occupation for many, more men were licensed than were actually in work. On the other hand, there were people dependent on the trade who were not cab drivers, being either ancillary workers, associated craftsmen such as coachbuilders, or dependent relatives. In 1864, for example, J.T. Dexter estimated that probably fifty thousand people were directly dependent on the cab for their livelihood, and although this figure is difficult to substantiate it may not be wide of the mark.[2]

The London growler. An engraving from the *Illustrated London News*, 1844

The cab driver of the nineteenth century was just as much a London 'character' as his twentieth-century counterpart, the taxi driver. He had a language of his own. To him, the hansom was not a gondola, but a 'shoful', a Jewish word for counterfeit, no doubt in reference to the fact that the hansom cab was by rights a 'chapman' cab, for Joseph Hansom's original vehicle was very different from those which eventually stormed the streets. An owner-driver was a 'mush', for they sprang up like mushrooms; while those casual, fair weather drivers who only took out a licence in the summer were 'butterflies'.

The account which is given here is essentially of the horse cab trade as it was practised in London. The provincial trade is briefly covered in the postscript, while the final chapter describes some of the momentous changes when the horse gave way to the horseless carriage.

This book is based on my 1991 London Ph.D. thesis, and I wish to acknowledge the support and advice of my supervisor, Professor F.M.L. Thompson, whose seminal lecture, *Victorian England: the Horse-drawn Society* (1970), was one of the inspirations for this study.

PICTURE CREDITS

The author and publishers acknowledge the following for permission to reproduce illustrations (references given are page numbers):

The Bodleian Library (John Johnson Collection), 31; The British Library (Science Reference Library), 37, 75, 140; The British Newspaper Library, Colindale, 67, 70, 73, 142; Buckinghamshire County Museum, 156; Greater London Record Office, 151; Greenwich Local History Library, 123; The Guildhall Library, 16, 52, 77, 91, 105, 118, 127; Hulton Deutsch Picture Library, 131; Metropolitan Police Museum Trust, 86; Public Record Office, 79, 88, 122, 134, 147.

Illustrations not listed remain the property of the author.

Chapter One

THE HACKNEY COACH MONOPOLY

Oh London is a fine town,
A very famous city,
Where all the streets are paved with gold,
And all the maidens pretty.

George Colman (1762–1836)

The streets of London may have been paved with gold, but they were often running with filth and choked with traffic. It had probably always been thus. For example, an Act of 1533 had set out to improve the paving of Holborn, which was 'of late so well and substantially paved,' but had become 'so noyous and so full of sloughs and other incumbrances, that often times many . . . subjects riding through the said street and way be in jeopardy of hurt and have almost perished.'[1] Early in the next century, the Venetian ambassador to the Court of Charles I, one Orazio Busino, held stinking black mud to be one of the special characteristics of London streets, which were often blocked by carts and waggons that had become bogged down.

It would have been more to the point had the streets been paved with stone. Some streets were, but the problem of matching roads to traffic, and traffic to roads, was as taxing in the past as it is now. Any improvement of the streets was likely to attract an increase in the number of vehicles using them, with the resulting traffic problem as great as ever. It was partly in order to preserve the paved streets and to reduce obstruction that, in the eighteenth century, proprietors of short-distance stagecoaches running to places on the outskirts of London were forbidden to pick up or set down passengers on 'the stones'. This prohibition highlights two aspects of the traffic problem at that time. In the first place, London had rapidly expanded and was continuing to do so. Secondly, the expansion had taken place without the simultaneous development of an effective administrative machinery . The concept of 'the stones' was one rough and ready solution to the problem of defining London after the town had burst through the confines of its medieval walls. Once that had happened there was nothing that could hold back the tide of London's growth.

As late as 1854 it was observed that, 'The area of the metropolis is more or less arbitrary, inasmuch as London cannot be said to be recognized by the law as one town, and its boundaries have never been fixed either by enactment or custom.'[2] The administrative problem was made worse by the fact that London did not expand into virgin territory, but instead gobbled up villages that already possessed an established parochial form of government. As London grew, these village vestries were absorbed, but were not replaced by any overriding municipal authority. The situation was further complicated by the fact that many parishes had acquired extra powers by Private Act of Parliament to grapple with the problems which they faced. The result was that by the middle of the nineteenth century around 250 Local Acts of Parliament had been passed, in consequence of which London was governed by some 300 local authorities, and around 10,000 commissioners exercising a variety of *ad hoc* functions.

Defoe estimated that, by the early eighteenth century, London stretched for 36 miles in circumference. It was too great in extent to be traversed by foot, although walking long remained one of the principal means of transportation. At the beginning of the Victorian period it is calculated that about 100,000 pedestrians a day crossed the river by means of London Bridge alone. Visitors to London were advised in 1853:

Don't stop on the pavement, move on as fast as you can, and do as the others do, that is to say, struggle on as best as you may, and push forward without any false modesty. The passengers in London streets are hardened; they give and receive kicks and pushes with equal equanimity.

The daily walk to work was part of the common lot; but as the city expanded, so demand grew for means of public transportation, and here was one of those services that needed to be tackled on a scale that surpassed the authority of the City Corporation.[3]

The first transport workers to be regulated were the watermen who plied their boats for hire on the Thames, for centuries the principal highway of London. The earliest Act dealing with them was passed in 1514. Further regulation in 1555 led to the formation of the Watermen's Company, which retained authority for the licensing of Thames watermen until 1908. It was in the early seventeenth century that the watermen found a champion in John Taylor, the 'Water-poet' (or 'literary-bargee' as one biographer disparagingly calls him). Taylor became a Thames waterman when he retired from the Navy with a lame leg. His injury did not prevent him from engaging in a number of madcap adventures (including a journey down the Thames in a brown paper boat using stockfish as oars), nor did it prevent him from churning out pamphlets, the titles of which fill nine columns of the *Dictionary of National Biography*.

Taylor sprang to the defence of the watermen in their competition with hackney coaches, which first appeared on the streets in any numbers in the 1620s. The early hackney coaches (from the Old French word, *haquenée*, used to describe an ambling nag) were hard to distinguish from gentlemen's coaches, and it is difficult to know precisely when they were first introduced. 'I do not inveigh against any coaches that belong to persons of worth and quality,' wrote Taylor in 1623, 'but only against the caterpillar swarms of hirelings.' These 'hellcart-coaches', as he described them, were at first to be hired only from their stable yards, but in 1634 a Captain Baily (like Taylor, an ex-seaman) placed four hackney coaches on a stand at the Maypole tavern in the Strand. So great did their number become that hackney coaches were soon subject to official restraint. In 1654, the number in London and Westminster was limited to three hundred, each paying a tax of 20s a year; and their regulation was placed in the hands of the Court of Aldermen. Eight years later the number was raised to four hundred, and a new body of commissioners was established to oversee the trade. This move was both unpopular with the owners and costly to operate, with the result that when the commissioners' powers lapsed in 1679 they were not renewed. However, the annoyance that ensued resulted in new commissioners being appointed by royal warrant in 1687.[4]

The frequency with which the regulation of hackney coaches was amended reflects the difficulty of controlling a service intended to serve the transportation requirements of a rapidly expanding metropolis. At last, in 1694, a body of Hackney Coach Commissioners was set up from which, in a direct line, control of hackney coaches, cabs and taxicabs has passed down to our own day. In that year five commissioners (among the first of whom was the poet William Congreve) were appointed to regulate hackney coaches in London. For their first year they were also given oversight of all stagecoaches in England and Wales, but this was then transferred to the newly formed Board of Stamps, a body with which the Hackney Coach Commissioners eventually came into serious competition.

The area which defined the London hackney carriage was laid down in 1694 and amended in 1710, when it was described as ' the Cities of London and Westminster and the suburbs thereof, and . . . all and every the parishes and places comprised within the weekly Bills of Mortality'. The Bills of Mortality consisted of the hundred or so parishes, in or near the City, which had compiled weekly lists of deaths since the sixteenth century and which represented an early attempt to define a 'metropolitan' area. No additions were made to the Bills of Mortality after 1726, but the definition of 'suburbs' was extended in 1771 to include certain areas beyond the Bills, namely the parishes of St Marylebone; St George, Hanover Square; St George the Martyr, Queen Square; and St George, Bloomsbury. The expanding districts of Paddington, Chelsea and Kensington, however, continued to lie outside the jurisdiction of the Hackney Coach Commission.[5]

The Act of 1694 increased the permitted number of coaches to seven hundred, but changes to the statutory maxima give only a crude indication of the actual hackney

Tom Rakewell is arrested for debt as he descends from his hackney chair in St James's Street. A plate from Hogarth's series, *A Rake's Progress*, 1733. That this is a public chair is apparent from the numbered plate to the rear of the side window

coach provision for two reasons. First, not all licences might be taken up, as was frequently the case in times of economic distress, when licences remained unallocated at the Hackney Coach Office. Secondly, it was open to the Treasury (to which the Hackney Coach Commissioners were responsible) to *reduce* the maxima, which they did on several occasions, usually at the instigation of the Commissioners (Appendix 1).

A typical chain of events was the following. In April 1802 the Commissioners suggested that the number of coaches should be raised by one hundred, on the grounds of 'the great additional extent of the Metropolis and its Suburbs', to which they added the more telling argument that licensing revenue would be increased. Since 1784, coaches had paid a weekly duty of 10s, a sum which remained fixed until 1853. The increased revenue of £2,600 a year on a hundred coaches was therefore no mean sum. Hackneymen were very conscious of this, and often threatened to quit the trade, causing a drain on revenue, unless relief was given them in times of distress. On this occasion the Treasury agreed, and the necessary legislation was brought in. The new maximum of 1,100 remained in force until 1813, when distress in the trade prompted the Commissioners to recommend a reduction. They claimed that many owners had been driven to the verge of bankruptcy by the high price of provender, and innumerable horses had died from poor feeding. Raising fares would do more harm than good, for 'many of the lower classes, who formerly rode in coaches [have] long since been precluded from that indulgence on account of the increased expense'. Licences were being given up on a daily basis, and there were already nearly a hundred unallocated. The remedy they therefore suggested was to accept resignations until the number had fallen to nine hundred. The Treasury gave its permission, and legislation followed in June 1814. In addition to reducing the total, however, this Act also provided for the licensing of up to two hundred chariots (a lighter carriage drawn by two horses), paying a reduced weekly duty of 5s. These vehicles proved popular, and their maximum number was raised to four hundred in the following year, at which time an unlimited number of two-wheeled vehicles, to be drawn by one horse, were also authorized. Although the latter vehicles were not termed as such in the Act they were, in fact, cabs – but it would be another eight years before any came onto the streets. The popularity of chariots, however, was considerable, and in 1817 the distinction between coach and chariot duty was abolished, the hackneymen being compensated by acquiring the right to transfer their licence plates between coaches and chariots at will. From 1817 to 1831 all changes to the permitted number of vehicles were made by the Treasury. When, in the course of time, cab licences came to be greatly desired, the patronage which the Treasury exercised became a cause for considerable controversy.[6]

It was helpful for a man to have a patron if he wished to apply for a hackney coach licence. In 1797 it was alleged that licences were generally granted 'to persons recommended by Ministers, and other Persons of Rank and Consequence, or by individual Commissioners'. In March of that year, for example, John King was granted a licence at the command of Prince Ernest August. A generation later Edward Jesse, one of the Commissioners, admitted that the granting of licences was, 'to a certain degree, a matter of favour and interest'. Applications were not disposed of according to priority on a list, and he frankly observed, 'I should certainly give [a licence] to a particular friend sooner than to a man I knew nothing of.' Such patronage was not uncommon, of course, and was justified in the eyes of the authorities by the need to ensure that coach proprietors were men of good character. Yet there was nothing like the outcry against this as there was against the issue of cab licences to nominees, for the latter were more limited in number and carried the expectation of far higher profits. Indeed, so anxious were the Commissioners to maintain the hackney coach revenues that they refused few applicants, and it was reported that, in the seven

A hackney coach. From a print first published in 1787

years between 1823 and 1829, only twenty-five applicants for hackney coach plates were turned down.[7]

The office of the Hackney Coach Commissioners, together with all its records and papers, was destroyed by fire in 1770; while other records from 1790 to 1799 were 'feloniously taken away and destroyed' by James Marshall, one of the messengers. None of the licence registers appears to have survived, although certain inferences about the issue of licences can be drawn from two extant minute books of the Commissioners, covering the six years from September 1796 to September 1801, and the five years from January 1807 to January 1812.[8] A total of 549 licences were issued in the earlier period, and 993 in the shorter, later period. There is some correlation between the turnover of licences and agricultural prices, which is not surprising in that provender was one of the principal working expenses, and one which frequently marked the difference between prosperity and distress. The years of high transfers, 1799–1800 and 1808–9 were years of bad harvests and high prices. The average annual price of oats shot up from 19s 5d a quarter in 1798 to 27s 6d in 1799, and to 39s 4d in 1800, a price exceeded only once between 1771 and 1916.[9]

Seasonal patterns are less obvious. In 1827 the writer John Jervis argued that the summer months, together with the Vauxhall season, were the best for hackneymen, and that February, March and April, when post-Christmas economies were made, were the worst. The autumn, when many people were out of town, was also considered poor.[10] Certainly, January, February and March saw the highest number of transfers in three of the eight years for which there is a complete record, and the second highest in another four. Perhaps we should not expect seasonal variations in prosperity to be so closely paralleled by resignations and revocations of licences. Asked whether fewer coaches plied in London when the town was empty than when it was full, Commissioner Edward Jesse told the Select Committee of 1830 that he did not know; all he knew was that the proprietors had to pay the duty monthly, and in advance.[11]

In fact, one can look at the whole question from the other side. What is striking is not so much that licences were resigned or revoked when times were hard, but that men were still found willing to take them up. Many men no doubt entered the trade in ignorance of its precariousness. Edward Jesse observed, 'A gentleman's servant saves up two or £300 and marries and he fancies he can do better with a coach than any other man: the workhouses are filled with hackney coachmen's wives and children at this moment.'[12] In the same year a correspondent for *The Times* claimed that many men were tempted into the trade with too little capital. They did all right for a time, until major expenditure came along, such as the need for fresh horses or coach repairs, whereupon they failed.[13]

Of the licences issued between September 1796 and September 1801, around a quarter were given up within three years; and of those issued between January 1807 and January 1812, the figure is over one-third. We do not know how many of these licences were held by a one-coach proprietor having a brief flirtation with the trade, but the indications are that a good many of them were. Others would have been licences taken by proprietors of longer standing, in a brief burst of expansion. The overall impression which the figures give is of a hard core of perhaps 45–60 per cent of established proprietors who remained in the trade for five years or more, and a large fringe group of men passing through in a transient manner.

In March 1827, as part of his campaign against the Commissioners, and no doubt in order to show the privileged position of large cab owners, Joseph Hume called for a list of the twenty largest proprietors (Appendix 2). Cab owners certainly headed the list. Vernon Abbot, with twenty-four cab licences, and William Boulnois, with eighteen, were the largest operators in the whole trade. Five proprietors possessed over half of all the hundred cabs licensed at that time, and seventeen owned one-eighth of the coach licences.This leaves us with 87.5 per cent of all coach licences owned by proprietors with four licences or fewer. Precisely how many hackneymen there were is impossible to say, for the only figure that we have is for April 1808, when there were 628.[14]

The information which we have on the seventeen largest proprietors of hackney coaches in 1827 indicates that over half of them were involved in other undertakings (Appendix 3). Four were funeral carriage proprietors who were required, by an Act of 1715, to take out hackney coach plates for mourning coaches and hearses. This law had been passed to prevent the common practice of undertakers hiring gentlemen's carriages from servants, without the knowledge of their masters. Not only was this to the detriment of the owner's coach and horses, but it was also prejudicial to persons licensed to keep carriages for hire.[15] The anomalous position of mourning coaches and hearses was removed by the Act of 1831, which made an essential part of the definition of a hackney carriage that it should ply for hire in the streets, which funeral carriages patently did not do!

We cannot tell if the four funeral carriage proprietors were also involved in regular hackney carriage work. Nor can we tell how important their hackney coach work was to the horse dealers, livery stable keepers and other horse tradesmen on the list. It is noticeable that only two of the seventeen coach owners also possessed cab plates; and there is no evidence that any of the others showed an interest in acquiring cabs until 1830, when eight were signatories of a petition to exchange and re-exchange coach plates for cab plates at will. The slowness of the hackney coach proprietors to take up cabs is a reflection of the extreme conservatism of the trade, a characteristic that was noteworthy throughout the nineteenth century.[16]

The amount of capital needed to enter the trade was quite small. Henry Clement, a hackneyman, claimed in 1830 that a coach could be started 'very decently' for £70. The vehicle itself would have cost about £30. Proprietors rarely built new coaches, and a large majority of the vehicles were said to be second-hand landaus. Mayhew was told that 'they were nearly all noblemen's and gentlemen's disused family coaches, which had been handed over to the coachmaker when a new carriage was made'. Coaches had to be inspected before a licence was granted, but it is clear that the examination was cursory. In 1830 there were four inspectors, all supposedly conversant with horses and carriages. However, as their former occupations had been butler, valet, gardener and land surveyor, this seems unlikely. Inspectors were supposed to ensure that coaches were wind and watertight. To the question, 'Does cleanliness form any part of your conception of the satisfactory state of a hackney coach?', William Powell, the Registrar, replied that it certainly did. But the fact that the question was asked suggests otherwise, and a leader writer in *The Times* held that 'There is certainly in no town in Great Britain, or on the continent, so dirty and rickety a vehicle as a London hackney coach.' However strict the inspection, there was no guarantee that the applicant would actually use the coach presented, for the switching of plates to inferior vehicles was frequent, a ploy which was adopted throughout the century. And, as was also to happen with cabs, a carriage that could not bear the light of day could always be brought out at night, to slink through the shadows.[17]

Clement argued that three horses, at about £10 each, were needed to operate a two-horse coach. A little earlier, John Jervis thought that horses might be purchased for between £8 and £20. Harness at £5 and stable utensils at another £5 made up Clement's total of £70. With his coach and horses, and rented stables to accommodate them, a man was ready for business. All that remained was to pay the licence registration fee of 45s and his first month's duty of £2.[18]

The low capital costs must have encouraged many men into the trade only to discover that the running costs could be high. The duty was one of the least of the running expenses; William Powell, Receiver and Registrar at the Hackney Coach Office, claimed that each day's share could be earned in ten minutes. The greatest part of the running costs was undoubtedly provender. Estimates of feed costs vary. Jervis, in 1827, thought that three horses could be kept for a year for £94 10s, which works out at just over 12s per horse per week. Henry Clement, in 1830, estimated that three horses would require 1½ bushels of corn at 6s, 1s worth of beans, 6d worth of chaff and 3d worth of straw (total 7s 9d), or about 18s per horse per week.[19]

A rise in the price of corn invariably put pressure on coach proprietors, and there was a temptation to reduce the amount of feed given. In both 1813 and 1820 the Hackney Coach Commissioners reported a distressing mortality of horses because of poor feeding. The untimely death of a horse could prove disastrous to a small proprietor unless he had been able to set money aside for a replacement. To get four years' work out of a horse was considered reasonable. A horse might therefore outlive a coach, which, often being second-hand, might only be expected to give service for a year and a half. In his calculations for the running of one coach, Henry Clement estimated £30 a year for the rent of a stable, coach-house and dwelling, bringing total running expenses in 1830 to between 15s and 16s a day, or between £273 and £292 per annum.[20]

The earnings against which these expenses had to be set varied seasonally, and it is impossible to get a precise picture, especially as the evidence comes mainly from the hackneymen themselves, ever anxious to show just how unprofitable the trade was. The estimates of four proprietors to the Select Committee of 1830 show a great

Livery stables at the old 'Black Bull Inn', Gray's Inn Lane. William Eskholm, a hackney carriage proprietor, operated from here in the early 1820s. By the 1850s it had become the livery yard of William Golding

variation. George Green complained that he was earning only 13s to 14s a day at that time (the end of May), whereas he claimed that 'we ought to earn at this season of the year 23s or 24s a day to support us in the winter'. Even his lower figures are higher than the estimates of the other three men, which ranged from 7s a day up to 10s a day.[21]

Two things are clear. Those hackneymen not involved in diversified aspects of the trade could not have been making much more than a bare living. Secondly, much depended on whether a man drove his own coach or employed a driver. For example, William James, a small proprietor with mews in Howland Street, considered that he would average 12s to 13s a day, whereas a driver would bring in no more than 9s 6d to 10s. He complained, 'If we send a man out with a good pair of horses and coach today, he is likely to keep it all day and all night, and send it home tomorrow by another man, without any money, and we cannot punish him for it.' He was not alone in complaining of the drivers' dishonesty. The agreements which were made between the hackney coach proprietors and their drivers are somewhat obscure, but it is evident that the bailee system, which later in the century became the customary arrangement for cabs, was only in an embryonic stage, and of doubtful legality.[22]

At one time the payment of a regular wage seems to have been the practice. William Hill, one of the Inspectors of Hackney Coaches, claimed that 'the old practice' was to pay drivers 10s to half a guinea a week, although he gave no indication of when this was. Clement argued that the payment of fixed wages had proved impossible because of the dishonesty of the drivers. What seems to have happened is that the owners *expected* a man to bring in a certain sum each day, and would no doubt dismiss him if he drastically or consistently fell below this; but having returned something like the sum expected, the man was suffered to keep any surplus for himself.[23]

Hackney coach proprietors were not the most innovative of men, but that was to be expected when existence for so many seems to have been a hand-to-mouth affair. The majority were in no position to take speculative risks, and their financial insecurity led to a deep-seated conservatism. Mistrustful of innovation, they remained content to operate in time-honoured ways. Thus for eight years after the Act of 1815 authorized the introduction of cabs, not a single hackneyman applied for a licence.

The chariots, first authorized in 1814, were taken up more quickly, but probably by the larger hackneymen rather than the small operators, and there were allegations that licences were granted to 'favourite owners' of the Commissioners. These lighter, four-wheeled vehicles had two forward-facing seats, with glass windows to the front and sides, and closely resembled the post-chaise. So close was the resemblance, indeed, that the Board of Stamps, responsible for the post horse duty from which hackneymen were exempt, strongly opposed them, for it was feared that the hackney chariots would be used for excursions to country places around London, undercutting the postmasters. The Hackney Coach Commissioners were no more enthusiastic. They were obsessed with the need to maintain a supply of covered vehicles for bad weather, and had a strong leaning towards what Commissioner Thomas Marrable described as 'a good old fashioned hackney coach'.[24]

The roots of innovation lay outside rather than within the trade. Petitions in favour of lighter vehicles were received in 1823 from residents of Pall Mall and St James; in 1827 from George Martin (a coachbuilder); and in 1828 from Martin Tucker, Abraham Van Oven, William Walker and Frederick Gye – all apparently speculators. The proposal of Gye is of particular interest, for it was supported by the Prime Minister, the Duke of Wellington, and was published as an appendix to the Select Committee of 1830. The proprietor of London wine and tea companies, Gye purchased the Vauxhall Gardens in 1821 and conducted them until 1840. From 1826 to 1830 he was MP for Chippenham. The scheme which he put forward in 1828 was to provide three hundred four-wheeled hackney carriages each drawn by one horse; one-third to be small coaches to carry at the current cab fares, one-third small chariots and one-third barouchets, principally for the summer season. The response of the Hackney Coach Commissioners to all these initiatives was as negative as ever. They reported that they

A hackney coachman and cad. The cad, or waterman, had the task of attending to the hackneymen and their horses at the stands

possessed no legal powers to license such vehicles and that, whatever might be their merits in certain circumstances, the hackney coach was generally to be preferred.[25]

The Commissioners were reluctant to allow the trade to be regulated by market forces if that would have the effect of putting a large number of hackneymen out of business. They were looked upon by the owners, and saw themselves, as 'protectors of the trade', and they took that role seriously. The Home Office, on the other hand, whose involvement with the hackney carriage trade commenced in 1838, saw itself rather as the protector of the *public*, a difference of emphasis which no doubt derived from that department's concern with public order. It could be said that the trade was under the thumb of the Home Office but under the wing of the Hackney Coach Commissioners, whose protection could take one of two forms: resisting the onslaught of vehicles eager to break into the ancient hackney coach monopoly; and holding the ring between various factions within the trade – between, for example, hackney coach owners on the one hand, and hackney stagecoach and cab proprietors on the other. Hackneymen faced competition from without and within, which makes the introduction of cabs a more complex issue than is sometimes supposed.[26]

Chapter Two

THE INTRODUCTION OF THE HORSE CAB

The first dozen cabs were introduced onto the streets of London on 23 April 1823. These 'cabriolets' were distinguished from the hackney coaches not only in construction and fares, but also from the fact that the drivers were said to be 'selected from gentlemen's servants only; who have produced good characters from their last places for sobriety and civility and are dressed in plain stable livery'.[1]

The character of the drivers reflected the character of their employers, for the first two cab proprietors were not hackneymen but gentlemen; and for ten years a small group of gentlemen – merchants, speculators and men of independent means – reserved for themselves a profitable monopoly of cabs, until the hackney coach monopoly itself was abolished in January 1833. Throughout that period the number of cabs on the streets remained under three hundred. Each licence was issued with the express approval of the Lords Commissioners of the Treasury, and the majority of them went to men with friends in high places.

A side-seat cab, driven by a cabman whose coarse features are in marked contrast to the refinement of his passenger. There were many complaints that the elegance of the new vehicles was not matched by that of their drivers

13

ANNO QUINQUAGESIMO QUINTO

GEORGII III. REGIS.

C A P. CLIX.

An Act to amend several Acts relating to Hackney Coaches; for authorizing the licensing of an additional Number of Hackney Chariots; and for licensing Carriages drawn by One Horse.

[11th *July* 1815.]

WHEREAS an Act was passed in the Fifty-fourth Year of the Reign of His present Majesty, intituled *An Act for the better* 54G.3.c.147. *Regulation of the Drivers of Licensed Hackney Coaches; for explaining and amending an Act passed in the Forty-eighth Year of His present Majesty relating to Hackney Coaches; and for authorizing the licensing of a limited Number of Hackney Chariots:* And whereas the Provisions in the said Act contained, for providing and delivering Tickets, have been found inexpedient; be it therefore enacted by the King's most Excellent Majesty, by and with the Advice and Consent of the Lords Spiritual and Temporal, and Commons, in this present Parliament assembled, and by the Authority of the same, That from and after the passing of this Act, so much of the said recited Act as relates to the providing of Tickets, as in the said Act mentioned, or delivering any such Tickets to Persons paying Fares, or as prohibits Complaints unless Tickets are produced, or accounting for any such Tickets, and all Provisions, Regulations, Penalties and Forfeitures in the said Act contained, in relation to such Tickets, shall be and the same is and are hereby repealed.

So much of said Act as relates to delivering of Tickets, &c. repealed.

II. And whereas the Hackney Chariots which have been licensed under the said recited Act of the last Session of Parliament have been found very useful

200 more Chariots may be licensed.

15 Y

Cabs were first authorized by the Act of 55 Geo.3. cap.159, although it was another eight years before the first vehicles actually appeared on the London streets

The two pioneers were Joseph Hoare Bradshaw, a London banker, and Benjamin Rotch, a barrister of Lincoln's Inn and a London patent agent. Rotch was typical of the adventurers who came to dominate the early years of the London cab trade. His grandfather, William Rotch, was born in Nantucket, Massachusetts, in 1734. He was the founder of the town of New Bedford and became a prominent whaling merchant. After the American Revolution, William's son, Benjamin sen., was invited by the British government to come to Milford Haven to establish the southern whale fishery. The family flourished and Benjamin came to own nine ships. William's grandson, also named Benjamin, was called to the bar in 1821 and was elected MP for Knaresborough in 1832, despite attempts to unseat him on the mistaken grounds that he was an alien. He was a wealthy and influential man, but he was not, as H.C. Moore claimed, a Member of Parliament at the time that he started his cabs.[2]

The hackneymen did not take kindly to the newcomers. In June a London magistrate declared that they were 'at open war with the cabriolets', and several cases of assault and wilful damage came before the courts. The introduction of the cab provides an excellent example of the reluctance of hackneymen to innovate. It was eight years since cabs had first been authorized, but no hackneyman had taken them up. Cabs required better horses than hackney coaches, involved investment in new vehicles and – perhaps most important of all – could only charge two-thirds of the coach fares. In the distressed times of 1815 it is not difficult to see why the hackneymen considered them an unsound investment.[3]

The year 1822, when the application for licences was made, witnessed the lowest oats prices since 1797, a factor which may have influenced timing; but how a banker and a lawyer came to interest themselves in cabs is not clear. The secretive manner in which they went about it suggests that their intention was to establish a monopoly of cabs. The original application was made in November 1822 by one Richard Fellowes, who described himself as 'gentleman' of Aldersgate Street. He argued that the growth of London and Westminster called for an augmentation of the number of hackney coaches and that, as the greater number of fares were paid by single individuals, two-wheeled vehicles to carry one or two passengers would be a great convenience. The cabriolet had originated in France, and was introduced to Britain in about 1810. It was a dashing vehicle, which W. Bridges Adams described as 'very convenient . . . for unmarried men to go out in at night'.[4] Fellowes insinuated that the Hackney Coach Commissioners had hitherto been reluctant to license cabs for public use, fearing that insubstantial second-hand private cabriolets would be employed. There is no evidence to support this; but the allegation might suggest that some hackneymen had shown an interest in cabs, but not to the extent of investing in purpose-built vehicles. Fellowes argued that second-hand cabs could be precluded by laying down a minimum width, which would eliminate vehicles originally built for private purposes; and he asked for twelve licences for an experimental period of three years.

Although Fellowes applied to the Treasury (the final fount of patronage), the board would not act without sounding out the views of the Hackney Coach Commissioners. The latter were not enthusiastic. They reported that they had no way of knowing if cabs would succeed commercially, as they had never been tried. They were prepared to support Fellowes's application for twelve licences, but not in such a form as to give him a monopoly. If they should prove successful, the Commissioners wanted the power to increase the number to fifty.

At some time between December 1822 and February 1823 it was revealed that Fellowes was only the managing clerk to the two real speculators. Bradshaw and Rotch now claimed the licences and increased their demand to twenty-four, to be made out in their joint names. The Commissioners not only refused this new demand, they now refused to license Fellowes at all, on the grounds that the other two men had a financial interest in the licences. Nor would they grant licences to Bradshaw and Rotch without an order from the Treasury, for the hackneymen had petitioned against the cabs, and the Commissioners were not prepared to injure their clients. After much wrangling they agreed to grant six licences to each of the real applicants, provided that they were kept separate. Bradshaw and Rotch appealed to the Treasury, claiming that they had already entered into joint agreements for a large number of vehicles. The Treasury would not budge on the question of numbers, but did instruct the Commissioners to issue twelve licences in their joint names, in contravention of the

The cabs introduced by Bradshaw and Rotch in 1823 were allegedly designed and built by David Davies, coachbuilder, of 15 Wigmore Street, London. This ink drawing in the Guildhall Library suggests a vehicle hardly different from the private cabriolets of the day

usual practice. The whole episode has every appearance of an elaborate ruse to maintain a commercial secret and to obtain a monopoly of cabs.[5]

If Bradshaw and Rotch claimed that their venture was by way of experiment, then it was a short one, for within seven months they were seeking to dispose of their plates. They made various excuses for their losses, but professed optimism that in other circumstances the cabs would yield 'a fair and even handsome profit to the proprietors'. They claimed that, having set at rest any doubts that might exist in the minds of the public, they wished to resign the trade 'into the hands of the same class of persons as had theretofore worked hackney coach plates'. The Hackney Coach Commissioners were not taken in by this attempt to save face, for they would not accept that Bradshaw and Rotch had performed a public service. Their venture was speculative, and they had made a speculative loss. The Commissioners reported:

[A]fter six months trial in the fine season of the year with the aid of novelty, but without the additional ruin of a profitless winter, this description of vehicle is found not to answer, and the proprietors are desirous of being permitted to sell their property with advantages that are inadmissible, and do not belong to them.

The trade did not revert to the hackneymen, as Bradshaw and Rotch rather patronizingly suggested. Instead, these pioneers were succeeded by a second wave of cab proprietors, many of whom were gentlemen like themselves. These men, admitted the Hackney Coach Commissioners in 1827, 'conducted the business with great regularity and good effect, although not to great profit'. Whether this is true or not, there clearly was the expectation of great profit; and the belief was shared by hackneymen and politicians alike that a handful of speculators were making a fortune out of a cab monopoly within the wider coach monopoly. The number of cabs was strictly limited by the Treasury until 1833, and there were never enough licences to satisfy those eager to operate them. The cries against the cab monopoly in the late 1820s swelled those of the opponents of the Hackney Coach Commissioners, who wished their office to be abolished. Ironically, the Commissioners were always lukewarm in their attitude to cabs, and the patronage which caused such an outcry was not in their hands, but remained firmly in the hands of the Treasury Commissioners.[6]

The hackneymen fought vigorously against this monopoly in their midst, for the principal proprietors of cabs were men of substance whose holdings of licences were greatly in excess of those typical of the coach trade. We do not know who all the proprietors were. In particular, we do not know which hackneymen took out cab licences even though perhaps half were owned by such men, albeit in very small numbers. However, it is possible to piece together portraits of some of the principal newcomers and they were worlds apart from the typical hackneymen. The immediate successors of Bradshaw and Rotch were William Boulnois, Vernon Abbot and J.E. Williams. These three between them possessed 48 per cent of all cab licences in March 1827, Abbot and Boulnois alone possessing 42 per cent.[7]

William Boulnois was a wine and spirit merchant with premises in Great Tower Street. He obtained his first licences from Rotch in 1824, when he purchased from him seven cabs and fourteen or fifteen horses. There appears to have been an understanding that he would have the plates transferred to him when Rotch handed them in at the office; and to secure them he paid around £240 for the 'bad cabs and indifferent horses'. By 1827 he had eighteen licences and was the second largest proprietor in the whole hackney coach business.[8]

The largest overall proprietor in the trade in 1827 was Vernon Abbot, listed in *Pigot's Directory* of that year as a livery stable keeper. A petition to the House of Commons in May 1828, complaining of the cab monopoly, refers to him as 'Captain Abbot', but there is no Vernon Abbot in the *Army Lists*, and the description is clearly a mistaken reference to Captain Christopher Abbot, a member of his family, who had acquired eight of his licences by October 1830. The third largest cab proprietor, J.E. Williams, with six licences in 1827, is not listed in any of the directories. Little is known of him, except that he, too, was mistakenly described as 'captain' in the petition of May 1828.[9]

Of those of whom something is known, the next two cab proprietors to enter the trade were C.J. Gerss and R.P. Staples. Gerss was a shadowy figure whose precise role is difficult to pin down. A foreigner, of unknown nationality but with business interests in South America, he applied for fifty licences in June 1827, claiming, like many other applicants, that he intended to introduce cabs 'on a new and improved plan'. The Hackney Coach Commissioners considered his application a sham, designed to obtain a considerable number of licences to the prejudice of previous applicants. What they did not know is that another person was involved in the application behind the scenes – Robert Ponsonby Staples. As in the earlier case of Bradshaw, Rotch and Fellowes, Staples may have been using Gerss as a front man in order to avoid publicity. A more likely explanation is that Gerss availed himself of the influence of Staples with the Treasury, promising him half of any licences he might obtain. Pressure for a favourable response on behalf of 'my friend Mr Staples' was exerted by Maurice Fitzgerald, Knight of Kerry, but as his note is undated it is not clear whether this was before or after he, himself, became a Treasury Commissioner on 31 July. In any event, the Hackney Coach Commissioners were instructed on 26 September to grant ten licences to Gerss and ten to Staples.[10]

Staples is by far the most intriguing of all the early cab proprietors, and the range of his speculative interests reveals the kind of venture that cab operation was assumed to be in the 1820s. In 1810, and apparently for some time prior to that date, Staples was a representative in Buenos Aires of the Belfast merchants Montgomery, Staples & Co.

In the following year he was appointed British Consul 'on the banks of the River Plate', but the Spanish government refused to accredit him. By 1812 he had set up a beef-salting establishment near Buenos Aires, and as supplies to the West Indies were interrupted by the war between Britain and the United States a speculative opening appeared in the supply of beef and flour to those colonies. In 1813 he was commissioned by the Treasury to purchase specie at Buenos Aires, from which dealing he must have made at least £4,000 for himself in salary. Although the Treasury curtailed this operation in 1814, Staples was again commissioned in 1818 to buy dollars for shipment to the Cape of Good Hope and Mauritius, for use in the public service. Denied a formal consulship, he nevertheless represented British merchants in Buenos Aires from 1816, and in 1819 assumed (quite without authority) the title British Commercial Agent, earning for himself a stern rebuke from the Foreign Office.

Staples returned to England in 1820, and then proceeded to the East Indies, Peru and Mexico, where he was appointed Consul at Acapulco in October 1823. He never took up residence there. Instead he exceeded his powers by negotiating a loan for the Mexican government, which he then induced the British Commissioner, Lord Hervey, to guarantee on behalf of the government. For this impropriety, Hervey was recalled and Staples dismissed. Whether he returned to England immediately is not known. In 1825 he was a director of the Famatina Mining Company, while his company, R.P. Staples & Co., was the agent for the Real del Monte Co.

The contemporary economist J.R. McCulloch described the South American mining boom of 1824–5 as 'a disgraceful era in our commercial history', in which 'the public gullibility, or rather its indiscriminating rapacity, was liberally administered to'. Among those eager to pander to that greed, and to make a quick killing, was Staples. Of the British speculators in Latin America in the early 1820s, Harriet Martineau wrote: 'Too many were eager for gain, making haste to be rich; and of these the sharpers of society made an easy prey.'[11]

Staples was one of the more prominent of these adventurers, and that he should have been interested in London cabs indicates the kind of speculative profits that were anticipated. The ten cab licences which Staples received in September 1827 must have been profitable, for in February 1828 he tried to obtain another thirty. The Hackney Coach Commissioners, arguing that the metropolis was already abundantly supplied with public carriages, opposed him, but they were overridden by the Treasury Commissioners, who ordered them to grant Staples a further ten. Staples now had more licences than his associate, Gerss, much to the latter's annoyance; and in April 1828 Gerss, too, applied for more, insisting that he was the inventor of the improved cabs, and making disparaging comments about the friendship between Staples and Maurice Fitzgerald, Knight of Kerry, MP for Kerry and Lord Commissioner of the Treasury from July 1827 to January 1828.[12]

Gerss was not without some political influence of his own, and he secured the aid of T. Hyde Villiers, MP for Hedon, and A.J. O'Neill, MP for Kingston upon Hull. O'Neill supported the application of Gerss in a private note to George Dawson, Junior Secretary to the Treasury, in which he expanded at some length on the whole question of patronage:

[Had] my application [been] made on the grounds of personal obligation I own that I should not anticipate a refusal – I have never asked the most trifling favour from the Government in which Mr Peel, yourself & what is called the Tory Party held office – Tho' I have invariably given and give the most decided support to that administration.[13]

The intervention of Hyde Villiers and O'Neill may have had some effect, for, in May, the Treasury instructed the Hackney Coach Commissioners to issue a further thirty-five plates, of which five were to be allotted to Gerss, but the lion's share – twenty – was assigned to Peter G. Fitzgerald, the fifth son of the Knight of Kerry. In November 1828 Peter Fitzgerald took on as partner Robert Fitzgerald, his older brother, in what was the most flagrant case of nepotism in the granting of cab licences.[14]

The taking of partners was a practice upon which the Hackney Carriage Commissioners frowned. It had been a long-standing prohibition which, together with a strict injunction against the private traffic in hackney coach plates, was aimed at maintaining accountability and protecting the revenues. In the event of arrears accruing, the Commissioners insisted that there be no doubts as to title which might complicate their recovery. The Treasury was perfectly aware that this was the practice, for it had been an issue when Bradshaw and Rotch had applied for joint licences, and it had come up a month before the Fitzgerald partnership was authorized, when Gerss had petitioned to take on a partner. He had claimed that his business interests made it imperative for him to travel to South America, and he therefore asked to be allowed to transfer all his fifteen licences to a partner, Joseph France, who was a clergyman. The Hackney Coach Commissioners objected, claiming that such partnerships were not permitted, and the Treasury appears to have upheld their opinion. Gerss attempted to dispose of his cab plates in an underhand manner, and eventually had them all revoked because of his 'fraud and duplicity'.[15]

Fitzgerald, Staples and Williams were more fortunate in their connections. Three weeks after the Fitzgerald partnership was confirmed, Staples applied for permission to enter into a partnership with W.H. May, a merchant in the City. The Commissioners again opposed the application, but were overridden by the Treasury. When Williams applied in 1829 to take on his 'trusty friend and relative', James Lock Cartwright, as a partner (owing to a 'domestic calamity' which would preclude his residence in London), the Commissioners merely recorded their long-held opposition to partnerships in general, but accepted that, as Fitzgerald and Staples had already been afforded this 'indulgence' by the Treasury Commissioners, there were no grounds for withholding it from Williams.[16]

The partnership issue illustrates the somewhat conservative attitude of the Hackney Coach Commissioners regarding business organization, paralleled later in the century by Metropolitan Police and Home Office antipathy to hire purchase. The partnership also illustrates the power of patronage at this time, for although the Treasury was often prepared to uphold the Hackney Coach Commissioners' policies, it was quite willing to override them when the interests of a favoured party were at stake

There were times when the Treasury was prepared to act unilaterally. For example, in December 1828 the board received a petition purporting to represent the views expressed at a meeting of hackney coach and chariot owners held at the Hercules Pillars, Lincoln's Inn Fields, on 20 November. It was claimed that the owners were in ' a most ruinous state of poverty and distress never before experienced in their business', and that this was caused by 'the partial and limited issue of two-wheeled carriages to persons not before in their trade'. The petitioners asked for a reduction in the number of licensed vehicles from 1,200 to 1,000, and the right to transfer their plates between coach, chariot and cab 'as the season or circumstances might require'. The Treasury did not follow the normal custom of referring the petition to the Hackney Coach Commissioners for report, but simply replied that they had the matter under their consideration. In fact, what was under their consideration was the abolition of the Hackney Coach Office, for they had already informed the Commissioners of their intention to introduce legislation in order to merge them with the Board of Stamps.[17]

The response of the principal cab proprietors to the hackneymen's attack was a united one, for a long memorial was submitted to the Treasury in January 1829, from Vernon and Christopher Abbot, Boulnois, May, Robert and Peter Fitzgerald, Staples and Roe. They argued that the clamour raised against them was an appeal against the opinion of the public who had supported the cabs. If hackney coach profits had fallen, this was due to the bad state of the carriages and horses employed, the lack of control over drivers and the practice of granting licences 'to individuals, who never can bear up against the accidents and casualties to which they are exposed'. The last point was a direct challenge to the Hackney Coach Commissioners' antipathy to corporate enterprise.[18]

The predicament of the Hackney Coach Commissioners was to get caught in the crossfire between the coach and cab proprietors, while at the same time being sniped at from the House of Commons. Their view, expressed with regularity and clarity from

1827 onwards, was that London was oversupplied with public vehicles and that the number of cabs should not be increased. 'We have . . . always thought,' they said, 'that the public would have been as well off without them.' The fact was that the Commissioners were in a most invidious position. The patronage question aroused very strong feelings, yet they exercised very little patronage themselves. Edward Jesse told the Select Committee of 1830 that he had not had a cab plate to give away for five years; while in May 1831 the Commissioners claimed that the only plates they had issued on their own discretion were those arising from vacancies caused by death or other cause, and that only two such vacancies had occurred in the previous ten months. It was the Treasury, not they, who exercised the patronage. The Treasury named the recipients, and the Hackney Coach Commissioners remarked somewhat bitterly that 'very improper persons have obtained licences in this way'. In the issue of cab licences (but not the less popular coach licences) the Hackney Coach Commissioners merely rubber-stamped decisions of the Treasury.[19]

Much of the turmoil sprang from the supposed profits made by the cab owners, for it was popularly supposed that these must have been high, or gentlemen would not have been interested in the trade.[20] There is no doubt that the capital required to establish cabs was greater than with coaches, as were running expenses. Whereas a hackney coach might be obtained for about £30, a cab cost between £60 and 75 guineas; and because the vehicles were worked so intensively, the owner had to have more cabs than he possessed licenses. Robert Fitzgerald had twenty licence plates, but he kept thirty-four cabs in order to cover breakdowns. Strong, sure-footed horses were required, both for safety and for speed, and they were worked in greater numbers than in coaches. Fitzgerald's twenty licensed cabs, for example, were worked by eighty-three horses. Hackney Coach Commissioner Edward Jesse estimated the cost of a cab horse at £15–20 in 1830; Roe and Fitzgerald, both cab operators, thought about £20 would be an average price. Roe had forty horses to work his ten cabs, which is about the same ratio as Boulnois and Fitzgerald. Henry Clement, the hackneyman who had claimed that a coach could be started 'very decently' for £70, reckoned that he should be able to start a cab for £100. Jesse thought about £150 was nearer the mark, but the three largest cab proprietors who gave evidence to the Select Committee gave estimates which worked out at £200–230 per cab. Allowing for the bias of both hackneymen and cab proprietors, it would seem that a cab must have cost at least twice as much to put on the road as a coach. John Jervis summed up cabs in 1827:

If the horse be ever so sure-footed, and the driver ever so skilful and steady, they are frightfully dangerous vehicles for town work, and will only be used by those who are rash enough to sacrifice safety for celerity and comfort for cheapness.

Lord Calthorpe's cabriolet. The two-wheeled hackney cab was based on the cabriolet, a vehicle imported from France early in the nineteenth century. The cabriolet was a popular vehicle with 'men about town', and necessitated not only the smartest of horses but a diminutive groom, or tiger'. From the volume on *Driving*, in the *Badminton Library*, 1890

Celerity was a key factor in their popularity. Boulnois told the Select Committee that people who used cabs generally did so for speed, and included merchants, professional men, lawyers and doctors.

The main difference in the running expenses between a cab and a coach arose from the more intensive working of the two-wheeled vehicles. Horses had to be better fed and their working life was shorter. Speed was the essence of the cab, and the horses were worked hard. Roe, who received his ten licences in May 1828, claimed to have had ninety-five horses pass through his hands by 1 April 1830, less than two years later. Of these, only forty-two remained in his possession, the rest having died or become unserviceable. The wear and tear on vehicles was also high. When Boulnois bought seven of Bradshaw's and Rotch's cabs after about eighteen months' use, they were allegedly in a very bad state. He, like other large proprietors, put maintenance out to contract, and had arranged with a coachmaker to repair his twenty-eight cabs, shoe his horses and maintain the harness for £1,150. At that rate (about £41 a cab) vehicles must have been written off in two years. Maintenance agreements such as these were doubtless one of the economies of scale enjoyed by large proprietors, others being stabling and, probably, the bulk purchase of fodder. Estimates of the annual expense of a hackney coach, which ranged from £238 to £292, must be compared with estimates for running a cab ranging from £400 to £450, or about 60 per cent higher.[21]

Clearly, cabs had to be worked very hard in order to offset these costs, especially as they could, by law, only charge two-thirds of the fares charged by coaches. Seasonal variations in earnings were every bit as extreme as those of the coach, if not more so, and the large proprietors accepted the argument of the Hackney Coach Commissioners that the cab was largely a fair-weather vehicle. Richard Box, a cab driver for Francis Roe, told the Select Committee of 1830 that drivers were expected to bring in 25s a day, or 17s to 19s in bad weather. Roe did not pay his drivers a wage, and it seems to have been the gentlemen cab proprietors who really developed the system of renting cabs to their drivers on a daily basis (the bailee system), which was described as commonplace in 1828.[22]

Wild guesses were made regarding the actual profitability of cabs, with those opposed to the small clique of gentlemen operators no doubt exaggerating their claims. For example, Joseph Hume talked of gentlemen cab proprietors having such numbers of cabs as would bring them in £10 to £20 a day. But in order to make that much a proprietor would have needed to run between fifty and a hundred cabs, which no man possessed. Edward Jesse put the figure at £100 clear profit per cab in 1830, an estimate which is broadly comparable with the figure of approximately £90, which can be inferred from Francis Roe's evidence. He calculated his profits to be not more than 5s per cab per day, which would produce a figure of about £91 a year, or £75 if the cabs were only worked for six days a week. There can be little doubt that cabs were far more profitable than coaches, and that a small group of men were making considerable sums from their operation. But their high returns were dependent on monopoly conditions, and the Hackney Coach Commissioners were decried as the patrons of monopolists. Without the one, it was argued, there would not be the other, and the public outrage at cab speculation breathed new life into attempts to have the Hackney Coach Commission abolished.[23]

Within a year or two of the abolition of the hackney coach monopoly the original gentry and merchant proprietors had all withdrawn. Their interest had been in the speculative profits to be made under monopoly conditions, and in this they had been aided by the patronage exercised by the Treasury, against the advice of the Hackney Coach Commissioners, whose first loyalty was to the regular body of London hackneymen. Once the trade had been thrown open after 1833, the only prospect of securing anything like a monopoly was with the aid of a patent or patents, but these were hard to protect as both Joseph Hansom and John Chapman were to discover.

Chapter Three

THE TRADE IS THROWN OPEN

The possibility of abolishing the Hackney Coach Office was first raised in the 1790s, when a general campaign of economy and retrenchment was launched in Parliament. Early in 1797 the Prime Minister, Pitt, set up the Select Committee on Finance, which produced thirty-six reports, of which the eleventh, in July 1797, recommended that the Hackney Coach Office be consolidated with the Hawkers and Pedlars Office, or that the work of both be transferred to the Board of Stamps, which was already responsible for the post-horse and stagecoach duties.[1]

One difficulty in the way of a merger was the fact that the Hackney Coach Office was not merely a revenue office, but possessed powers of summary jurisdiction over licensed hackneymen, and such police powers did not fit comfortably with the activities of the Board of Stamps. By October 1797, therefore, the Treasury had decided that the powers of the Hackney Coach Office should be transferred instead to the Commissioners of Taxes, and that the regulatory powers should cease. In future, offences against the hackney carriage legislation would be tried solely before the courts. These proposals caused alarm among the hackneymen, of whom 115 petitioned the Treasury in December. Licensing and regulation, they argued, were so bound up with each other that they could not easily be separated. They looked upon themselves as a trading company, paying a rent for the liberty of the streets, 'out of which their own board is paid for regulating them, protecting their rights and privileges, and for sustaining the general prosperity of the employment'. The Hackney Coach Commissioners were not unsympathetic to this view. Like the Metropolitan Police after them, they accepted a responsibility for the protection of the public, but they were far more inclined to adopt the paternalistic role of protecting the trade. Indeed, it might well have been this partiality which aroused feelings of antipathy towards them from those who wanted greater coercion of hackneymen. The Commissioners likewise opposed the confinement of summary powers to the justices. The proprietors alleged that their experience of the magistrates was a bitter one, for they were treated like criminals, 'with much rigour and hostility', and were subjected to excessive penalties. The Commissioners did not go that far, but they did argue that the public would suffer if they had to resort to the criminal courts for redress, for the better rank of people, especially ladies, would 'feel repugnance to encounter the crowds and descriptions of people with which public offices are generally beset'.[2]

As it happened, the matter was not proceeded with, but the Select Committee on Finance floated a more ambitious scheme in their twenty-eighth report on the Police and Convict Establishments, issued in June 1798. The report drew heavily on a plan by Patrick Colquhoun and Charles Pool to establish a Board of Police Revenue, which would exert control over a variety of 'dangerous and suspicious trades'. All persons employed in certain trades which were considered to be at moral risk would be compelled to register with the consolidated board. Altogether, eighteen occupations were identified, which included, besides hackneymen, horse dealers and livery stable keepers, auctioneers, pawnbrokers, slaughterhouse keepers, dealers in a variety of waste and scrap materials, and hawkers and pedlars. The criminal reputation of hackneymen was based on their alleged assistance to burglars and their utterance of counterfeit money.[3]

Colquhoun drafted legislation in 1799, but it was not proceeded with. However, in 1800, the Hackney Coach Commissioners were given the task of registering (but not licensing) hackney coach drivers and the watermen at coach stands, a venture that appears to have been so successful that in 1805 Sir John Sinclair suggested that they be given control of another troublesome group – domestic servants. This was not to be, but the existing enlargement of their duties helped the Hackney Coach Commissioners to justify their existence for a little longer. Ever on the defensive, they argued in 1801, and again in 1807, that their new functions meant that they could no longer be reasonably considered the same board as that which the Select Committee of Finance had sought to abolish in 1797. Three years later, in 1810, they again escaped extinction when they were merged with the Hawkers and Pedlars Office. A considerable economy was effected. In 1797 the Hackney Coach Office had a staff of forty-two, whose total salary bill was £3,866 and who were responsible for the collection of £26,176 in revenue. By 1827, with the addition of only two more staff, revenue was nearly tripled (£70,974), with 56 per cent consisting of receipts from hawkers' licences.[4]

The 1820s brought the Commissioners little comfort. The firm grip which the Treasury Board maintained on the issue of cab licences brought them many enemies and few friends. Throughout the decade they were the target of fairly persistent sniping in the House of Commons from Joseph Hume and a small group of Radicals who made the issue of monopolies their own. There was a growing mood of *laissez-faire*, made all the stronger in the case of hackney carriages by the fact that one of the original arguments for a monopoly was losing its force. Street congestion had underpinned the demand for a limitation on the number of public carriages, but as old streets were widened and new roads opened, the case for a hackney coach monopoly was weakened. However, it was not until May 1830 that a Select Committee was set up (under the chairmanship of Sir John Wrottesley, the Reforming Whig member for south Staffordshire), charged with examining the working of the Hackney Coach Office, as well as the state of public carriages in the metropolis and the laws affecting them. The membership of the committee, which was packed with Whigs and Radicals, together with the choice of witnesses, could only have led to one outcome.

Five hackneymen gave evidence, of whom three, at least, are known to have been refused cab licences. These included George Green and Charles Saggers, who had petitioned the House of Commons, in the most bitter terms, for the abolition of the Hackney Coach Office in 1829, and again in 1830. Two other witnesses had axes to grind. George Shillibeer had been vainly seeking cab licences since 1825, and had subsequently turned to omnibus operation in the face of opposition from the Commissioners; while George Cloud was the proprietor of a short stagecoach. He had been convicted ten or twelve times by the Commissioners for taking up passengers on the 'stones'.

Only two of the five Commissioners were called to give evidence. Edward Jesse had been appointed in 1814, at the age of thirty-four. He held the sinecure of Gentleman of His Majesty's Ewry, and was Deputy Surveyor of the Royal Parks and

George Cruickshank's engraving of a 'coffin cab' makes very clear the origin of the name for this variant of the side-seat cab

Roads. His sole qualification for being in charge of London's horse-drawn public transport was a fondness for pets and a belief, according to his biographer, 'that quadrupeds at least could [not] be denied immortality'. Thomas Marrable (appointed in 1817) was also Secretary to the Board of Green Cloth and received a pension as a former Clerk of the Kitchen's Office. The Senior Commissioner, Colonel Charles Wade Thornton, had been appointed in 1808, after retiring from the army on full pay two years previously. Thornton had served in the Royal Artillery since 1779 and had had his right arm shot off at Lannoy during the Flanders campaign. At the time of the Select Committee he was also Lieutenant Governor of Hull Castle, and *aide-de-camp* to the King. Not surprisingly, he was the least frequent attender of all the Commissioners, appearing at the Office on only twenty-eight days in 1829. It is not clear why he was not called to give evidence. It may be that the committee members wished to hear from someone more involved and with a more open mind. If that was the case, Jesse would have fitted the bill. There are indications that he had never seen eye to eye with his fellow Commissioners on a number of issues, for he favoured admitting stagecoaches onto the 'stones', increasing the number of cabs and allowing the lighter flies to ply.[5]

The Committee began taking evidence on 17 May and reported just over three weeks later. Its recommendations were hardly surprising. The thirty-year-old proposal to transfer the revenue duties of the Office to the Board of Stamps was revived. No limitation of the number of licences issued was recommended, and licences were to be transferable between all classes of vehicle, with the constraint that the number of people to be carried in each description of vehicle should be determined by the Commissioners of Stamps. Drivers and watermen at the stands were to be licensed. The magistrates were to have jurisdiction over all complaints under the proposed Act, and the Committee recommended that a special court should be established to hear such cases. New fares were proposed, and extended limits of the metropolis for the purposes of back fare were advocated.

Legislative action was delayed, first by the death of the king and secondly by the fall of the government in November. Hume criticized the delay on 8 July 1831, and the Bill was finally introduced at the end of that month, over a year after the report had been published. The Bill was not an easy one to frame, for it consolidated some twenty-eight Acts of Parliament, and several major amendments were made during its passage through Parliament. Thus a recommendation of the Select Committee that, for three years, the licences should be issued to existing proprietors, 'and to such other persons as shall agree to take out not less than three numbers', was dropped. So, too, was the suggestion that drivers should be licensed and badged. The former recommendation was designed to prevent a flood of one-number men from entering the trade once the limit on numbers was removed, and was replaced by a temporary limit, for one year, on the number of licences issued. The latter suggestion, which was one of those police measures frequently advocated in the previous thirty years, was dropped as 'impracticable'.

The Act which emerged – the London Hackney Carriage Act of 1831 – was to be the foundation of all subsequent cab legislation, and parts of it remain in force to this day. The Hackney Coach Office was abolished, and all licences issued by that Board were to cease from 5 January 1832. Within a month of that date, proprietors were to deliver up their plates to the Board of Stamps, who would in future issue licences. That body did not take over the regulatory powers of the Hackney Coach Office, which in future were to be exercised solely by the magistrates. The Bills of Mortality lost their defining role as far as hackney carriages were concerned, and new limits of five miles from the general Post Office were introduced.

A breathing space of one year was provided, during which the number of licences was to be kept to a maximum of 1,200, preference to be given to existing proprietors. After 5 January 1833, licences were to be issued without limitation of number. Only two classes of vehicle were henceforth to be recognized – those drawn by one and those drawn by two horses, and in consequence the streets were opened to a variety of carriages, some of which their promoters had in vain tried to persuade the Hackney Coach Commissioners to allow. Omnibuses (though not regulated under this Act) could also ply in London after January 1833, when stagecoaches acquired the long sought after right to take up and set down on the 'stones', or the paved streets of the capital, which had previously been reserved for hackney coaches.

The last few months before the Act came into effect witnessed a great flurry of activity, as the Treasury Commissioners jostled to exercise patronage, albeit short-lived, before it was abolished. Lord Nugent, one of their number, dramatically exclaimed: '[We] have sacrificed our patronage in cabs on the altar of our Country'. George Shillibeer, the originator of the omnibus, was one of those who received cab licences in the dying days of the monopoly, although even then he nearly missed out. He claimed to have been applying for cab licences since 1825, but the first extant application is of November 1827. He was unsuccessful then, and again in January 1828. In June of that year he wrote to George Dawson, Junior Secretary of the Treasury, regretting that his patron, Alexander Baring, MP, was 'unfortunately . . . not in the habit of voting with his Majesty's Ministers'. In July he pressed the Assistant Secretary for a more favourable response, bemoaning the fact that 'a Foreigner totally unconnected with the Business' (Gerss) had been granted fifteen plates. He applied again in November, but devoted his energies in the following year to the omnibus, which most of the Hackney Coach Commissioners had also tried to block. When at last he was promised ten cab licences, only to discover that there were none available, he was aided by the personal intervention of Edward Jesse, who wrote to the Treasury:

I know little of Mr Shillibeer except that the public are much indebted to him for a new and useful description of carriage and he is, I think, one of those persons who ought to receive every encouragement. It was on this ground only that I recommend him for cabriolet licences.[6]

Commissioners Thornton, Jesse and Marrable were not granted compensation when the Hackney Coach Office was closed, on the reasonable grounds that they already received substantial public incomes. The former clerks and messengers were given either gratuities or pensions, with the exception of William Powell, Receiver and Registrar of the Hackney Coach Office, and William Quaife, a street keeper, who were transferred to the Board of Stamps to deal with hackney carriage work.[7] The Quaife family had made a good living out of hackney coaches. James Quaife sen., the surveyor, was the compiler of a semi-official handbook of hackney coach fares, and must have been as knowledgeable as any man in London on the subject. He had worked in the office for thirty years, where the employees included his wife, son, brother and nephew. The Quaife family was heavily involved in the practice of collecting the hackney coach duties from proprietors for a commission of 1s a month. About half of the proprietors paid in this manner. It made sense to keep on the right side of the Quaifes who, it was even alleged at the time, ran what we would call a protection racket.[8]

One member of the Hackney Coach Office staff successfully managed to privatize his job. William Hill (former inspector and assistant to the surveyor) soon found employment with the Cabriolet Union. This was an association of the principal gentlemen cab proprietors, set up to fill the regulatory vacuum which soon became apparent. Its purpose, ran the advertisement announcing its formation in September 1832, was

to make such arrangements as would, in their opinion, insure the respectability and good conduct of the Drivers in their employ, as well as supply to the Public the accommodation and information which the abandonment of the Hackney Coach Office has withdrawn from them.[9]

As if to stress the links between themselves and the former Commissioners, the Union took an office at 24 Essex Street, next door to the former Hackney Coach Office. Not content with this, application was made to the Treasury for the use of the official records of the abolished Commission. The Commissioners of the Treasury, whose *protégés* these proprietors were, acquiesced in this further attempt to procure a privileged position within the trade, and instructed the Board of Stamps 'to give . . . any information on those points which the records of the late Hackney Coach Office afford'. The Board interpreted this as an instruction to hand over the books themselves, for in May 1833 (by which time the Cabriolet Union appears to have been dissolved) an apparently unsuccessful attempt was made to secure their return.[10]

A cab belonging to the Cabriolet Union, *c*. 1832–3. This print does little to support the Union's claim that it supplied a better class of cab and driver

The short life of the Cabriolet Union is indicative of the pressures which were faced by the gentlemen pioneers. Towards the end of 1832 a number of them began to pull out of the trade, and the columns of *The Times* contained numerous advertisements of proprietors 'declining the business', including the offer of a business comprising forty-three cabs and seventy horses. On 26 September the Board of Stamps agreed to transfer Francis Roe's plates, and three days later a similar undertaking was given to George Shillibeer. On 1 October the Fitzgeralds dissolved their partnership, explaining their reasons for quitting in a petition to the Treasury in September 1833. They claimed that the operation of the Act of 1831 had so depreciated the trade that they found that no profit could be made from it. They sold their share to their partner, J.H. Rayner, who possessed greater capital, and had decided to carry on in the hope that Parliament would see the necessity of further amending the law.[11]

The changes brought about by throwing open the trade in January 1833 were soon apparent. There was an increase in the number of public carriages upon the road, a swing from hackney coaches to cabs and omnibuses, and loud complaints of a 'cab and omnibus nuisance'. Board of Stamps figures for January 1834 show that the number of licensed hackney carriages had gone up from the previous limit of 1,200 to 1,703 (an increase of

40 per cent), although the figures do not distinguish between hackney coaches and cabs. In addition there were 423 short stage carriages on the streets and 376 omnibuses. In April the hackney coach proprietors petitioned for a reduction of duty to 5s a week, blaming their distress on the competition of omnibuses and short stages, reduced fares and the effects of free trade. They claimed numbers to be between 1,700 and 1,800, and it is quite possible that the higher figure had indeed been reached by the end of the year, for in November it was cited in a letter to *The Times* from a cab proprietor. He noted that there were at that time over 1,000 cabs, when 165 had previously sufficed. If this was the case, then the balance had already swung to cabs within a year.[12]

The subsequent decline of hackney coaches was rapid, and by 1845 (when there were 2,400 cabs) there were fewer than 200 hackney coaches left.[13] In *Sketches by Boz*, Dickens vividly portrayed the decayed state of hackney coaches in their declining years:

There is a hackney-coach stand under the very window at which we are writing; there is only one coach on it now, but it is a fair specimen of the class of vehicles to which we have alluded – a great, lumbering, square concern of a dingy yellow colour (like a bilious brunette), with very small glasses, but very large frames; the panels are ornamented with a faded coat of arms, in shape something like a dissected bat, the axletree is red, and the majority of the wheels are green. The box is partially covered by an old great-coat, with a multiplicity of capes, and some extraordinary-looking clothes; and the straw, with which the canvas cushion is stuffed, is sticking up in several places, as if in rivalry of the hay, which is peeping through the chinks in the boot. The horses, with drooping heads, and each with a mane and tail as scanty and straggling as those of a worn-out rocking-horse, are standing patiently on some damp straw, occasionally wincing, and rattling the harness; and now and then, one of them lifts his mouth to the ear of his companion, as if he were saying, in a whisper, that he should like to assassinate the coachman.

Whether the hackneymen died out or transferred to cabs is not clear. It was observed in 1845 that the hackneymen

were too bigoted and inactive to become cabmen; and those who were not prudent enough to save up a 'bit of money' during their days of prosperity, most likely ended them in the workhouses of their respective parishes. Their downfall was but little regretted.

Too much reliance cannot be placed upon statements such as this, for it is clear that many did make the transition, although their holding of cabs remained small. For many, too, their association with the cab trade must have been a brief flirtation, as had been the case since hackney coaches began. For example, a correspondent in *The Times* in December 1834 suggested that of the 1,400 new licences issued by that date, some 900 had been given up through an inability of the proprietor to carry on.[14]

The abolition of the hackney coach monopoly removed all impediment to the introduction of omnibuses, the number of which increased to 620 by 1838–9. The transition from monopoly conditions to free trade, and the rapid expansion in the number of cabs and omnibuses on the streets, soon led to complaints of a nuisance. In May 1833 the House of Commons tabled a petition signed by 384 inhabitants of the City of London, pleading that public carriages be subjected to stricter control and inspection, and that no more than necessary be allowed to ply. They argued that the reckless conduct of drivers and the general increase in street obstruction damaged them in their occupations, and 'must ultimately ruin the retail trade in the City and the leading thoroughfares'. On 24 May, Benjamin Rotch presented an identical petition signed by 304 inhabitants of Oxford Street; and on 5 July another copy from 219 residents of the Strand. These three petitions, praying that the House would take measures 'for putting the public carriages of the Metropolis upon such a system as shall secure their becoming a convenience and accommodation, instead of a nuisance and annoyance', were clearly orchestrated – no doubt by Rotch himself. Since his brief flirtation with cab operation in 1823 (which seems to have been unrecognized by his contemporaries), he had become a magistrate and a Member of Parliament, in both of which offices he sought to put the trade in order. In September 1834, Rotch sentenced a cab driver to six months in prison (the last three to be in solitary confinement) for theft from his master. He remarked that there should be legislation for the better control of drivers, for the masters 'were robbed and the lives of the public constantly endangered by about 1,500 of the most lawless ruffians in existence'.[15]

Inevitably the rapid expansion of cabs and omnibuses led to problems, but it is equally clear that the issue made good newspaper copy. An article in the *Westminster Review* suggested that 'The moment anything is done in England for the comfort or convenience of the numerous classes, it makes its appearance under the title of a nuisance.'[16] Nor is the view that cab and omnibus obstruction damaged retail trade very persuasive. A correspondent in the *Morning Chronicle* argued: 'a lady's carriage, standing for an hour at the door of the haberdasher's shop, occasions more interruption to the business of the street than twenty omnibuses'. In any case, the writer continued, the argument of City tradesmen that street obstruction damaged them was a sham, for loss of trade was due more to the opening of better shops in the West End and to the general westward drift of population.[17]

It is not surprising that the movement for greater control of public carriages should come from the City or that a former Lord Mayor should be the driving force. Sir Matthew Wood was a self-made chemist and druggist, who had served two terms as lord mayor between 1815 and 1817. In 1820 Wood came to prominence as a champion of the hapless Queen Caroline. From 1817 until his death in 1843 he represented the City in the House of Commons, where Henry Brougham dubbed him 'Jackass' Wood, and said that 'he never rises but to make a roar of laughter'. Lord Denman, however, spoke of his 'uncommon perseverance and activity', qualities which Wood certainly displayed when it came to reform of the hackney carriage laws.[18]

Between 1834 and 1838 Wood introduced a total of five Bills to regulate cabs and omnibuses. There was little consistency between them, and he lurched from one solution to another as he attempted to drum up support. In the wake of the London Hackney Carriage Act of 1831, which effectively deregulated the public carriages of the metropolis, Wood tried to weigh them down again with a mass of regulations. Inevitably those Radical reformers who had thrown open the trade were implacably opposed. Henry Warburton, an ardent advocate of free trade and a member of the 1830 Select Committee, complained of the 'extreme minuteness' of Wood's legislative proposals, and argued that he grossly exaggerated the extent of the problem:

When the worthy Alderman gets any subject into his legislative microscope he fancies that those hairs which appear to all the rest of the world as down, are nothing less than enormous claws – such is the power of his oxyhydrogen microscope.[19]

Early cabs had curtains which could be pulled across to protect the passenger in the event of rain. From H.C. Moore, *Omnibuses and Cabs*, 1902

The determined opposition of the small group of radicals who had secured deregulation of the trade; lack of support from the government; and the general apathy of most Members of Parliament towards a question which elsewhere in the kingdom would have been in the province of a town council, meant that Wood got nowhere until 1838.

Although Wood may have exaggerated its extent, there was a real problem, for the Act of 1831 had indeed left something of a vacuum when it came to policing the public carriages, and the Board of Stamps was very conscious that it had not inherited the judicial powers formerly exercised by the Hackney Coach Office. This had been made abundantly clear in October 1832, when Henry Bartholomew, the fifteen-year-old son of a Keppel Mews cab proprietor, knocked down and killed Lady Caroline Barham. Reporting the inquest in its leader column, *The Times* noted that hardly a day passed without a cab accident, and argued that the law ought to ensure that proprietors employed 'careful and proper drivers of these at all times dangerous carriages'. Lady Barham's relatives petitioned to have Bartholomew's licences revoked, but the Board declared itself powerless to act. Only after repeated family pressure, the seeking of the Solicitor of Stamps' opinion, and the receipt of certificates of conviction for this offence and another for wanton and furious driving, did the Commissioners agree to revoke Bartholomew's two cab licences. This appears to have been the only instance of such action being taken down to 1836, the period for which records are extant.[20]

Central to the issue was the question of whether the driver or the proprietor should be held responsible. The 1831 Act had decided on the latter, on the grounds that drivers were impossible to trace. Licensing of drivers was a logical solution, but licensing would have to be backed up by requiring the drivers to wear a badge, and this was a particularly sensitive issue, for badging carried strong overtones of criminality and pauperism. Opponents of further regulation took the unacceptable (but entirely logical) line that as the driving of private coachmen was no better than that of the public carriage drivers, they too should be badged – in effect, general driver licensing should be introduced into London.

Wood finally got a Bill through in August 1838. It had a life of only five years before it was repealed by the London Hackney Carriages Act of 1843, which was a Home Office measure. Its one enduring provision was the licensing of drivers and conductors, at first by a Registrar of Metropolitan Public Carriages and from 1850 by the police. One might reasonably ask why the latter had not been brought in at the very beginning, for the Metropolitan Police Force had been established in 1829, two years before the Hackney Coach Office had been swept away. That question, however, relates to the wider one of the nature of the police function. Not everyone felt that the control of traffic was part of it, and the chequered relationship between constables and cabs is a subject taken up below.

Chapter Four

'HANSOM CAB' OR 'CHAPMAN CAB'?

To most people the horse cab conjures up one picture – that of the hansom, the popular image of which owes much to Sir Arthur Conan Doyle. In 1892, when *The Adventures of Sherlock Holmes* was first published, nearly 66 per cent of London cabs were hansoms, rising to a peak of 69 per cent five years later.[1] When cabs were first introduced in the 1820s, a number of different designs had appeared on the streets, though all were based on the private cabriolet of that time. None was very satisfactory, and cabs acquired a reputation as dangerous vehicles. In the early 1830s the hansom cab (the 'gondola') and the four-wheeled clarence cab (the 'growler') appeared at roughly the same time. These two vehicles set a new standard, so much so that no viable alternatives to them were to appear in London until the advent of the motor cab. The hansom is one of those eponymous articles like the sandwich, the hoover and the biro. But the design as we know it owed more to another man, John Chapman; and there is some justice in asserting that Sherlock Holmes ought really to have requested Dr Watson to summon a chapman.

The appearance in 1942 of many of Chapman's original papers clarified the picture somewhat, but left many questions unanswered. Hansom's claim to the original invention of the safety cab had already been challenged, although the assertion made in 1932 (at the time of the fiftieth anniversary of his death) that the true inventor was Edward Bird cannot be substantiated. Bird was allegedly the secretary of the Misses Gottwaltz, postmistresses of Birmingham in the 1820s. Bird's son claimed that his father presented drawings of his unpatented invention to his brother-in-law, Edward Welch, who was then Hansom's partner. There is no evidence to support this claim, which only escapes incredibility because of the difficulty of explaining how Hansom, a Birmingham-based architect of Owenite leanings, should have been drawn towards improving the horse cab.[2]

Hansom's patent of 1834 is a rather curious document, for although it is described as for 'an improved vehicle for the conveyance of various kinds of loads on common and other roads', it in fact sets out *three* quite different vehicles in the specification – an incongruity that was later to present some legal difficulties. One vehicle was the passenger carriage with which we are familiar, consisting of an almost square body (not inappropriately likened by some writers to a large packing case) with 7 ft 6 in

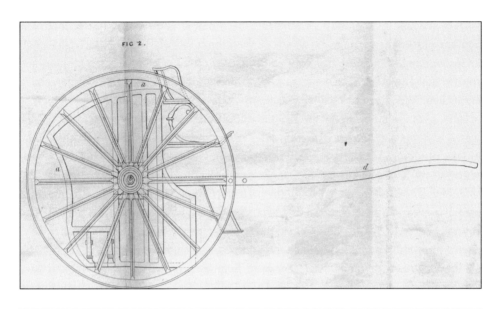

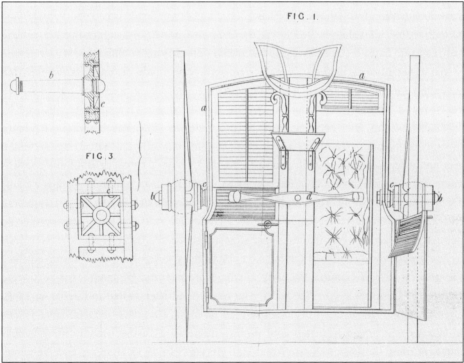

The drawings in Hansom's patent specification of 1834 show just how different his original cab was from the one which later bore his name

wheels attached to the body's framework by a pair of stub axles. The second was another passenger carriage in which conventional wheels were replaced by giant hoops working through friction rollers, having the effect of eliminating both hubs and spokes, and allowing the passengers to pass through the 'wheels' and into the vehicle at the side. This ingenious device was to prove quite unworkable! The third vehicle is usually ignored, but may contain the clue to Hansom's interest in vehicle design. This was a two-wheeled wagon, on stub axles, the purpose of which was to shift large blocks of stone. This may have been the vehicle which first engaged Hansom's interest, and from which the passenger carriage developed. In 1831 Hansom had submitted a design for a new Birmingham Town Hall, which was accepted by the town commissioners, but on condition that he entered into a bond on behalf of the builders. He was later to regret this but claimed that, as a young man (he was then aged twenty-eight), his ambition at gaining such a commission overcame his caution. It proved a great mistake, for the builders' financial difficulties soon led to his own bankruptcy. Part of the problem seems to have been the high cost of transporting marble from Anglesey prior to the railway. It would thus have been quite natural for Hansom to turn his attention to methods of bearing large and heavy loads on a road vehicle, and to realize that his solution – to lower the centre of gravity by supporting the vehicle between stub axles – could be applied to passenger-carrying vehicles.[3]

Whatever his original motivation, Hansom soon made attempts to exploit his invention for the purposes of a hackney carriage, and had a prototype built by John Fullylove, a Hinckley coachbuilder. Moore suggested that Hansom was financed by William Boulnois, the second largest cab proprietor in 1827, but there is no evidence to support this claim. Boulnois was himself the inventor of a closed carriage having a rear entrance which, for a while, competed with Hansom's cab. The Boulnois cab was sometimes referred to by contemporaries as 'a slice off an omnibus' because of its shape. The driver sat in front, and the rear door made it much easier for passengers to enter. However, where they could enter they could also exit, and these cabs became so popular with fare-dodgers that they had almost disappeared by 1841.[4]

The group who introduced the hansom cab to the metropolis was far removed from the general run of London hackney carriage proprietors. Hansom's backers were Dempster Heming and J.S. Needham. The former had been called to the bar in 1808, after which he had successfully practised law in India. He possessed extensive estates in Warwickshire, and also had coal-mining interests. Hansom became his business manager after the Birmingham Town Hall disaster. In 1835 Heming and Needham established a private bank at Hinckley (where Hansom is said to have originated his cab) with Needham as the active partner.[5]

Hansom was an enthusiastic follower of the socialist and philanthropist Robert Owen, and was a prominent supporter of the Birmingham Builders' Union of 1833–4.

He attracted a number of midland Radical activists to his new cab venture, including the Birmingham Member of Parliament, Thomas Attwood, and William Greathead Lewis, the founder of *Lewis's Coventry Recorder*, who, in 1819, had received a two-year prison sentence for seditious conspiracy.[6]

John Chapman was from the same mould. He was born in 1801, the son of a Loughborough clockmaker who, in 1816, became president of the Loughborough Hampden Club, one of many Radical groups regarded by the government of the day as subversive. John Chapman became its secretary, and later helped to establish the Loughborough Permanent Library. He entered his father's workshop, but in 1823 established a partnership with his brother William, formed to manufacture lace-making machinery. Although the export of machinery was illegal at the time, the partners conducted a large business with France, while John lobbied Westminster for a repeal of the laws. In the recession of 1833–4 he had machines seized by the Customs on at least two occasions. The authorities may have been alerted by Nottingham lace-makers, angered both by Chapman's lobbying at Westminster in favour of free trade, and by his continued support of local Radical politics. The double blow of trade depression and confiscation led to the firm's ruin, and the brothers lost their factory and all their possessions.[7]

It was thus that, in the late spring of 1835, Chapman left his pregnant wife and four daughters and journeyed down from Loughborough to London in search of work. An able writer, he sent papers to the *Morning Chronicle*, but found that journal interested only in what he described as 'personal politics'. In vain he tried to secure the patronage of Dr John Bowring, the Radical Member of Parliament for the Clyde burghs, and subsequently one of the founders of the Anti-Corn Law League; and he contemplated applying for the posts of factory inspector and 'junior collector' at a gasworks. He tramped around the London engineering workshops, and considered a job with a Manchester machine manufacturer. His fortunes changed when he sent a mechanical paper to Joseph Clinton Robertson, the founder of the *Mechanics' Magazine*, and one of the instigators of the London Mechanics' Institute. With a shared interest in technical and educational matters and a sympathy of political views, Chapman soon struck up an acquaintance with Robertson, who first tried to find him employment with the Eastern Counties Railway (with which he was associated) and then introduced him to Hansom and his partners. Chapman described this event in a letter to his wife in August 1835:

> I was introduced to them by Mr Robertson: and as you know, did considerable work for them, and was a great deal consulted by them. I opposed some of their plans and opinions and they have found me in every case right. It was some time before I knew clearly the relative situation of the parties among themselves. I found at last

that there would be two concerns, one at Hinckley (Mr Hansom's own) and one in London to be *in the end* possessed by a Company. Mr Hansom, when last here, engaged me at 2 guineas a week *probably* to go to Hinckley, but said that he could not complete the arrangements for beginning for a week or two. He has since noticed me in a letter to Mr Lewis deferring the thing shortly – he said another week, which is nearly expired – Mr Lewis, Mr Heming and Mr Needham are engaged in the project for a Company with every prospect of speedy success: they are about taking very large premises for keeping their horses and making their carriages: the Mews they are in treaty for are near Regent's Park and are at a rent of £200 per year. Their proceeding with business does not depend on the forming of a Company, but if the Company be formed, their preparations will be transferred to it: most of the steps in the business Mr Lewis has told me of as they have occurred, and upon many he has consulted me: though not under a regular arrangement with him, I have seen him and assisted and advised with him almost every day for the last fortnight.

In his anxiety to reassure his absent wife, Chapman may have exaggerated the extent to which the partners took him into their confidence, but his very detailed letters home provide evidence not only of the boundless optimism that Hansom's patent would make their fortunes, but also that even before a company was formed, factionalism was already present.[8]

The adventurers needed an engineer of Chapman's calibre in order to turn Hansom's ideas into a vehicle that could cope with the strains of regular public use. 'They are afraid,' Chapman wrote, 'of venturing it upon a pavement least its failure (which with such use is extremely probable) should be a discredit to the invention.' Chapman's own doubts about the design were confirmed when he made a model of it. He found himself in a difficult position, for while Hansom's associates in London urged him to develop the design, the inventor himself remained in Hinckley, showing little enthusiasm for the project. Chapman offered to return to Leicestershire to see Hansom, hoping at the same time to visit his wife and the newborn daughter he had yet to see; but Hansom wrote that he was far too busy to be depended upon to give any considerable assistance. Thus, urged on by Lewis and Robertson, the initiative for developing the cab passed to Chapman, and he soon produced a design which retained the stub axles and front-driving position of Hansom's patent; modified the safety frame; and replaced the box-like body with one more closely resembling the cab as we know it.

Though still only engaged on a casual basis at 10*s* a day, Chapman was elated by his prospects:

The employers are wealthy – they have in hand a project whose success is certain and need not be long deferred – they *can* push their design independently of all others – though the concurrence of others would render the business of greater magnitude – large expenses have been incurred and are incurring which can only be repaid by perseverance – the projector and only mechanical man amongst them declines taking an active part in the management thro' excess of other engagements – they have confidentially employed, consulted and actually engaged me, and *no one else*. Against this you have to set the fact that though engaged I am not yet in actual permanent employment and the general uncertainty attending everything not yet actually done. Judge dearest and tell me whether or not I ought to seek out elsewhere or for the present abide by this: our friends are of the latter opinion.[9]

Mrs Chapman advised caution, but his mind was made up:

[As] the only eligible application of the principle has originated with me, may I not justly look for greater consideration in the proceedings than I should have had in an old affair? Is it merely a freak of my faulty hopefulness when I say I confidently look for comfort after a short time?[10]

Chapman was indeed rewarded with the post of secretary when The Safety Cabriolet and Two-wheel Carriage Company was set up early in 1836, with a nominal capital of £100,000. Among the first directors listed in an early prospectus were Heming, Needham, and Ebenezer Fernie (Managing Director of the British Commercial Life Assurance Company). W.G. Lewis was managing director but, surprisingly, Hansom was not among the officeholders. Instead he was described as having granted to the company 'an exclusive licence for the making and employing of his carriages, whether for public hire, or private use'. The popular story is that Hansom disposed of his rights in the cab for £10,000 but was never paid. This cannot be substantiated and appears unlikely, for the prospectus states that the provisional agreement with him was 'of such a nature as to make his remuneration entirely dependent on the success of the Company in working his invention'. This would suggest a percentage of the profits, or some kind of royalty for the use of his patent.[11]

As far as can be ascertained, none of the directors had any previous experience of the cab trade, despite Chapman's belief that two large cab proprietors were to be taken on as directors, including the former owner of the mews they were renting. The directors seem to have divided fairly equally between provincials and Londoners, a fact which appears quite soon to have fostered a partisan spirit which acted greatly to the detriment of the company.[12]

The intention was to start operations as soon as £7,000 had been raised, whereupon up to fifty cabs would be launched. Figures were produced to demonstrate that a profit of at least thirty per cent could be anticipated, but running expenses were clearly

An improved hansom cab, before the position of the driving seat was modified by John Chapman. From H.C. Moore, *Omnibuses and Cabs*, 1902

underestimated. Premises capable of accommodating over a hundred horses were secured in York Mews, Baker Street, and the company announced at the beginning of May 1836 the imminent commencement of business. However, although a trial cab had been running since the previous November, it was still to be another three months before operations commenced in earnest, and even then (on 1 August) only five cabs were put on the road.[13]

By this time the defects of Hansom's design, despite the improvements made by Chapman, were already apparent. The narrowness between the safety frame and the large, and often dirty wheels made it difficult for passengers to get in and out. The solution of this problem by placing the driver behind, rather than on the front of, the roof, was discussed even at this early stage, but for a number of reasons it was decided to push ahead with existing plans; and immediately after the first five cabs were started the directors ordered a large number of frames to be cut out. The defects extended beyond inconvenience to the passengers. Hansom's safety frame alone weighed four hundredweight, and a heavy burden was placed on the horses. Although the body was attached to the safety frame by springs, the framework itself was unsprung, with the consequence that the horse was struck whenever the carriage was going fast and came to an obstacle. Sometimes the weight was thrown suddenly on the horse's back, sometimes on the belly-band, so that, as Chapman put it, 'the poor animal was so beaten upwards, downwards and sideways, that he was very quickly worn out'. The body springs frequently broke, as did the axles, and the large wheels proved expensive to maintain. It was demonstrated that in 1838–9, for example, 43 per cent of the cost of maintaining the company's cabs was attributable to wheels. In consequence of these difficulties the company soon found itself in a bad way; so much so that, if Chapman is to be believed, by August 1837 (if not earlier) the shares had become almost worthless.[14]

Chapman threw himself into the cab trade at the deep end. In the summer of 1835 he was offered the post of 'secretary and mechanist' at a salary of four guineas a week, but he soon added to his duties by taking on the work of superintendent.[15] It was typical of Chapman to attempt to broaden his knowledge in this manner. Whenever he set out to master a new subject he always returned to first principles, so that it was said of this former lace-machinery manufacturer and future aviation pioneer that, in his cab days, 'he learned so much about London cab horses that no dealer could deceive him'.[16]

The problem with two-wheeled vehicles was that they had to remain in balance, with or without a passenger, or the horse would soon become fatigued. Chapman speedily realized that the key variable was the driver, who might be placed before, above or behind the body of the vehicle. With the driver placed forward, the vehicle could not be in balance both empty and with a passenger. If it was to balance when empty, the axle had to be placed very far forward, with the result that when loaded there was a preponderance of weight behind, with consequent pressure on the horse's belly-band. If it was to balance with passengers, their absence would throw the weight of the driver onto the horse's back. If the driver was placed above, the passenger seat had to be kept low. The axle had to pass under the passengers' feet, but no common cranked axle could accomplish that, except with very small wheels. Small wheels, however, would place the centre of gravity far above the axle. This was dangerous, for 'a small inclination forward occasions a fearful increase of pressure on the back of the horse: a slight stumble or check . . . puts the driver and sometimes the passengers in great danger'. Chapman correctly saw that all these problems disappeared if the driver was placed behind. The vehicle could be made to balance without passengers but, if present, they could be over the axle, which would not affect the equilibrium. The driver could be placed lower than he would be if on top of the roof, thus lowering the centre of gravity. Finally, the axle might be placed under the passengers' seat, rather than their feet, which would allow for the use of larger wheels.[17]

The question of driving from behind was much discussed in 1836 by Chapman, Lewis, and a large shareholder of the company, W.S. Gillett, who was himself something of an inventor. Gillett was a frequent visitor to York Mews, and in November persuaded the others to fix a seat temporarily to one of the cabs so that the plan might be tried. The consequences of this were far-reaching, as the new design had yet to be patented. Although the experimental cab appears to have been on the streets for no more than twenty minutes, there was a danger that competitors might see it and, furthermore, that it might be considered a 'prior user'. This might invalidate any subsequent patent, as later litigation was to show.

When, in December 1836, a patent was taken out, less than complete frankness was shown by the parties either to each other or to the company. Lewis and Chapman first applied for financial assistance to Attwood, who was a banker. When he declined, Chapman (apparently without Lewis's knowledge) turned to Gillett, who insisted that *his* name be inserted (on the ground that he had thought of driving from behind) and that Lewis's name should be excluded, as *he* was not an inventor at all. Thus the patent (No. 7266) was taken out jointly in the names of Gillett and Chapman, and in that order, although Chapman always claimed that he alone was the true inventor of driving from behind.[18]

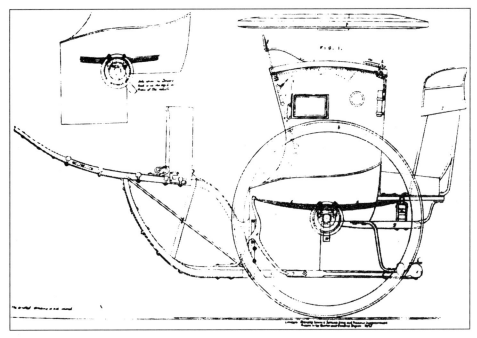

Side view of Gillet and Chapman's cab, from their patent specification of 1836. This shows very clearly the heavy safety frame that was designed to prevent the vehicle tipping forward if the horse slipped, but was later abandoned due to the great addition which it made to the cab's total weight

It is hardly surprising that when the directors of the company discovered that their secretary, together with a substantial shareholder, had taken out a rival patent, they were furious. Chapman was accused of having a conflict of interests, but there was little that the company could do other than accept a licensing agreement from him. Hansom took no noticeable part either in the development of his own patent or in the negotiations over Gillett and Chapman's, and he appears to have withdrawn totally from active participation in the company's affairs at this time. Chapman seems to have got on better with fellow inventors than he did with businessmen – after all, Nottingham businessmen had only recently helped to bankrupt him. Consequently his dealings with Hansom, a fellow bankrupt and inventor, were much more frank and open. In a letter sent a week before his patent had been sealed, Chapman wrote to Hansom:

I am far from thinking myself at liberty to injure your interests in any way, but you will probably not dispute that any profit which may arise from the new patent, beyond that which would have arisen from yours, I have as good a right to bargain with the Company as though I was independent of them; and I doubt not that you will think it fortunate that the new carriage was originated with one disposed to preserve and improve your interests rather than to injure and supplant them.[19]

However angry the directors of the company may have professed themselves to be, Chapman's patent was in fact a godsend to them, for not only did it solve the technical problems of Hansom's carriage, but it also solved certain potential legal problems by rendering Hansom's patent to all intents and purposes obsolete. Doubts already existed as to whether it would ever stand up in a court of law. Four months prior to Chapman taking out his patent, William Carpmael, the leading authority on patent law, had reported that he had serious doubts as to the validity of Hansom's patent because of the incongruity of the title and its objects. Although he suggested a way out of the legal deficiencies, he felt that there would at all times be doubts as to the patent's standing. The company was therefore in a predicament. They possessed a vehicle which, despite its deficiencies, was arguably the best in the trade; but it was protected by a seemingly defective patent. Piracy of Hansom's cabs was thus a very serious threat. Chapman had now given them access not only to a better vehicle, but to a stronger patent.[20]

The way ought to have been open for the company to embark on a profitable career, but this did not happen. Relations between members of the board with each other and with Chapman were dogged by suspicion and acrimony. The company was lumbered with between forty and fifty old cabs originally built to Hansom's specification as modified by Chapman, and now converted yet again to accommodate driving from behind. This imposed upon the wooden frames strains which they were not designed to bear, and the bodies rapidly deteriorated as rain seeped in through the cracks which opened up. With such depreciating stock, the way was left open for competitors to pirate Chapman's patent and to put newer, brighter cabs upon the road.[21]

In an attempt to set matters straight, Hansom was called back to give advice, but his cautious approach, whereby some twenty cabs would be renovated each year and only half a dozen new ones would be built, antagonized Chapman, who favoured an immediate replacement of the total stock. After much wrangling, Chapman resigned from his position as secretary to the company in February 1840. His freedom brought him no great fortune. Although he successfully established his patent before the courts he had little success in securing the payment of damages, and he was no more successful in selling licences to manufacture his cab.[22]

Neither Hansom nor Chapman made any money out of cabs. Hansom went on in 1842 to found the *Builder*, but, lacking the capital to develop the journal himself, was bought out at the end of the year for a small sum. Chapman carved out a new career in characteristic manner. For a while he assisted W.S. Henson in his aeronautical experiments, and then directed his interests towards India, where he was instrumental in launching the Great Indian Peninsular Railway.[23]

The declining fortunes of the Patent Safety Cabriolet Company (the change of name dates from November 1838) are less easy to document. The company is listed in the *Post Office London Directory* until 1848. It reappeared at the same King Street Address in 1850, but now called 'Hansom's Patent Cabriolet Company', under the proprietorship of Edwin Leaf. He had been associated with the original company, of which he appears to have been a director in 1838. In 1851 the company's premises were in the occupation of Peter Fearnhead, who is listed elsewhere as a livery stable keeper. By 1855 all trace of the company at King Street had gone.

In the light of subsequent cab companies, the Patent Safety Cabriolet Company cannot be judged a complete failure. For one thing it survived longer than most. It was also almost certainly the largest cab concern in London, running between forty-five and fifty cabs at the end of 1839. While we have no figures for other proprietors against which a comparison can be made, the number is more than double that of each of the three largest cab proprietors in 1827, and there is no evidence that any other operator came anywhere near the company in the number of cabs which it ran. James Bardell, sixth largest cab and coach proprietor in 1827, was running seven coaches and two cabs in 1827. In February 1840 (by which time he appears to have moved up in the rank order) Bardell was allegedly running three hansom cabs and was preparing twelve more, but was obviously lagging behind the Patent Safety Cabriolet Company.[24] However, the rub was that all of these cabs were pirated vehicles, built without licence from the patentees. Bardell was described as one to whom the trade looked up, and all the while he pirated hansom cabs, others were encouraged to follow. With patents which the courts did little to protect, the Patent Safety Cabriolet Company was at a disadvantage, for here is a very real example of a pioneer suffering from its early start. Hansom's patent represented a sharp break in two-wheeled cab design. But while it remained an untested vehicle, it was a disastrous move to invest immediately in fifty bodies, for Chapman's improvements followed so quickly that the company was forced to work with converted vehicles with all the attendant problems of wear and tear and structural failure.

The dream of possessing a patent monopoly was to be shared by others later in the century, many of them strangers both to the cab trade and to London. The 'Hinckley party' of the 1830s was to be matched by the 'Birmingham Gang' of the 1880s. Both groups had an improved vehicle; both saw it spread through the trade with little profit to themselves. The courts proved reluctant to protect patent rights, but the real enemy of the would-be monopolist was the ease of entry into the trade. In this respect, Hansom's and Chapman's innovations came a decade too late. Had their inventions come at a time when the issue of cab licences was restricted, the fortunes of the company might have been very different.

Chapter Five

THE CAB BUSINESS

Until the Metropolitan Police took over responsibility for licensing in 1869, it is difficult to obtain firm figures for the number of hackney carriages operating in London, although the broad trend is clear. As might be expected, the opening of the trade in 1833 led to an immediate and rapid expansion. Numbers rose from 1,200 to 1,703 within a year, and had risen to over 2,400 by 1844. By September 1851 there were 3,548, rising to 5,119 in June 1861. From 1870 onwards figures were published annually in the Reports of the Commissioner of the Metropolitan Police (Appendix 4).[1]

Even the Metropolitan Police figures have to be treated with some caution, for a cab might be presented for a licence more than once in any particular year. If a cab was involved in an accident some months before it was required to undergo its annual inspection, rather than overhaul and repaint the cab then, only to have to repaint it yet again in order to pass the inspection, the proprietor might decide to surrender the licence, have the work carried out, and relicense the vehicle upon completion of the repairs. The result would be that two licences for the same vehicle would be issued in a period of twelve months. It was suggested in 1911 that reducing the number in the official returns by around 500 would fairly represent the number of cabs actually working the streets.[2]

What is immediately noticeable from the police returns is that the number of licences issued for four-wheeled cabs remained remarkably stable from the late 1870s down to the middle of the first decade of the twentieth century. In the twenty-eight years from 1881 to 1908 there were only five years in which the number varied by more than 200 from the mean figure of 3,778. It was the number of hansom cabs which fluctuated most, taking the total to its peak of 11,519 in 1898, and pulling it down to little more than one-eighth of that figure by 1914.

The expansion in the number of hansom cabs in the 1870s and '80s was associated with the introduction of improved vehicles (especially the rubber-tyred Forder), whereas the four-wheeled cab did not undergo technical development to anything like the same degree. The growler was a vehicle much used for station work, and the railway-generated trade tended to even out demand. Growlers plodded on with the railway travellers, their families and their piles of luggage, while the hansom cab was much more affected by developments in other forms of transport such as the omnibus

The hansom cab horse. An engraving from *The Leisure Hour* of 1892, which reminds us of the quality of many of these animals

and underground railway, and by improvements in communications such as the telephone. The decline of the hansom cab was both earlier and faster than that of the four-wheeled cab, although both eventually succumbed to the motor taxi.

It is much more difficult to determine the number of proprietors, for there is no equivalent series of figures relating them. But from anecdotal, often journalistic, evidence, together with the occasional official estimate, a picture emerges of a trade which, like that of the hackney coachmen before it, was dominated by small masters. Drawing on the 1851 Census, Gareth Stedman Jones has demonstrated that 70 per cent of proprietors in the cab trade ran establishments employing between one and five persons, while a further 10 per cent ran firms of between five and nine employees. In June 1861, figures returned by the Board of Inland Revenue revealed a similar picture. The 5,119 licences issued for metropolitan hackney carriages were held by 2,026 proprietors, of whom 1,327 held only one licence and 1,942 (96 per cent) held ten or fewer. Only one proprietor held more than forty licences, and that was Thomas Tilling, with seventy-nine. The position thirty years later was little changed. Although by 1893 the total number of cabmasters had increased by more than half, 2,967 of the 3,168 proprietors (94 per cent) still possessed ten licences or fewer.[3]

Whereas in both periods roughly two-thirds of all proprietors were owner-drivers with one cab, by 1893 some twenty-eight had succeeded in establishing substantial businesses of fifty cabs or more, while three had taken the lead with over one hundred each. These three concerns were the London Improved Cab Company Ltd, the partnership of Phillips and Brickland, and the firm of Thomas Gunn. The London Improved Cab Company was the most successful of a number of cab companies formed in the 1880s. It was incorporated in 1887, and operated 287 cabs by June 1894. Most cab companies were ephemeral, and the majority of the larger operators were men who had worked themselves up in the trade. Giving evidence to the Home Office Committee of Enquiry of 1894–5, W.E. Cooper observed that 'The cab trade has to be conducted on very economical lines, and by thoroughly practical men. Nearly all the large proprietors in London have originated from drivers.' Cooper was an example of just such a person. He commenced driving in about 1876, and became a proprietor three years later. By 1894 he was in partnership with a man named Goode and operated twenty-two cabs. The firm of Goode & Cooper successfully made the transition to motor cabs and expanded in the twentieth century, still existing as a subsidiary of the London General Cab Co Ltd. Thomas Gunn provides another good example. He was born in 1828, and at the age of twenty-one became the proprietor of a cab. By 1851 he had acquired a second, and after the Great Exhibition he increased his stock to five. The Exhibition of 1862 enabled him to expand from twelve to seventeen cabs, and between 1862 and 1868 his fleet grew to nearly fifty. For nearly twenty years he shared the privilege of the Midland Railway at St Pancras with another operator, and he tried his fortune at omnibus operation in addition to dabbling in house property. By the early 1880s he was running just over one hundred cabs.[4]

The success of men such as Gunn and Cooper was no doubt the spur that drove many drivers to take the plunge into cab ownership. It was not difficult to make the transition, although it was hard to make the change permanent, and many would-be proprietors slipped back into the ranks of the driver. An article in *All the Year Round* in 1863 spoke of 'struggling men, who either strive and continue, or break and relapse into their old position of drivers, horsekeepers, conductors, or something even more anomalous, according to the season and the state of trade'. Small proprietors were known in the trade as 'little mushes' (or mushrooms) because of the suddenness with which they sprang up; but like mushrooms, they could just as quickly wither away.[5]

The position of owner-drivers became no more secure as the century progressed. A correspondent in the *Hackney Carriage Guardian* in 1887 questioned the decision of so many drivers to become one-number men, claiming that financially they were not much better off. Independence and ambition were the principal driving forces, and proprietors lost many of their steadiest drivers as a consequence. That the more reliable men were drawn towards ownership made most people look upon the owner-driver with considerable favour. John Garwood, Secretary of the London City Mission, considered them to be 'the most respectable portion of the drivers', a view which was endorsed by Henry Mayhew.[6] Owner-drivers were not without their critics, however. In 1866, for example, the Commissioners of Inland Revenue complained that they were responsible for keeping up the number of shoddy vehicles on the streets:

> There can be no doubt that this trade is at present in a condition almost peculiar to itself; that capital is repelled from embarking in it, and that the number of needy men who set up a single cab and drive it themselves is increasing every year, while that of the large proprietors is diminishing. In any other kind of business this state of things would not long exist. Open competition would secure for the cabs the most custom and the best prices, and the dirty and rickety cabs would soon vanish from our streets. But the necessary conditions for this self-adjusting process are wanting. The prices are fixed by law at a uniform rate, and the public, for the most part, exercise rarely their right of selection when a cab is called; at all events sufficiently to drive the inferior vehicle out of the trade.[7]

In the 1880s there was an upgrading of hansom cabs, which may well have led to a flood of inferior, second-hand cabs becoming available to owner-drivers and small proprietors at knock-down prices, thus helping 'little mushes' to maintain their hold. The purchase of a second-hand cab always remained an option for the man embarking on the trade, but as more and more cabs came onto the streets the price of new ones also fell sharply. At the time of the abolition of the hackney coach monopoly, a cab might cost between £60 and 75 guineas. By the 1850s a new cab could be purchased for around £30 to £35, while a second-hand cab was estimated at around £26. Writing in 1861, Mayhew gave £40 to £50 as the price of 'a clarence built in the best manner', while, in 1864, J.T. Dexter quoted £48 as the average price of a cab, whether four-wheeled or two-wheeled, £55 being the maximum price and £45 the minimum. There had always been complaints about the varying quality of cabs, but by the middle of the 1890s the range appears to have been enormous. James Scott, Secretary of the London Improved Cab Company, put it vividly in 1894 when he said that 'There is as much difference between the best and worst cab property on the London streets as there is between the Saloon Car and the Cattle Wagon on our Railways.'[8]

It was always necessary for the proprietor to be able to cover for vehicles temporarily taken off the road for repairs. Dexter estimated that eleven carriages had to be kept in order that ten might always be running. The proportionate cost would be greater for the small proprietor, but the one-number man could cover himself by the willingness of coachbuilders to hire out cabs at the rate of about 10s a week. If kept in good repair, a cab might last anywhere from six to eight years, but much depended on

MEMORANDUM OF AGREEMENT.

183*6* *January 20 wad* Mr. *Thomas gooding* has hired Street Cab of James Emms, Carriage Manufacturer, No. 17, Richmond Street, Bartholomew Square, at *14 shillings* per Week each, to be paid in advance. Mr. *Thomas gooding* is to pay for all damage done to the same, of every description whatsoever ; Mr. Emms finding Fair wear and tear only, Mr. is to work with no other Name nor Number on the said Cab, but No. *1435* If he changes the Stable and standing of Cab, he must give Mr. Emms notice of the same, in case of non-payment Mr. Emms shall be at liberty to take the Cab wherever and when he shall think proper so to do.

Thomas Gooding

Witness

An agreement of 1836, whereby James Emms, coachbuilder, hires out a cab to Thomas Gooding at 14*s* a week. Many owner-drivers relied on such arrangements when their own cab was undergoing repairs. This also encouraged men with little capital to enter the trade, although such sub-letting was frowned upon by the authorities

the quality of the original vehicle, the standard of maintenance and the manner in which it was driven.[9]

Infinitely greater skill was needed in the selection of a horse. With twenty years' experience in the trade behind him, Edwin Dyke declared in 1892 that the cab business

is almost as much a matter of speculation as backing horses, to use a sportsman's phrase, because a proprietor may go to a cab sale and purchase half a dozen horses, each horse averaging £20, and out of that half dozen horses only one horse will become what is technically known as a 'cabber,' and consequently he may lose largely on that purchase, and on the other hand he may purchase for half their value, that is, given the market value of the horses – but they may turn out twice as valuable as the price he and the market itself put upon them; consequently in that way it is a very speculative business.[10]

'The mortality of horses,' wrote Dexter, 'is one of the chief causes of the failure of small proprietors, many of whom are compelled by their reverses to seek employment.' Infectious diseases, such as glanders, could wreak havoc on an unfortunate owner. The Horse & Vehicle Insurance Company reckoned that 75 per cent of the claims on account of glandered horses were attributable to the disease

METROPOLITAN

Drinking Fountain & Cattle Trough

ASSOCIATION.

Supported entirely by Voluntary Contributions.

OFFICES:

VICTORIA HOUSE, 111, VICTORIA STREET, WESTMINSTER, S.W.

President—His Grace the Duke of Westminster, K.G., etc., etc.
Chairman of Committee and Treasurer—Joseph Fry, Esq.
Secretary—M. W. Milton.

THIS IS THE ONLY SOCIETY FOR PROVIDING

Free Supplies of Water for Man and Beast in the Streets of London.

The relief which it affords both to human beings and dumb animals is incalculable.

If it had not been for the operations of this Society, thousands of people, young and old, who now quench their thirst at the Fountains, would probably be driven to the public-house, and if it were not for the Troughs, the amount of suffering amongst the multitude of dumb animals continually crowding round them would be inconceivable. Half-an-hour spent at one of them during the heat of the summer would do more to secure sympathy and support for the Association than any words which the Committee can use, they therefore very earnestly solicit liberal contributions, and trust the work will not be permitted to languish for want of funds.

Annual Subscriptions and Donations will be thankfully received by the Bankers, Messrs. Ransom, Bouverie, & Co.; Messrs. Barclay, Bevan, & Co.; or at the Office by

M. W. MILTON, *Secretary.*

FORM OF BEQUEST.

"I give and bequeath the sum of   to be paid (free of Legacy Duty) out of such parts of my personal estate as can be lawfully applied for that purpose unto the Treasurer for the time being of a Society called or known by the name of The Metropolitan Drinking Fountain and Cattle Trough Association, to be at the disposal of the Committee for the time being of the said Society.

The Metropolitan Drinking Fountain and Cattle Trough Association, founded in 1859, brought great relief to animals; but the fear of their horses catching a contagious disease, such as glanders, made some proprietors forbid their drivers to make use of them

having been contracted at a public trough. Drivers were advised against watering their horses at such places, and so great was the risk that the Improved Cabs Club (an association of Forder cab owners formed in 1882) had a rule dismissing drivers caught doing so.[11]

In the first three decades after the abolition of the hackney coach monopoly the price of horses does not appear to have changed significantly, around £20 being an average price. The fall in price which some felt would follow the spread of railways did not materialize. Edward Sherman, the coach proprietor, claimed that the price of coach horses had been maintained by the increase in branch coaches serving railway stations and by 'the extraordinary quantity of omnibuses and cabs' in London. From the 1860s the price of horses began to increase. William Sheather, a cab proprietor with forty cabs and a hundred horses, gave evidence before a House of Lords Select Committee on the Supply of Horses in 1873, that a horse which would have cost him £20 ten years before now cost him 35 guineas. Much of this price increase was due to the Franco–Prussian war, when both belligerents sent agents to this country to purchase horses, and some 30,000 were exported. Thereafter the price seems to have levelled off, with £37 10s quoted as an average price in 1883, and £34 in 1894.[12]

The life of a cab horse was generally between two and three years, but a hansom cab horse which was past its prime might be relegated to a four-wheeler, or from a day

The Show of Cabs and Horses at the Alexandra Palace in 1875 marked the beginning of the meteoric rise of the Forder cab. The presence of 'Tiger' (top right) showed that a cab horse might, with care, give eighteen years' service

cab to a night cab. It is clear, however, that with care and good luck a horse could be worked for much longer. At the Alexandra Park cab show in 1875 there were sixteen entries for the best cab horse which had been at work for not less than eight years, and first prize went to a horse that had been in constant service for seventeen years. Generally, two horses were used in rotation to work a cab, but in practice it was necessary to provide for replacements in case of sickness or injury. A ratio of between two-and-a-half and two-and-a-third horses per cab was generally applied. The owner of a single cab, therefore, would be put to the expense of maintaining three horses if he was to enjoy any measure of security.[13]

The depreciation of cabs and horses was a significant running expense, and many proprietors met their downfall because they failed to take this into account. Rent, duty and taxes, and feed were the other key items for which the proprietor had to budget. It is hard to find figures for rent which can be compared with any degree of accuracy. There were many variables, including location and the quality of accommodation. Only the very largest proprietors ever possessed purpose-built yards, the vast majority operating from stables in converted mews, scattered throughout the capital. The description of Walworth cab yard in the 1890s is typical:

As you walk along the busy thoroughfare which leads from the Elephant to Peckham, if you are of an observant nature and happen to hit upon the right time of day, you will see a procession of hansoms of all grades turn sharp round into what appears a cul-de-sac devoid of houses. If you have had any previous acquaintance with these matters, you know at once by the broken state of the road, where the water lies in pools, that you are in the region of some cabyards, and that the cabmen are going to change their horses. Walk down a little way, and you will see other roads leading off at right angles. Having left the din of the streets behind, you begin to hear the blacksmith's hammer, and smell the farrier's heated iron. Another cab drives up behind you, and as it splashes you from your head to foot you turn into what proves a real cul-de-sac. There is a smithy on one side, where men are busy making shoes. It is not the ideal smithy associated with the spreading chestnut tree, but a little tumbledown shed, in which the men work in a clearing made among the lumber of broken vehicles, and heaps of rusty iron work. Immediately opposite is the yard-gate of the owner of five cabs and eleven horses. One of the cabs, quite a respectable hansom, is left in the alley just outside the gate.

You do not wonder why it is left there when you see the yard, because if it was inside it would be next to impossible to get round it to go up to the house. The most curious feature of the place is that almost everything is made of wood. There was only a little house here once, but odd places have been built up all around; a combination of curious structures that might be described as 'a thing of sheds and patches'. One is a stable with a loft above it – the home of the eleven horses, At the top of the wooden ladder is a wooden box well glazed, which the proprietor uses as a counting house and post of observation – the dog's kennel is hidden away underneath within easy reach of the stable door. Another lean-to at the side of the dwelling is the harness room; another shed some few feet away is the granary. The cabs evidently remain outside all night, for there is no place where they could be stowed away . . . Open the door [of the stable] and you leave light and air behind. Walk through a puddle of water, keeping close to the horses' feet, and you see them in their boxes. There are six of these, and if you express surprise that they should suffice for seven horses, you learn that London stables are worked on the 'Box and Cox' arrangement – that the whole family is never at home at once. But it is the diminutive size of the stalls that surprises you most, for it seems absolutely impossible that the animals can lie down in them. You remark this, and are informed that they manage very comfortably. If, still incredulous, you suggest that none are lying down, though having been out all night, the ostler points triumphantly to the fact that the floor is covered with a thin layer of shavings, and clinches the argument by remarking that they would not be likely to 'waste money on bedding if it was not used.' . . . With that you are glad to escape, for the place is dark, damp and evil smelling; the roof is close down on the horses' heads, and you are in too close proximity to the horses' heels to be pleasant.[14]

The largest single element in operating costs, and that which was subject to most fluctuation, was feed, and a rise in the price of horse feed could put great pressure on proprietors. To harvest fluctuations must be added external factors, such as the Crimean War, which forced prices up sharply; while the opening up of world trade in grain from the later 1870s had the effect of bringing prices down. The absence of any continuous series of accounts, such as exist for a bus company like the London General Omnibus Company (LGOC), makes it difficult to be precise about trends in the cost of feeding cab horses; but a comparison of the LGOC figures with those which exist for cabs would confirm that feeding was an area where considerable economies of scale might be achieved. Barker and Robbins have demonstrated that the LGOC reduced their feed costs (which amounted to about half the company's total expenditure) by such measures as the introduction of steam-driven machinery; centralized, large-scale processing; and the substitution of imported maize for home-grown oats. Such economies, combined with a fall in agricultural prices, meant that the cost of feeding (and bedding) a stud of twelve horses fell from more than £340 per annum in the mid-1870s to between £280 and £300 per annum in the latter part of the decade. From then on, though, it occasionally rose above £300, it sometimes fell in good years to as little as £260. This is equivalent to approximately 10s 10d per horse

The growler horse was generally accepted to be inferior to that of the hansom. It would have been such horses that General William Booth, the founder of the Salvation Army, had in mind when he wrote *In Darkest England and the Way Out*, in 1890. Seeking a metaphor for the lowest standard of welfare that the poor might aspire to, he rejected the 'gaol standard' as an unrealistically high ideal. Instead, he settled on the 'cab horse standard'. From *The Leisure Hour*, 1892

per week at the highest rate, and 8*s* 4*d* per horse per week at the lowest. The latter figure corresponds well with the 8*s* 6*d* charged in 1894 to its feeding account by the London Improved Cab Company, the largest cab concern. James Scott, the secretary, felt that 10*s* was a fair average price for fodder, but commented that 'Small proprietors could not buy it at that price. We buy in large quantities at the ship's side, and bring it up to our place in barges.'[15]

In most commercial relationships, employers pay their employees a wage, which they count as one of their production costs. They then set a price for their product or service which will cover those costs and provide them with an acceptable profit. The cab trade differed from this practice in two important respects. In the first place, the cab owner was not ordinarily free to fix a price for his services to the public, for fares were laid down by law. Secondly, the owner lacked control over his drivers on the streets, and had no accurate knowledge of the amount of fares which the driver collected. Consequently, the payment of a wage was speedily abandoned, and for the straightforward employer/employee relationship was substituted a 'bailee' system, whereby the owner, in effect, hired the cab to the driver, and left the latter to make what he could from fares and tips. In other words, the owner, being deprived of the power to fix the price to the ultimate consumer, fixed instead the price which the driver had to pay for the day's hire of the cab. The owner was thus given a more assured income, although there was no guarantee that the driver would pay the full hiring price at the end of the day. The proprietor possessed few legal sanctions. The London Hackney Carriages Act of 1843 laid down that only written agreements between proprietors and drivers were enforceable, and the better drivers refused to sign them. The main hold which a proprietor had over a driver was that he could refuse the man a cab until he had paid off his arrears (known in the trade as 'shorts') but this could only be applied if there was another driver to take his place, otherwise the cab would lie idle. When times were easy, reliable drivers were not likely to fall behind with their payments, When times were hard, it was more difficult for a proprietor to replace a man who was in arrears.

Drivers who were persistently unreliable might find themselves blacklisted. This practice had existed from at least 1830, and from the late 1860s some of the largest proprietors banded together in a Protection Society which operated 'The Red Book'. By the 1890s an alternative device, known as 'chairmarking', seems to have been preferred. This consisted of endorsing a driver's licence in some secret way, known to the masters, in order to indicate that a driver was in arrears, or was otherwise unreliable or dishonest. One of the devices allegedly used was the writing in words, rather than in figures, of the dates of a man's entering and leaving. The colour of ink used was also thought to contain hidden messages. The magistrates proved powerless to intervene, even if they were willing, which many were not. One magistrate in 1894, for example, described the practice as being neither prohibited by statute nor 'against honour or morality'. Beasley, the union leader, thought that only about twenty or thirty masters resorted to chairmarking, but the men's anxiety was exacerbated by the very vagueness of the practice, whereby any mark on the licence might be considered of cabbalistic significance.[16]

Edward Jesse, one of the Hackney Coach Commissioners, stated in 1830 that he understood the price at which a cab was let to be about one guinea or 25s a day. He made no note of any seasonal variation in price, but this had become established by at least the middle of the century. In 1853 sums ranging from 16s to 18s were quoted as the 'in season' price for a two-wheeled cab, falling to between 11s and 16s 'out of season'. At this time, four-wheelers could be had for between 12s and 14s 6d in season, and between 9s and 12s 6d out of season, the lower sums reflecting the lower earning power of what was, in any case, often a markedly inferior vehicle. Throughout the 1860s, hiring prices appear to have been fairly stable, at around 14s to 16s for a hansom cab in the summer season, and 7s to 10s in the winter.[17]

By the 1880s a much more subtle gradation of prices had developed, reflecting some of the social high spots of the London Season. G.R. Flower, Vice-chairman of the Hackney Carriage Mutual Benefit Society and Editor of the *Hackney Carriage Guardian*, outlined the annual calendar in 1887. In January the price was 12*s*, falling to 11*s* in February and March. After the Boat Race there was a gradual rise of 1*s* at a time until the highest price (ranging from 15*s* to 18*s*) was reached in Derby Week. After the Eton and Harrow Match the price fell 1*s* at a time until mid- or late August, when it reached 11*s* where it remained until November (though frequently 5*s* to 8*s* was accepted from old servants). In November, if the weather was favourable, 12*s* was demanded, but some yards continued at 11*s* until the Cattle Show Week, when the price was raised to 12*s* until January. It should not be thought that the calendar was immutable, and the fixing of the changeover dates, as much as the hiring price itself, was often a source of contention between proprietors and drivers. W. Chapman, a representative of the owners, held that 'You cannot tell in advance when the season and the work will be at its best.' In 1893 Gordon wrote that

The amount paid by the man for a day's hire varies with the vehicle, the master and the season. It is much less really than it is nominally, owing to the numerous occasions on which allowances are made for bad luck and bad weather. Continuous wet is not cabmen's weather; what they like is a showery day, or, what is better, a fine morning and a wet afternoon, or a series of scorching hot days when people find the other means of conveyance too stuffy for comfort.[18]

The London Season provided a fairly regular tide of demand for cabs which was shadowed by the hiring price, but there were other fluctuations, external to the trade, which affected earning capacity. The International Exhibitions of 1851 and 1862, when thousands of visitors were attracted to London, led to more cabs being introduced to meet the demand, and there were great fears of public extortion. The prospect of a similar exhibition in 1871 is alleged to have brought a further 1,500 cabs onto the streets. 1875, however, was described as a slack year, when many small proprietors surrendered their plates; while the onset of economic depression at the end of the decade led to twenty years of difficult times, recovery from which was nullified by the introduction of the motor cab. *The Centaur* described 1880 as 'a most disastrous year', and drew attention to an interesting paradox: the general stagnation in the economy actually led to an increase in the number of cabs licensed, as casual entrants to the trade attempted to eke out a living. Within the trade there was increased competition from a new breed of improved cabs, and there was growing competition from tramways, cheap omnibuses and the underground railways. Frequent complaints were made that the trade was overcrowded, in consequence of which the temporary

12   CAB FARES
To and from the Metropolitan Railway Stations.

TO	L. and N. Western		Great Western		Brighton and S. Eastern		London and Blackwall		South Western		Great Northern		Eastern Counties	
	s.	d.	s.	d.	s.	d.	s.	d.	s.	d.	s.	d.	s.	d.
Adelphi Theatre, Strand	1	0	1	6	1	6	1	6	0	6	1	6	1	6
Albany, Piccadilly	1	0	1	6	1	6	1	6	1	0	1	6	2	0
Albany Street Barracks	0	6	1	6	2	6	2	0	1	6	1	0	2	6
Aldersgate Street, Barbican...	1	6	2	0	1	0	1	0	1	⸱	1	0	1	0
Angel, Islington	1	0	2	0	1	6	1	6	1	6	0	6	1	0
Audley St. South, Mount St.	1	0	1	0	2	0	2	0	1	6	1	6	2	6
Baker Street, King Street......	1	0	1	0	2	0	2	0	1	6	1	6	2	0
Bank of England	1	6	2	6	0	6	0	6	1	0	1	6	0	6
Basinghall Street	1	6	2	6	0	6	0	6	1	0	1	6	1	0
Battersea Bridge, Beaufort St.	2	6	2	6	2	6	3	0	2	0	3	0	3	6
Bayswater, Black Lion.........	1	6	1	0	3	0	2	6	1	0	2	0	3	0
Bedford Square	1	0	1	6	1	6	1	6	2	0	1	0	1	6
Belgrave Square	1	6	1	6	2	0	2	0	1	6	2	0	2	6
Berkeley Square.................	1	0	1	0	2	0	2	0	1	6	1	6	2	0
Bishopsgate St. Houndsditch	2	0	2	6	0	6	0	6	1	0	1	6	0	6
Blackfriars' Bdge. Chatham Pl.	1	6	2	0	1	0	1	0	0	6	1	0	1	0
Blackwall Term. Fench. St...	2	0	2	6	0	6	0	...	1	6	1	6	1	0
Bloomsbury Square	1	0	1	6	1	6	1	6	1	6	1	6	1	6
Bond Street, Piccadilly	1	0	1	6	1	6	1	6	1	0	1	6	2	0
Botanic Gardens, Regent's Pk.	1	0	1	0	2	6	2	0	1	6	1	0	2	6
Bricklayers' Arms, O. Kent Rd.	2	0	3	0	1	0	1	6	1	0	2	0	1	6
British Museum	1	0	1	6	1	6	1	6	1	0	1	0	1	6
Brompton Square	2	0	2	0	2	6	2	6	2	0	2	0	2	6
Brunswick Square	0	6	1	6	1	6	1	6	1	6	0	6	1	6
Bryanstone Square.............	1	0	0	6	2	6	2	0	2	0	1	6	2	6
Buckingham Gate, St. James's	1	6	1	6	1	6	2	0	1	0	2	0	2	0
Camberwell Green	2	6	3	0	1	6	2	0	1	6	2	6	2	0
Cambridge Square, Hyde Park	1	6	0	6	2	6	2	6	2	0	1	6	2	6
Camden Town, Park Street...	0	6	1	6	2	0	2	0	2	0	1	0	2	0
Cavendish Square	1	0	1	0	2	0	2	0	1	6	1	0	2	0
Chancery Lane, Holborn	1	0	2	0	1	0	1	0	1	0	1	0	1	0
Charing Cross, the Statue ...	1	0	1	6	1	6	1	6	1	0	1	6	1	6
Cheapside, Wood Street	1	6	2	6	0	6	0	6	1	0	1	0	1	0
Chester Square, Pimlico	2	0	1	6	2	0	2	0	1	6	2	0	2	6
Christ's Hospital...............	1	6	2	0	1	0	1	0	1	0	1	0	1	0
Clerkenwell Green..............	1	0	2	0	1	0	1	0	1	0	1	6	1	0
Corn Exchange	2	0	2	6	0	6	0	6	1	0	1	6	1	0
Commercial Docks. Plough Br.	3	0	4	0	1	6	2	0	2	0	3	0	2	6
Covent Garden Theatre	1	0	1	6	1	6	1	6	0	6	1	0	1	6
Cremorne Gardens..........	2	6	2	6	2	6	3	0	2	0	3	0	3	6
Custom House....................	2	0	2	6	0	6	0	6	1	0	1	6	1	0

Many users of cabs were visitors to London, either on business or for leisure. For the convenience of their customers, Parkins and Gotto, wholesale and retail paper and envelope makers, printed a list of cab fares in their annual almanac and price list. The example shown dates from 1860

boons of earlier years, such as the Fisheries Exhibition of 1883, the Inventions Exhibition of 1885 and the Golden Jubilee of 1887, brought little relief.[19]

The complexities of the fare tariff, which included fares by time as well as fares by distance, coupled with the extra charges which might be made for additional passengers and luggage, makes it almost impossible to calculate with any real degree of accuracy how far a cab might have to travel in order to cover the hire charge, and before the driver started to earn anything for himself. The distance would have been considerable, however. With a fare tariff of 1*s* for the first two miles and 6*d* for each mile or part of a mile thereafter, a driver might have to travel for around 24 miles in the low season or 36 miles at the height of the season simply to pay the proprietor. To this would have to be added the 'dead' mileage between the yard and the places where passengers might be expected, together with the unremunerative mileage returning empty to a stand or crawling in search of fares.

Fixing the price at which a cab was to be let inevitably became a matter of strain, and led to periodic industrial strife. Strikes in 1882 and 1891 forced masters to reduce their prices temporarily. On 15 May 1894 a mass meeting of cabmen was held at the

Cab stock – both horses and vehicles – was regularly auctioned through one of the great London repositories, such as Rymill's in the Barbican and Aldridge's in St Martin's Lane, shown in these engravings from the *Illustrated London News*, 1883

Novelty Theatre, where a strike resolution was carried. By 17 May the union claimed that some 7,000 cabs were lying idle, while 4,000 (whose owners had agreed to the men's demands, or which were operated by owner-drivers) were running with the union's permit. The men's demand was for a maximum price of 15s and a minimum price of 13s, with the abolition of all yard money, currently running at between 1s and 3s a day.[20] 'Yard money' consisted of miscellaneous stable charges which the cab driver was expected to pay in addition to the price of his cab. He would have to pay for some items, such as nosebags and mats, which were liable to wear and loss. He might also be required to pay for certain breakages, such as those to window glass. There was an element, known as 'box money', which was used to pay court fines. The most contentious payment, however, was that to the yardmen, who were employed as horse-keepers and cab washers. Their payment was shared between the proprietors and the men. The drivers' contribution was effectively a tip, reflecting the ability of the yardman to affect the driver's earning potential through his control of the cleanliness of the cab, and the health and well-being of the horse. Yard money was such a cause of friction that several proprietors, including the London Improved Cab Company and Thomas Tilling, tried to stamp the practice out altogether.[21]

The strike dragged on for three weeks before masters and men called on the Secretary of State to mediate. Asquith (in what was an unprecedented action for a Home Secretary) agreed, although he was clearly not without misgivings. The issues were complicated, and there was little prospect of pleasing everybody, especially as the facts were hard to ascertain. 'Cab masters', claimed Alfred Mills, Secretary of the United Cab Proprietors' Protection Association, 'have not much time to keep an elaborate set of books.' The drivers tended to exaggerate the profits of the owners, who for their part tended to overestimate the men's earnings in fares and tips.

Settlement was eventually reached on 11 June, when a seasonal scale of hiring charges was fixed, to run until April 1895; but the charges proved difficult to apply and impossible to enforce. The Asquith Award may have given the horse cab trade a few years of comparative peace at a time when internal conflict was no longer to be viewed with equanimity. Motor cabs began to appear in 1903, in which year the union leader, Sam Michaels, viewed the trade with pessimism:

We recognise [the horse cab business] as a dying trade; we stand in the position of the physician anxious to sustain life in a valuable patient; nothing could be worse than a strike, and if the masters force it upon us it will mean throwing a bucket of cold water over our patient and killing him.[22]

Chapter Six

IMPROVED CABS AND LORDLY CABMEN

The hansom cab, as improved by John Chapman, proved to be a design classic. In the eighty years before it was introduced, hackney carriages had been transformed many times. The lumbering hackney coach faced the competition of the lighter chariot, while both joined battle with the cab, a vehicle which went through a number of forms before Hansom and Chapman together revolutionized it. Yet, eighty years later, when the horse cab was in its death throes, it would take a practised eye to distinguish the hansom of that day from its predecessors. Admittedly, what the eye might not see the ear would have heard, for by that time most hansoms had exchanged their steel rims for rubber tyres.

The growler proved to be even more resistant to change. In 1873 the Metropolitan Police Commissioner observed that 'The four-wheeled cab, for its special uses, appears to be incapable of improvement, except as regards fitting and condition.' Growlers, which did much railway work involving the carriage of heavy luggage, were required to carry much heavier loads than hansoms. The problem for coachbuilders was to combine strength with lightness. They found that draught was lighter the closer fore and hind wheels were placed together, hence the somewhat limited knee room inside the vehicle. There were several unsuccessful experiments, such as a cab with a fixed front and a dropping leather hood at the rear. Passengers had liked such vehicles, but they carried insufficient luggage, and drivers could not make them pay. In 1885 the *Daily Telegraph* was quite scathing:

> The four-wheel cab, as we at present know it, is a type of stagnation in a world of activity; indeed, it is an emblem of decline in an age of almost universal progress. While all else in the vehicular world has improved with the rolling years, the London 'growler' has alone retrograded.[1]

Efforts were made to improve cabs. Carriages as a whole proved a prolific field for inventive activity, ranking fifth out of ninety-seven categories of patent issued between 1750 and 1851.[2] Improvements to the cab could take two forms: changes in design, and general improvement of the quality of construction or fittings. Most improvements took the latter form, such as the introduction of the rubber-tyred wheel,

The New Patent Curricle Tribus appeared in the *Illustrated London News* in October 1848, and was one of those short-lived, improved cabs which *Punch* described as having their portraits taken before they die

but there were a number of attempts to alter the basic form. Of the many examples, two must suffice here. The first was the 'Tribus', patented by a Westminster coachbuilder named Harvey and introduced in 1844. The 'Tribus' carried three passengers and was entered from behind. This arrangement harked back to the Boulnois cab of the 1830s ('the Bilkers' Cab') but had the merit that the driver was placed at the rear and thus had control over the entrance, and exit, of the passengers. A successor to this cab, 'Harvey's Patent Curricle Tribus', was featured in the *Illustrated London News*, but an interesting response from *Punch* warns us that such 'improved' vehicles could be ephemeral in the extreme, and might not exist beyond a demonstration model:

> [Improved cabs] appear in the *Illustrated News*, but are never carried out. They run through all the coffee-houses in the world inside its columns, and then, as if their journey was completed, they suddenly pull up, go home, and you never see anything more of them. They only come out to go in again. The poor things have their portraits taken, and then die.[3]

Such a fate awaited a cab designed by Joseph Parlour, and first exhibited by the Bideford coachbuilding firm of John Abbot at the 1885 Inventions Exhibition. This was a four-seated, two-wheeled cab with sliding doors at the rear. It was described by *The Times* as 'most comfortable and convenient . . . [and] a substantial improvement upon the hansom', and was licensed by the Metropolitan Police as a hackney carriage. But like other exotic types it did not catch on.[4]

The second avenue to improvement was to concentrate on the general quality of construction and fitting out. It was in this direction that the government pushed for reform. From 31 December 1869, the weekly duty on cabs was abolished, the intention of the Home Office being that some of this saving of between £15 and £19 a year should be passed on to the public in the form of better cabs. As a further nudge in that direction, the police inspection of vehicles was tightened up, and new regulations came into force on 1 January 1870, imposing strict standards of construction. Finally, the Metropolitan Public Carriages Act of 1869 allowed proprietors to fix their own rates of fare, which were to be specified on the licence and prominently displayed on the cab. It was hoped that cab owners would provide superior cabs at a higher fare, but results were disappointing, and in March 1871 the flexible fare scheme was abandoned, having failed to meet its objective.[5]

The problem was that a cab is the most anonymous of vehicles. The chances of a would-be passenger finding a particular cab are remote in the extreme, and the cab driver has little opportunity of nurturing a regular clientèle. Unlike the jobmaster who hired cabs by the hour or the day from a yard, the cab proprietor plying for hire on the streets had no chance of building up a marketable goodwill. As today, most passengers – business passengers especially – wanted to find a cab quickly, and their main consideration was speed of journey. They were not likely to spend time on the slim chance of finding a cab of superior quality, especially if the improvements were matters of internal comfort that could not be seen from the outside (particularly if the vehicle was moving). If they looked at anything, it was more likely to be the horse, the principal determinant of speed. Where comfort was at a premium, and especially when the need for a vehicle could be ascertained in advance – as in the case of ladies planning shopping expeditions, or people needing a cab for the theatre – recourse was more likely to be made to a jobmaster. Improved cabs which did not succeed as hackney carriages might enjoy success as jobmasters' vehicles, or as private vehicles purchased by professional men, such as doctors. Elegance in cab design usually meant lightness, and a light cab could stand up less well to the rigours of public use. Furthermore, rents in London were so high that most cabs were kept in the open, rather than under cover in a coach-house. The weather soon led to their deterioration, which would have been a further disincentive to introduce a fancy vehicle.[6]

All in all, it did not pay the cab proprietor to run a particularly elegant cab. His improved needle in the general haystack just would not be looked for. The return to the small proprietor on his additional outlay was therefore likely to be limited. The driver might gain, for while a passenger was unlikely to seek out an improved cab, he was quite likely to give a larger tip to the driver of such a cab if he chanced upon one. If the proprietor was also the driver, these earnings would accrue to him; otherwise his only hope was to try to impose a higher price on his men, not always an easy thing to do.

The view was sometimes put forward that joint-stock enterprise might succeed where private capital failed. A leader in *The Times* in January 1870 took the line that the public wanted improved cabs, and declared that 'We cannot suppose that in these days of keen competition and speculative enterprise the demand, once generally felt and recognised, will long exist without creating the supply.' Records survive of at least twenty attempts to form cab companies in London between 1846 and 1871. Most companies aimed to provide cheap cabs with civil drivers, and offered the impossible dream of better cabs at lower fares. The Six Days Cab Company proposed in addition 'to afford their servants the opportunity of moral and religious instruction, by entirely abolishing all SUNDAY WORK'. None of these companies survived for more than a year or two.[7]

The tide began to turn in the mid-1870s. The initiative again came from the Midlands – in this case, from Wolverhampton, the home of the coachbuilding firm of Frederick Forder. Unlike earlier improved cabs which had no permanent impact on the trade, the Forder-style hansom was to sweep all others from the streets, with the result that by 1890 the design was described as ubiquitous. The change of fashion which Forder introduced had, in less than two decades, rendered every earlier hansom virtually valueless.[8]

The Forder fortunes rose rapidly following the firm's foundation in 1864. In 1868, the Society of Arts offered gold and silver medals for improved cabs, but the response was disappointing. In 1872 they revived the idea but substituted cash prizes. The work which led to Forder's crucial patent (No. 3563, of November 1873) seems to have been done in response to this competition, for the defects which competitors were challenged to remedy were precisely those which it addressed: 'want of room, the difficulty of getting in and out, by reason of interference of large wheels, and the want of ventilation when the windows are closed'. Forder first extended the body in width and depth over the axles. He then angled the doors towards the middle, which gave greater leg room. When opened, they folded against the wheels, thus shielding the passengers from mud when they entered or alighted. Louvres at the front allowed a free flow of air, even when the windows were shut, and a smoother ride was given by a novel arrangement of the springs, to which the body was attached, not by metal shackles but by leather 'robins' or links.

Sixteen firms competed for the prize, but when judgment was given an outright winner could not be found, and the prize money was therefore shared equally between four coachbuilders: two from London, Thorn from Norwich, and Forder. Royal

An advertisement in the *Hackney Carriage Guardian* for 'The Genuine Forder' is indicative of the problems which the original builders had in protecting their patent

patronage secured Forder's advancement, for the Prince of Wales ordered an improved hansom cab for his private use. Shortly afterwards the firm became his warrant holders, the cab being known from then on as the Patent Royal Hansom. Forder received a medal at the London International Exhibition in 1873, a special gold medal at Manchester in 1874, and first prize in the Manchester Cab Competition of 1875. In that same year the firm won first prize for hansom cabs in the even more prestigious Cab Show at Alexandra Palace. Three of the four main prizewinners were provincial. Forder and Thorn won first and second prizes respectively in the hansom cab class, and John Marston of Birmingham won first prize for four-wheelers. However, *The Times* reported that the Alexandra Palace exhibition failed to gain the support of the large cab proprietors, 'who have a great stock of cabs, and do not wish to assist in anything which may help to render that stock useless to them'.[9]

The early 1880s witnessed a revival of speculative interest in the cab trade reminiscent of the 1820s, when gentleman-adventurers attempted to rule the trade. Cabmen's journals, such as *The Centaur* and the *Hackney Carriage Guardian*, frequently complained about the new intruders. In January 1884 *The Centaur* wrote that 'this craze among Lords to be Costers and Cabmen is past my comprehension'. In fact, the influx of the blue-bloods is not incomprehensible. Their motives were clear, though not always identical. Some saw genuine commercial opportunities in providing the travelling public with a superior vehicle and an improved service; others needed to make a living in the one area where they had knowledge and skill – namely horses. Yet others saw opportunities to look after the pence of personal expenses while their pounds were being staked at the gaming tables.

The timing is significant. The reorganization of the regiments of the line in 1881 saw many army officers pensioned off. At the same time the agricultural depression pressed heavily on the aristocracy, as prices fell and rents were difficult to sustain. Thirdly, the appearance of the Forder cab appeared to render the time ripe for the introduction of a better class of vehicle.

The pioneer of this patrician interest in the cab trade was the London General Cab Company, which was incorporated in 1875. The first company secretary and general manager was Major General Charles Louis, former Colonel Commandant of the Royal Marines. Louis had just left the army after serving nearly forty years, and having been severely wounded in the Crimean War 'by the explosion of an infernal machine'. A list of shareholders in 1880 shows them to have been small in number but select in character. They were also young. Sydney Buxton (later Earl Buxton and Governor-General of South Africa) was the largest shareholder and was aged twenty-six. The earls of Pembroke and Milltown were thirty and forty-four respectively. Sir David Salomons, the future motoring pioneer, was twenty-nine. The Honourable William Lowther, MP, was a grand old man of fifty-eight but his nephew, the Earl of Lonsdale (a cab proprietor in his own right), was only twenty-three.

Within a couple of years the company had a fleet of eighty-five cabs, and took on a professional manager; but the aim of operating superior cabs proved impossible to sustain, even though it apparently enjoyed the privilege of the Great Northern Railway. The company rapidly lost over £12,000 but, by exerting the strictest economies, just about managed to break even by 1884. That seems to have been the peak of its success, for it went into voluntary liquidation three years later.[10]

The Chelsea Cab Company and the Leinster Cab Company were no more successful. The Chelsea was incorporated in 1882 in order to take over the cab business which had been run from Albert Yard, Kensington, by Captain Livingston Thompson, late of the 11th (Prince Albert's Own) Hussars. Thompson was a partner of Frederick Forder, and operated ten of his improved cabs. In order to expand the business, Thompson sold his interest to the Chelsea Cab Company in 1882. With the exception of Forder, all of the subscribers to the company were military men, and included (apart from Thompson) Lt.-Col. Alan Gardner, late of the 14th Hussars, and former ADC to the Lord Lieutenant of Ireland, together with three other former cavalry officers. The company's debts soon mounted, however, and in 1884 it went into liquidation.[11]

The same fate befell the Leinster Cab Company, the offspring of Lt.-Col. William Brind of the 103rd Foot (Royal Bombay Fusiliers); Major Ponsonby Shaw of the 95th (Derbyshire) Regiment; and Colonel Granville William Paget. Brind had started his service career with the Navy. He had been wounded in the Crimea, and took part in boat engagements in China in 1857. Transferring to the Indian Army, he saw action in the Indian Mutiny, and again in the China War of 1860. On his retirement from the army in 1881, he set up with Paget as a cab proprietor, running a fleet of eighteen Forder cabs with a stable of forty-five horses. It soon ran into trouble. The stock was sold off in January 1884 (the quality of the horses being indicated by the extraordinarily high prices which they fetched) and the yard was taken over by Lord Shrewsbury.[12]

The regular hackney cab proprietors claimed that impecunious army officers and aristocrats were beguiled into the trade by exaggerated ideas about its profitability. This they allegedly picked up from conversations with cab drivers who, knowing nothing of the overheads involved, spoke glowingly of the amount of money they took in a day. Expenses were inevitably higher if the proprietor planned, as the newcomers did, to run cabs that were a cut above the ordinary. Superior cabs had to be worked by superior horses and driven by superior drivers, and they required superior maintenance. But they could not charge a superior fare once that short-lived experiment had been abandoned in 1871 as impractical. Only a very large fleet of such cabs could fight off the competition, but this dream, shared by several cab companies, proved impossible to realize.

Some gentleman proprietors were prompted by other motives, notably the prospect that they could offset their own costs as prolific cab users by purchasing a well-appointed cab or two and setting them to ply for hire when they were not using them. This was the aim of, among others, Viscount Mandeville; Hugh Lowther, later fifth Earl of Lonsdale (once described as 'almost an Emperor but not quite a gentleman'); and Sir John Dugdale Astley, Bart. Viscount Mandeville, who succeeded to the title of Duke of Manchester in 1890, was born in 1853. Between 1877 and 1879 he purchased a number of cabs which he licensed in the name of his driver, who was allowed to ply with them when he did not require them for his own use. He was bankrupted in 1889. Hugh Lowther, four years his senior, was almost reduced to that state. He had a passion for horses and, when he became fifth Earl of Lonsdale at the age of twenty-five, it was said of him that he 'started collecting horses like a schoolboy collects postage stamps'. Although it was claimed that he had started the craze, his cab operations are the least clear of all, although his charitable patronage of the trade was well publicized. More is known of Sir James Dugdale Astley. He was of an older generation (having been born in 1828) but had many of the characteristics of the perpetual youth. Not for nothing was he generally known by his nickname of 'The Mate', for he was a great sportsman and gambler, an athlete and manager of athletes, and an inveterate racing man. When Astley started running cabs in the early 1880s, he gave his driver 25*s* a week in standing wages, and received from him 10*s* a day when the cabs plied for hire. He claimed that 'with . . . three nags I could work both cabs well, and my riding cost me comparatively little'. His so-called 'nags' were in fact his less successful racehorses. Therein lay his downfall, for racehorses and hansom cabs do not mix. In 1884 one of his thoroughbred 'nags', in harness to a hansom, mistook Piccadilly for Epsom Downs. It bolted, and knocked down a vanman, seriously injuring him. Astley had damages of £125 awarded against him, and promptly gave up the business.[13]

Many of the aristocratic cab proprietors were members of The Pelican Club, a drinking and gaming den in Gerrard Street (of which Astley was first chairman) that attracted most of the larger-than-life members of the sporting aristocracy. The membership has been described as 'a body of rumbustious young men who, apart from

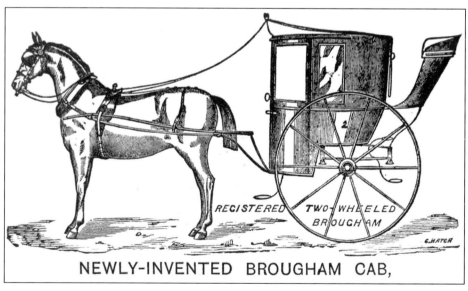

NEWLY-INVENTED BROUGHAM CAB,

Hayes & Son was a prominent firm of coachbuilders, based in Stamford and Peterborough. The 'Newly-Invented Brougham Cab' was illustrated in a catalogue of *c.* 1880. The lightness of the vehicle made it unsuitable for public carriage use, but it was described as 'exceedingly well-adapted for the purpose and use of Medical Practitioners'

shared high spirits and *joie de vivre*, also had in common a chronic condition of lack of ready money'.[14] No one fits this description better than George William Thomas Brudenell-Bruce, Viscount Savernake and 4th Marquess of Ailesbury.

In 1884, shortly after he started up horse cabs, Savernake married the actress Dolly Tester. That he should be one of the first aristocrats to make such a liaison in the late nineteenth century is entirely characteristic. *Vanity Fair* spoke of his launching 'into a career of irregularity of all kinds'. In addition,

> His habits, his associates, his dress, and his deportment became the astonishment and horror of the society to which by birth he belonged, but which he had shaken off; and he, whose ancestors had refused dukedoms, adopted himself into the people whom the smart term common, and gave himself up to horse-racing, boxing, cock-fighting, ratting, and all the sports that pharisees do most condemn.

His biographer claimed that 'He would bet on anything', and by the age of twenty-one he had amassed debts in the region of £175,000. A cousin claimed that 'He chose deliberately to mix with blackguards, having found that in that class alone was he treated with deference.'[15]

While not for one moment suggesting that it was the mouthpiece of blackguards (although the general public might regard it as such), it has to be noted that the cab trade press dealt less harshly with Savernake than with other aristocratic proprietors. This may have been because, alone among the four, he appears to have seen cabs less as playthings, and made a serious attempt to run a cab yard. Savernake (then aged twenty-one) commenced running Forder cabs early in 1884, operating out of the Harp Yard, Kendall's Mews, Marylebone. The *Daily Telegraph* spoke approvingly of him, describing his hansoms as 'not only admirably appointed, but excellently horsed and skilfully driven'. It continued:

> [T]here is no reason in the nature of things why a young man of honestly horsey tastes should not learn to take as much pleasure in the personal management of a cab-yard as in looking on, perhaps helplessly, at another man's management of his training stable. Moreover, if he must keep horses, it is certainly much to be preferred that he should keep them for the benefit of the large and mostly respectable public who use hansoms, than that of the smaller and very 'mixed' class of persons who make their living by the turf.[16]

The attitude of the *Hackney Carriage Guardian*, which regarded the mass of aristocratic operators as 'titled sharks', was patronizing rather than aggressive towards Savernake:

Now, although we are by no means pleased to see members of the aristocracy dabbling in cabs and horses, knowing from experience that it invariably means loss to all parties concerned, there is one redeeming point in connection with Lord Savernake. We believe from the accounts reaching us, that he supplies his cabs to the drivers at a reasonable price per day, and while that is done we have perhaps no right to object to him losing a few hundreds or thousands of pounds in the cab trade.[17]

Tempting as it is to see these men as a throwback to the early days of cab operation when the trade was a gentlemanly preserve, motivation would seem to be different. In the early, monopoly days there were large sums to be earned, but it cannot be supposed that the likes of Mandeville, Lowther, Astley and Savernake expected to make a fortune, or even much of a profit. They were generally young, raffish and hard up. A well-turned-out hansom cab would have appealed to their sense of dash, and, if they could offset some of the cost, so much the better. They cannot have been a serious threat to the cab trade, although publicity given to their superior vehicles may have jolted the complacency of the regular proprietors. There was one aristocrat, however, whose threat was of an altogether different magnitude. This was Charles Henry John Chetwynd-Talbot, 20th Earl of Shrewsbury.

In many ways, Shrewsbury was like the others. He was in his twenties, he liked to gamble and he was fond of horses. *Vanity Fair* observed that he had 'some of the finest animals to be bought for love, money or credit'. It was claimed of him that he had been 'to all intents and purposes born in a manger', and he was considered by many to be the best whip in England. Unlike the others he had already succeeded to his title at the time that he started cabs. And unlike the others, he did not dabble. He took to the cab business – and later to the motor car business (he was the Talbot half of Clément-Talbot) – in a very serious way.[18]

Shrewsbury started up two cabs round about 1882, the year that he married. How fast he built up his fleet is not clear, but it is significant that by January 1884 he was receiving considerable publicity in the press on account of some of his cabs being fitted with solid, india-rubber tyres. He saw the potential of fitting rubber tyres to improved Forder cabs, and it was this combination that was to rock the trade. The rubber tyre changed the economics of operating improved cabs. It offered a more comfortable ride, and the public could immediately identify a cab so fitted – by sound as much as by sight. Furthermore, unlike other improvements which added little, if anything, to the life of a cab, rubber tyres (by reducing vibration) made a considerable difference, both to the wheels and to the body. In 1888 it was estimated that rubber tyres made wheels last three times as long. Wear was a problem. In the early years a pair of tyres might only last about four-and-a-half months. By 1894 they might be expected to last six or seven.[19]

The List of Applications for Shares will close on Monday next at 4 p.m.

As evidence of the profits to be obtained from a well managed Cab Building Company, FORDER and COMPANY, LIMITED, has just announced its intention of paying a Dividend of 10 per cent., besides carrying forward an additional 3 per cent.

THE "VICTORIA-HANSOM" CAB COMPANY,
LIMITED.
(Incorporated under the Companies' Act 1862 to 1883.)

"It is certainly a remarkable vehicle. Closed, it is a Hansom; open, a Victoria; at once useful, light of draught, beautifully upholstered, with India-rubber tyres and C springs. Londoners should hail such a vehicle with joy."—*Pall Mall Gazette.*

CAPITAL £100,000 in £1 SHARES.
PAYABLE
2s. per Share on Application,   3s. per Share on Allotment.

3s. per Share on the 2nd April, 1887, and the Balance by Calls as required, at intervals of not less than two months.
Shareholders desiring to pay up in full on allotment have the option of doing so, and will receive interest at the rate of 4 per cent. per annum on calls paid in advance.

DIRECTORS.
J. FORTESCUE HARRISON Esq., J.P. (Director of the Provident Life Office), 41, Ovington Square, S.W., *Chairman.*
ERNEST S. INMAN, Esq. (Director of the International Marine Insurance Company, and late Manager of the Inman Steamship Co.).
MAJOR-GENERAL V. GILBERT, C.B., 6, Baron's-Court Road, S.W.
COL. F. CORNWALLIS MAUDE, C.B., V.C., Gatton House, East Bergholt, and 5, Park Place, St. James', S.W.
WYNDHAM PORTMAN, Esq., Allipore House, Sutton, Surrey.
LIEUT-COL. CHARLES E. W. ROWORTH, Gloucester Villa, Croydon.
J. CORRY FELL, Esq., M. Inst., M.E. (Messrs. J. C. Fell and Co., Manufacturing Engineers), 1, Queen Victoria Street, London, E.C.

The 'Victoria-Hansom' Cab Company was incorporated in 1887 with the intention of exploiting the patent for an improved hansom that was capable of conversion to an open carriage. 'Londoners should hail such a vehicle with joy', the *Pall Mall Gazette* is quoted as saying. But they did not, and the company was wound up in 1888

In January 1884 Shrewsbury transferred his business to the Earl Street, Westminster, premises formerly occupied by the Leinster Cab Company, and by the middle of the year he was running thirty-one cabs. Profits were around £140 a week. Two years later he sold off his stock to the Star Cab Company Ltd, in preparation, it was alleged, for putting a fleet of one hundred improved hansoms and a few four-wheelers onto the streets, and to establish a fresh stable of 250 horses, many of which he would personally break. This expansion certainly took place, for in June 1888 Shrewsbury sold his business – including 134 cabs and 325 horses – to a new company for the sum of £55,000, of which £35,000 was in cash. The Shrewsbury and Talbot **ST** Cab and Noiseless Tyre Company was set up to acquire rubber tyre patents and to give Shrewsbury monopoly control over their use on cabs.[20]

The Earl of Shrewsbury was approaching the peak of his business optimism, reached later in that same year when, in association with Forder Brothers, he promoted the Compagnie Générale des Hansom Cabs à Paris. But Parisians never took to the hansom, and remained wedded to their *fiacre*. Tristram observed that 'In the City of Civilization Shrewsburys were put to shame'. The company went into voluntary liquidation in just over a year-and-a-half.[21]

He had greater success with his London company, although it became apparent that one half of this hybrid venture would be more successful than the other. The cab side did not come to much. At the annual meetings of 1889 and 1890 the misfortunes of the business were ascribed partly to a loss of horses from disease, but this was nothing like the whole story. At one time Shrewsbury's turn-outs had been considered the smartest; now they were among the shabbiest. This may have contributed to the labour troubles with which he was plagued. When he had commenced business, drivers were prepared to pay a higher rate for their cabs because of the increased number of fares they expected to take. But with cabs that had failed to maintain their original standard, and with increased competition from other improved cabs, they demanded a reduction in the price. There was a serious dispute in the early summer of 1891. Shrewsbury, in what seems to have been a characteristically impulsive gesture, put all his horses up for sale. There was a suspicion in the trade that he had bought some back in, and had sent them out to grass, but the action, according to the financial journal, *The Lighthouse*, had left the company like the proverbial ship without a rudder. Only the noiseless tyre side of the business had yielded profitable results, bringing in more than £8,000 in the financial year to 1892. Shrewsbury successfully defended the company's patents, but could not fend off competition altogether as other manufacturers took out their own patents and entered the market. In 1900 the assets and goodwill of the company, together with those of the Challiner and Willoughby Carriage Tyre Company, were sold to a new company, the Shrewsbury **ST** and Challiner Tyre Company Ltd, which had some success with motor tyres and was eventually bought out by Dunlop in 1926.[22]

Judged merely by its ability to survive as long as it did, Shrewsbury's venture would have to be regarded as one of the more successful cab companies. They were precarious ventures, firstly because they were at the mercy of their drivers. Secondly, cab, omnibus and tramway companies were in ill repute with investors for it was alleged that in no class of undertaking had there been more swindling in the promotion. *The Lighthouse* claimed in 1888 that the public were 'fighting shy of such securities'. The *Hackney Carriage Guardian* was equally dismissive: 'Taking cab companies on the whole, it cannot be denied that such enterprises have ever been a disastrous failure.' It argued that top-heavy administration together with the weight of excessive capital were the cause.[23]

At the end of the century, therefore, the cab trade was organized very much on the same basis as it had been in the 1830s, with approximately two-thirds of cabs owned

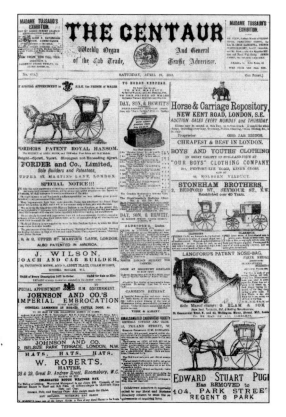

The Centaur appeared between 1879 and 1885, and was the mouthpiece of the Amalgamated Cabdrivers' Society. Its advertisements show how quickly other manufacturers adopted the improvements introduced by Forder

by owner-drivers, and most of the remainder in the hands of small proprietors. The basic design of vehicles remained the same, but cab stock generally had been transformed, especially by the spread of the india-rubber tyre. However, the success of such improved cabs had not led to the dominance of large concerns, partly because the patents upon which several companies hoped to base their fortune proved difficult to defend. This is not to say that cab builders did not see the potential that lay in the formation of large, corporate fleets; and the partnership between vehicle manufacturers and corporate cab operators was to continue into the motor era. That the majority of horse cab companies enjoyed little success was also due to the want of practical experience of the trade on the part of management. More than a knowledge of horses on military manoeuvres or the racetrack was needed to run a successful cab business. The fortunes of a cab operator lay very much in the hands of the drivers, and it was operators who had risen from these ranks who had their fingers more effectively on the pulse of the trade. Only Lord Shrewsbury showed any marked business acumen. He became at home with the motor car as he had been with the horse, carrying his family name of Talbot into motoring history.

Chapter Seven

THE POLICE AND THE CAB TRADE

To this day the cab trade of London is unique in that it is regulated directly by central Government. The department which originally had responsibility was the Treasury, working through the Hackney Coach Commissioners. From 1838 the Home Office gradually acquired control, and that department remained responsible until 1984, when regulation of taxis and hire cars passed to the Department of Transport.

The Home Office exercised its control through the Metropolitan Police, which still maintains a Public Carriage Office. However, police powers over hackney carriages were acquired only gradually, and the suspicion continued to be felt by many people – both inside and outside the force – that this was not 'real' police work. Consequently, the regulation of the cab trade by the Metropolitan Police throws light on the history of policing as well as the history of urban transportation.

The Metropolitan Police Act of 1839 added a range of public order functions to the role of the police, including the regulation of omnibus routes during divine service; street obstruction and nuisances; and furious driving. It is conceivable that, had the measure to license hackney and stage carriage drivers passed through Parliament a year or two later than it did, this function would have been taken on by the police at the outset. However, we have seen that the long-suffering Sir Matthew Wood eventually succeeded in getting a regulatory Act of Parliament passed in 1838, when there was no Bill before the House to widen police powers.

It thus happened that Wood's Act of 1838 invested the Home Secretary with the power to appoint an *ad hoc* official, the Registrar of Metropolitan Public Carriages, the post being given to Daniel Whittle Harvey, MP for Southwark. Harvey was a Radical politician and attorney who founded the *Sunday Times* in 1822. He had a long-standing battle with the Inner Temple, which refused to admit him to the bar because of alleged malpractice. Extravagant living placed him in financial difficulties, and he was therefore glad to accept the office of Registrar of Metropolitan Public Carriages, which seemed something of a sinecure. He remained in office for less than a year; for this man who attracted controversy like a magnet found himself again in difficulties as he was a paid officer of the crown while still a Member of Parliament. Within a year he gave up both the registrarship and his parliamentary seat, landing instead the office

LEFT
In a Hackney Coach,

ON WEDNESDAY AFTERNOON, 16th September,

That took up in BRIDGE STREET, BLACKFRIARS, and set down in West Smithfield,

A Lady's Black Silk Bag,

containing a £100 Bank Post Bill, a Purse and Money, Silver Knife, Smelling Bottle, Bracelets, and other small articles. Payment of the Bank Post Bill is stopped.

Whoever will bring the Bag and its Contents to Mr. CREASE, 53, West Smithfield, shall receive £5 REWARD.

Mrs. Davison, Printer, 37, Duke St. West Smithfield.

An undated handbill, c. 1835. James Crease & Son of 53 West Smithfield were colourmen in the 1820s and 1830s. A Lost Property Office was maintained by the Hackney Coach Commissioners, and later by the Metropolitan Police. Among articles lost, which the chief Commissioner reported in 1895, were '£700 in a banker's bag, an astronomical telescope, bicycles, a bantam cock, a cat, a canary in a cage, chairs, cylinders of compressed gas, dogs, electric batteries, foot-warmers, a horse's brain in spirits, opium, perambulators, rifles and guns, a sewing machine on stand, swords, stage properties, soldiers' kits, a suit of chain mail, various mail, various tools used by workmen &c. &.'

of first Commissioner of the City of London Police, which he held until his death in 1863. Harvey was succeeded as Registrar by Hensleigh Wedgwood, grandson of Josiah, the potter. He had been appointed a London police court magistrate in 1832, but resigned five years later when he decided that his religious convictions were inconsistent with the administration of oaths. As with Harvey, appointment as registrar was a welcome escape from financial difficulties, but both men took their responsibilities seriously and threw themselves into their work with gusto.[1]

Both Harvey and Wedgwood took an expansive view of the functions of the Registrar of Metropolitan Public Carriages, seeing the office as having regulatory as well as a purely licensing duties. The registrar was concerned with the licensing only of hackney and stage carriage drivers, conductors and watermen, and had no jurisdiction over proprietors, whose vehicle licences were issued by the Board of Stamps. Both men were aware of the difficulties to which this could lead, especially during the six years that the office was located in Princes Street, at a considerable distance from the Board of Stamps office in Somerset House. To seek redress from a driver, an aggrieved passenger had to prosecute the cab *owner*, necessitating tedious enquiries at two offices. Harvey attempted to use his own staff to do the legwork for complainants, and tried in vain to get the Metropolitan Public Carriage Office established as a court, where a magistrate could hear public carriage cases on stated days of the week.[2]

It was Hensleigh Wedgwood who noted a serious anomaly in the law relating to the appointment of cab standings, which was to lead to the first formal involvement of the Metropolitan Police with the London cab trade. He pointed out that Section 18 of the 1838 Act imposed a penalty on hackney carriages plying for hire 'elsewhere than from some Standing or Place appointed for that Purpose'. However, authority existed only for the appointment of standings in the City. Wedgwood may have had it in mind that he should be granted the power to establish standings outside that area, but the Home Office had other ideas.[3]

The ensuing London Hackney Carriages Act was a sloppy piece of legislation and a recipe for chaos. It confirmed the office of Registrar of Metropolitan Public Carriages, but confined his activities merely to licensing drivers, conductors and watermen. Perversely, it required the Commissioners of the Metropolitan Police to appoint cab standings, but gave them no disciplinary powers. With two authorities for hackney carriages, people did not know where to turn, although the registrar appears to have figured more in the public eye. Wedgwood (like Harvey before him) had an empire to build, and showed far greater interest in the trade, taking a far more proactive line.

The Commissioners did not relish the task of appointing cab stands, and soon found a reason for doing little, for the law appeared to deny them power to intervene in areas covered by Local Acts of Parliament, passed for the appointment of improvement commissioners. The whole of the Whitehall, Westminster, Finsbury and Lambeth police divisions were thus excluded, together with three-quarters of Camberwell and half of St Marylebone. Those parts which were not under Local Acts tended to be the less populous, outlying districts where standings were less needed. Richard Mayne, the commissioner most involved with hackney carriages, loathed his new responsibility. It was a task guaranteed to bring him into conflict with members of the middle class whose support he needed. Most cab users wanted a nearby cab stand – but not in their back yard. They wanted one tucked away in a neighbouring street; never in their own. A surviving outletter book of the Public Carriage Office from 1850–3 is full of complaining letters on the subject; and in many of his replies Mayne described how unpalatable his task was. In 1851, for example, he wrote that 'The appointment of the Standings was the most obnoxious job I have ever had to get through.'[4]

It is clear that two rival authorities for the cab trade could not coexist for long. Wedgwood's forwardness in repeatedly suggesting improvements to the administration of the cab service must have proved irksome to Mayne, and his tendency to build an

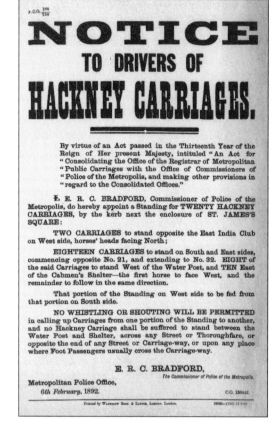

The Commissioner of the Metropolitan Police not only appointed standings, but had the power to decide how many cabs might stand there. The prevention of whistling and shouting was, no doubt, a vain hope. (PRO, Mepo 2/4817)

empire did not win favour with the Treasury, which was always searching for economies. In the three financial years ending in January 1850, income from licences averaged £2,460, while the expenses of the Metropolitan Public Carriage Office averaged £1,423, or 57.8 per cent of receipts. In January 1849 the Treasury therefore proposed that savings could be made by transferring the work of the registrar to the Metropolitan Police, and this was effected by the London Hackney Carriage Act (13 and 14 Vict. c7) of 1850.[5]

Mayne took up his new duties on 5 April, and soon found that they were more arduous than he had bargained for. By February 1851 he was complaining that he had not anticipated such a burden and that he 'would gladly be relieved from the office'. He had expected that, once the annual renewal of licences in June had been completed, the work would die down; but he found that applications continued to be numerous. He may have exaggerated the volume of work, for he was angling for a salary increase (which he received), but he justified this by pointing out how the Exchequer was benefiting from the new regime. He claimed that the expense of the registrar's office was saved, and that receipts were increased. He offered two explanations: more effective administration prevented frauds, while persons in outlying parts of the Metropolitan Police District had, for the first time, been made to take out licences.[6]

In fact, the income from the licence duty on public carriages was 30 per cent higher than it had been in the previous year, although Mayne could not claim all the credit for this. Of far greater significance was the Great Exhibition, which inevitably led to an increase in the number of omnibuses and cabs placed upon the streets. There was much concern that unsuspecting visitors to London would be exploited by unscrupulous cab drivers. The public, it was said, lacked adequate safeguards, for 'the most notorious ruffians within the ken of the detective force, madly tooling their dog horses in rickety and leaky vehicles, and respectable men driving good animals in decent carriages, take up their places on "the rank" on nearly equal terms'. The police made a determined effort to weed out undesirables, and the licences were suspended of eight hundred cabdrivers who were brothel keepers, notorious drunkards or 'otherwise improper persons to be intrusted [sic] with the public service'.[7]

From the latter half of 1851 there were demands for a reduction of fares from 8*d* to 6*d* a mile. Faced with over-capacity when the Crystal Palace closed, omnibus proprietors slashed their fares. Cab fares held up, however, and when one proprietor, W. Thompson, advertised cabs at 6*d* a mile he was obliged to withdraw them after he had received threats, insults and anonymous letters. *The Times* fulminated against 'dark influence' in the cab trade, which had 'invariably interposed and driven us back to the hard bargains of monopoly and combination'.[8]

By the beginning of 1853 the view seems to have been accepted that the wings of the cab trade needed to be clipped, and in April, Henry Fitzroy, the Under-secretary of State at the Home Office, introduced a Bill which the *Illustrated London News* proclaimed would herald '[a] New Revolution in Cabs'. Fitzroy, the paper boasted, was 'the first to mount this English barricade, which had driven back with fear so many stout legislative hearts'. It went on, 'The tyranny of Cabdom is no longer to exist! . . . . Never was a tyranny more hated, and yet more patiently submitted to! A cabman was supposed to be the servant of the public, and yet he was everyone's master.' Such hyperbole might be considered mere cabman-baiting, of a very familiar type. But it does seem to convey a spirit of vengeance against cabmen; and vengeful legislation is never good legislation. For the first time cabs would be brought under strict control by the Metropolitan Police, whose powers were to be greatly extended.[9]

Not only was the Bill flawed, the manner in which it was passed into law left the ensuing Act vulnerable when it came under pressure from the trade. The Bill proposed to reduce by 25 per cent the fares payable by distance (from 8*d* to 6*d* a mile). It also abolished 'back fare' – a provision of the 1831 London Hackney Carriage Act whereby cabs discharged beyond the limits of the metropolis, and unlikely to pick up a passenger on the way back, could charge a supplementary fare for their return journey. Yet these assaults upon the cabmen's pockets were made without any investigation of their true earnings, despite attempts to send the Bill to a select committee, where the matter could be investigated.

The Act (16 and 17 Vict c33) was intended to deliver the trade a short, sharp shock. Section 1 prohibited the Board of Inland Revenue (the successors to the Board of Stamps after 1849) from issuing a licence to a proprietor unless he could produce a certificate that the cab (or omnibus) had been inspected by the Commissioners of the Metropolitan Police and had been found in a fit and proper condition. Section 2 empowered the Commissioners to inspect a vehicle and its horse or horses at any time, and to suspend the licence if they were found unfit for public use. Section 4 reduced fares to 6*d* a mile and abolished back fare. Section 5 required the proprietor to display the legal fares both inside and outside the cab, and obliged the driver to carry an authorized book of fares and to produce it for the information of any person hiring the cab. Section 7 compelled a driver to drive his cab to any place required by the hirer up to 6 miles, or for a period of one hour. This section, coupled with the abolition of back

CABBY'S CABALISTICS.

A COLLECTION of cab tickets given under the New Act by some of the London Cabmen would be a curiosity of hieroglyphics which might puzzle the ingenuity of the ablest to decipher or elucidate. We beg to present the public with a *fac-simile* of the latest specimen we have received, and we shall be happy to give any reasonable reward to anybody who will furnish a key to the mystery.

Perhaps some members of the Cab Protection Society may charge us with injustice to the much abused and particularly abusive cab fraternity for having put forth only a one-sided view of the ticket, and to meet this accusation we give the other side, for the benefit of all who may be able to make anything out of it.

We can fancy some future LAYARD employed in a fruitless attempt to find the meaning of these inscriptions, or some remote GELL endeavouring to do for a Cab Ticket what his antiquarian ancestor succeeded in accomplishing with regard to Pompeii, the ruins of which enabled him to conjecture what the city was in its perfect condition.

Punch was hardly exaggerating when it pointed out the deficiencies of the provision of the 1853 Fitzroy Act that cab drivers were required to give the passenger a ticket. Not only were tickets frequently illegible, but some cabmen picked up the dropped tickets of their fellow-drivers and gave these out

fare, had the effect of obliging a driver to travel 6 miles beyond the limits of the metropolis, if called upon to do so, with little chance of securing a return fare. Section 8 required the driver, on each hiring, to deliver a ticket to the hirer with the number of his cab printed thereon. This proved quite unworkable, and soon fell into abeyance. Passengers tended to throw the tickets away, and they were often picked up and used by other cabmen, with the result that summonses frequently failed because they were taken out against the wrong proprietor. Under Sections 12 and 13 the Commissioners of Police were to appoint hackney carriage attendants to take the place of watermen at cab standings. This was a thinly disguised attempt to establish quasi-constables at the standings under the control of the police authorities. In case of dispute, Section 18 enabled a hirer to require a driver to proceed to the nearest magistrate's court or police station to allow the matter to be decided without the necessity of a summons being taken out. The section did not afford the same right to the driver. All told, the Fitzroy Act was a tough measure. But tough measures do not always work in practice.

The Act immediately ran into troubled waters. On 20 July *The Times* reported a case heard the previous day at Bow Street. A Mr Bond, residing in Fulham, was in dispute with a cab driver named Phillips over a fare from his home to the Strand. Because of traffic stoppages, Phillips had been obliged to take a more roundabout route than usual (the reasonableness of which the passenger did not deny); but Bond was adamant that the journey was no longer than 3 miles, while Phillips insisted that it was more than 4, and attempted to charge accordingly. When Bond refused to pay, Phillips suggested that he should drive Bond to Bow Street, where, under Section 18 of the Act, the question could be immediately settled. That the driver made this suggestion is indicative of his confidence in his own judgment of distance. However, things did not turn out as he had anticipated. Mr Henry, the magistrate, lacking the official book of distances which had not yet been published, offered to have the distance measured if each party would pay 5s into court. This Bond was prepared to do, but Phillips, who claimed that this was his first job of the day, had no money with which to pay. As a result, Henry was reported as saying that he would take Bond's word as to the distance, and sentenced Phillips to a fine of 40s, or one month in prison. Bond was taken aback by both the suddenness and the severity of the sentence and asked Henry to reconsider, for the cabman had at no time been uncivil. Henry refused to listen. 'The object of the act,' he said, 'in enabling passengers to go at once to the police court was not to dispense with the penalties, but to save the complainants the trouble of applying for a summons.' Phillips was packed off to gaol.

The severity of the sentence shocked the public. On the day following the report, a letter in *The Times* spoke of 'the manifest injustice and hardship of the decision,' and argued that, 'If such decisions as these are to prevail, we shall soon have to complain of a scarcity of public conveyances in our streets.' This was a correct reading of the situation, in that a lock-out of cabs occurred within a week. The Phillips case was promptly taken up in the House of Commons, where John Bright likened it to one that 'might have happened in Russia or Turkey'. Public concern refused to abate, despite attempts by Henry and by Palmerston, the Home Secretary, to suggest that it had been misreported. Phillips wrote to *The Times* on 23 July, to say that, his fine having been paid by friends, he had been released from prison. He had the disputed distance independently measured, and this showed that, whereas Bond had held it to be no more than 3 miles, and he had claimed that it was over 4, it was in fact more than 7. He also petitioned the Treasury and the Home Secretary for redress, and when a police measurement showed the distance to be longer still, Palmerston had no option but to pay him compensation.[10]

By then the damage had been done. On Wednesday 27 July, with little or no warning, the cab proprietors withdrew their vehicles from the streets, plunging London into its first major cab strike. The attack mounted against the Act had the advantage of surprise, and also caught the government on the defensive. The failure to refer the Bill to a select committee weakened the government's position, especially as the Dublin Public Carriage Bill, currently passing through the House, had been more thoroughly debated, and also contained the right of appeal denied to the London cabmen. The threat of an omnibus strike, and disaffection over pay among both the Metropolitan and City Police placed the government under yet further pressure. It is not surprising that Fitzroy quickly offered concessions to the cabmen, although he was strongly criticized in some quarters for apparently giving in too soon.

The suddenness of the strike placed Fitzroy in an awkward position, for he had already been moving towards some sort of compromise, but now appeared to be caving in to pressure. On Monday 25 July he had received a deputation from the proprietors, and although he remained convinced that the 6*d* fare was viable and would not, therefore, be altered, he conceded that something might be offered in lieu of back fare. At their meeting two days later, the proprietors adopted a proposal that, for any distance beyond a radius of four miles from the General Post Office or other central point, 1*s* a mile should be paid. A clause to this effect (but substituting Charing Cross for the General Post Office) was added to a second Bill that very evening, as was one allowing 6*d* to be charged for each passenger over the number of two, which was another of the proprietors' demands. Thus, in less than twenty-four hours from the commencement of the strike the cab owners had secured two of their main points. They did not succeed in everything, however. The government stuck in its heels over the demand for a 1*s* minimum fare, while an amendment to allow a right of appeal (a point on which the cabmen felt strongly after the Phillips case) was voted out at the third reading. It was at that stage, too, that an anti-strike amendment was passed subjecting a proprietor to penalties if he withdrew a cab for two consecutive days without just cause.[11]

BEFORE   AND   AFTER.

"Vell, Summons me! I ain't a going to take Sixpence! You call yourself a Gentleman, I s'pose?"

"O! Don't Summons me, Sir! Consider my poor wife and children, there's a kind Gentleman."

The hope that the Fitzroy Act of 1853 would control cabmen once and for all was to prove illusory. From *Punch*, 30 July 1853

As an exercise in bringing the cabmen to heel, the legislation of 1853 proved a lamentable failure, but it is important in marking the point at which the Metropolitan Police acquired control over all aspects of the hackney carriage trade, although the actual issue of licences remained with the Inland Revenue department until 1869. The additional powers acquired by the police in 1853 were the appointment of hackney carriage attendants and the inspection of vehicles and horses. Watermen (the attendants at hackney carriage standings, charged with keeping order and supplying cabs and horses with water) had, since 1831, been the first group of hackney carriage workers to be licensed and obliged to wear a badge. In 1843 the duty of licensing watermen was transferred from the Board of Stamps to the Registrar of Metropolitan Public Carriages, who was also authorized to lay on water and standpipes, the water rate, however, being borne by the men. In 1850 these powers were transferred to the Commissioner of the Metropolitan Police. The watermen recouped the water rate by charging the drivers for water, and were also paid by the drivers for their services. In

1853 it was alleged that drivers were paying a sum of around £15,000. Consequently it was argued that the replacement of watermen by waged Hackney Carriage Attendants would compensate for the reduction of fares to 6d a mile.[12]

There was, however, another reason why the phasing out of watermen and their replacement by quasi-policemen (akin, in some respects, to traffic wardens in our own day) found favour in official circles. The responsibility of maintaining order at hackney carriage standings was mitigated by two factors. In the first place, the livelihood of watermen was dependent on sums received from the very drivers whom they were supposed to control. One who was considered to be excessively strict could therefore be starved into submission by drivers conspiring to boycott his stand. A second reason for their not being overzealous is that, generally speaking, they came from the ranks of former-cabmen. The 'professionalization' of watermen, therefore, may be considered as paralleling the professionalization of the police force itself, as an attempt was made to separate those who kept order from the communities which they policed.[13]

Mayne had it in mind that the post of hackney carriage attendant might suit army or police pensioners, but Palmerston, the Home Secretary, was more interested in economy than strict discipline. Consequently the majority of new attendants seem to have been former watermen. In April 1854 Palmerston sanctioned 217 attendants, of whom 145 were to be 'first class' earning 17s a week and 72 second class, at 15s; but by the following February only 195 men had been appointed, all at the lower grade. Not surprisingly, the new attendants were hardly more effective at controlling cabmen than their predecessors, and they were phased out in favour of police constables from 1869.[14]

The problem of appointing hackney carriage attendants was symptomatic of police attitudes to this branch of their work, which was not considered a mainstream activity, and the inspection of cabs presented further opportunities for disagreement. Mayne was in favour of setting up a permanent establishment under an 'Inspector of Public Carriages' (an office not recognized by law) while the Home Office was ever eager for economy. In the event, it agreed to the temporary appointment of Colonel Paschal, a former officer of the King's German Legion who had fought at Waterloo, and who had acted as liaison officer with foreign police forces during the Great Exhibition. Paschal inspected around 3,500 cabs in 1853, with the assistance of the seventeen Divisional Superintendents. Two years later, Mayne secured the appointment of four permanent officers (two inspectors and two sergeants), who formed the nucleus of what came to be known as the Public Carriage Office.[15]

In addition to the requirement to inspect public carriages, the Metropolitan Police Commissioner also had the power to lay down regulations for vehicle construction. In 1858, for example, cabs were required to have knobs and straps fitted to their windows, as well as iron frames fitted to the roof for the accommodation of luggage. These requirements, originally issued from time to time as separate orders, had, by the 1870s, been codified into *Notices to Proprietors as to Conditions for obtaining a Certificate of Fitness*. These could influence the overall design of cabs as well as their quality, and were eventually to be of crucial importance in determining the paths along which the motor cab developed.[16]

The high hope of a general improvement in cab stock was frustrated, however. There was no guarantee that a plate affixed to a cab which passed inspection would not be transferred by an unscrupulous proprietor to an inferior vehicle. The use of a stencil plate to mark the month as well as the year of inspection was introduced some time before 1881, but some owners found a method of transferring even this. There was less guarantee still that the horse presented for inspection would be the horse regularly employed with the cab. The substitution of a satisfactory horse for an inadequate one at the annual inspection meant that it was principally on the streets that unfit horses had to be spotted, for public carriage inspectors, unlike sanitary inspectors, lacked general powers of entry into stables. This limitation meant that the

The Public Carriage Office in Scotland Yard, built in 1874 and demolished in 1909

most likely place where an unfit cab or horse could be observed was at a standing, and public carriage attendants were instructed to report to officers on duty at the divisional police stations any unfit horses or carriages which appeared on their stands.[17]

Shortly after Mayne's death, Paschal retired from the police force in 1869, leaving the Public Carriage Office in some disarray. The new commissioner, Edmund Henderson, placed the work under an assistant commissioner, delegating the day-to-day running of the office to a subordinate officer, originally of the rank of chief inspector. Three men held this position from the 1860s down to the First World War: Edward Ware, until his retirement in 1894; William Beavis from 1894 to 1902; and Arthur Bassom from 1902 onwards. These men came to exert an enormous influence over the administration of the cab trade, for their advice frequently formed the basis of Home Office policy. Yet there can be little doubt that the Public Carriage Office, dealing with traffic rather than crime, was considered something of a backwater within the Metropolitan Police. When Ware was promoted from chief inspector to Superintendent in 1887, it was noted that he would have been recommended for that promotion some years earlier, had he been in another branch. The work was not sought after by rank-and-file police officers, and on more than one occasions difficulties were experienced in securing volunteers to take up public carriage duties.[18]

It paid the Metropolitan Police (quite literally) to keep the line between hackney carriage duties and general police work as hazy as possible. Prior to 1869, vehicle licences were issued by the Board of Inland Revenue upon production of a certificate of fitness issued by the Metropolitan Police, but no fees passed through police hands. The licences of drivers and conductors were issued by the Metropolitan Police, but these fees were passed on to the Inland Revenue. The police, therefore, derived no income from licence fees, but instead were paid a fixed sum of £12,100 a year to cover the expenses of inspection and supervision of public carriages.[19] In his Budget of 1869, however, the Chancellor of the Exchequer, Robert Lowe, repealed the weekly duty on hackney carriages. Later in that session a short Bill was pushed through setting the parameters within which the Home Secretary could fix annual licence fees. Under Section 6.1 of The Metropolitan Public Carriages Act, 1869, the Home Secretary was empowered to license public carriages at an annual fee not to exceed two guineas, while Section 8 gave him the power to fix licence fees for drivers and conductors up to a limit of 5s per annum. In each case the fees were to be paid to the police receiver, and were to be carried to the account of the Metropolitan Police Fund. Section 12 entitled the Secretary of State to appoint such officers and constables of the Metropolitan and City Police Forces as were necessary to carry out the provisions of the Act, and to award the receiver, from the moneys raised by licence fees, such sums as were necessary to cover the costs.

The Act did not require a separate account to be kept of public carriage revenues,

FARES FOR HACKNEY CARRIAGES
AND DISTANCES
WITHIN A CIRCLE OF FOUR MILES RADIUS FROM CHARING CROSS MEASURED BY AUTHORITY OF THE COMMISSIONER OF POLICE.

London, Brighton, and South Coast Railway,
(LONDON BRIDGE STATION)

A Metropolitan Police fare table of 1861. This one is printed on paper, but they were also printed on enamelled panels for display in public places. (PRO, RAIL 414/559)

which provided the receiver with significant accounting opportunities to offload as many police costs as possible onto the hackney carriage revenues. A.R. Pennefather, the receiver from 1883, maintained that the Treasury had allowed the control of these funds to pass to the police in order that they might provide more effectively for the regulation of street traffic.[20] The obstruction of metropolitan street traffic was certainly seen as a particularly pressing problem in the 1860s, and was the subject of several public enquiries. So bad was the situation that Henry Mayhew observed that one could 'walk over the roofs of vans and buses as readily as over the united up-raised shields of the Roman soldiers outside the walls of some beleaguered city'.[21]

The Metropolitan Streets Act of 1867 greatly extended the traffic powers of the

The engraving *A City Thoroughfare*, by Gustave Doré, first appeared in *London: a Pilgrimage*, published in 1872. It is a brilliant evocation of the turbulent London streets, in which a police constable holds high his arm with all the desperation of a drowning man

police at a time when the force was fully stretched. In 1866 there were Reform riots in Hyde Park, while in the following year Fenian agitation culminated in the Clerkenwell bombing in December.[22] When Henderson took over from Mayne, he therefore inherited considerable problems. The years 1868–70 witnessed a great expansion of the force, and also presented Henderson with the opportunity to rethink police procedures. The annual transfer to the Metropolitan Police Fund of around £20,000 in public carriage licence fees could not have come at a more appropriate time. However, it would be a mistake to see the intention of the government as merely to supplement police revenue, for it has to be noted that the annual licence fee for a public carriage was set by the Home Secretary at a sum below the legal maximum – at £2 rather than two guineas. This led critics subsequently to assert that it had been the intention of Parliament that licence fees for public carriages and their drivers and conductors should be set at a level that simply covered costs.[23] But how could you estimate costs when the activities of constables on the street were constantly changing? Pennefather described the problem as he saw it:

> Anyone who cares to observe can see that, in miles upon miles of busy crowded streets, the duty of the Police is at one moment to move on a crawling cab; the next to move on a loitering bus; the next to stop all traffic in order to allow foot

TWO DROPS OF COMFORT.

Publican. "P-O-ON MY WORD! THINGS IS COMING TO A PRETTY PASS!"
Cabby. "LOR' BLESS YER, GUV'NOR, YOU AIN'T NO CALL TO BE AFRAID. WHY, MR. BRUCE HE TRIED
TO REFORM *THE CABS!* WELL! 'ERE WE ARE!—HAS WE WOS!—NO BETTER, AN' NO WUS!!"

The problems of steering a Licensing Bill through Parliament diverted the Home Secretary's attention away from reforming the cab trade. As a later Home Secretary, R.A. Cross, put it in 1879, 'Beer and Cabs had better be left alone as far as possible'. From *Punch*, 15 April 1871

passengers to cross the road; the next to attend to some accident or collision; and in a thousand other ways to keep the streets clear, and facilitate the passage of everyone – How is it possible, in the midst of all this, to say what proportion of the man's services is chargeable to 'Cab revenue'?[24]

But the crucial point was that, under the terms of the Metropolitan Public Carriages Act of 1869, the receiver did not even have to try! No separate account of public carriage monies was kept, and any surplus that accrued might be used to offset general police expenditure. Henderson hit upon another idea. One of the early reforms which he introduced in 1869 was that of 'Fixed Points', whereby a constable was ordered to patrol around a stated place to which he was required to return at regular intervals, so that the public would know where to find him, or he could receive instructions from a superior officer. If hackney carriage standings were designated as fixed points, two birds could be killed with one stone, for the services of the hackney carriage attendant could be dispensed with. In the course of the next few years, therefore, all the hackney carriage attendants were phased out, to be replaced by police constables charged against the hackney carriage revenues.[25]

At first, the attempt to subsidize general police duties from the hackney carriage

Taking out cab licenses at the Public Carriage Office. An engraving from the *Illustrated London News*, December 1886

revenues aroused little controversy, but the question came to greater prominence in the 1880s when the cab trade experienced a period of distress, and when, at the same time, a power struggle developed between successive commissioners and the receiver. Matters came to a head in 1894, when the Home Office set up a Departmental Committee of Enquiry into the Cab Service of the Metropolis, which came to the conclusion that it was the intention of Parliament, as well as being right in principle, that the expense of administering the Cab Acts should fall upon the trade. It was recommended that in future the accounts of the Cab Fund should be kept distinct from those of the Metropolitan Police Fund, and that the revenue collected should not exceed that which was sufficient to cover the cost of the service. It was not considered a practical possibility to fix the licence fee at a level that would lead to an exact balance against expenditure, but any surplus should be applied to improving the conditions of the trade by, for example, providing shelters and covered standings. This recommendation was greeted by Pennefather with the utmost disdain. 'In my opinion,' he said, 'it is a monstrous thing that men earning good wages, as cabmen for the most part do, should appeal for outside support, either charitable or otherwise, to supply them with shelters.'[26]

With Home Office connivance, Pennefather loaded the hackney carriage accounts with every conceivable charge, in an attempt to balance the books and avoid a surplus. In 1905, for example, it was decided to charge £20 per annum for every police station where accommodation was provided for hackney carriage inspectors, irrespective of the nature of that accommodation. At Battersea it was reported that the public carriage inspector was accommodated in 'a wooden box about 9ft × 4ft, never cleaned, seldom lighted (a halfpenny candle would last a month) and never heated'. It was only used for two hours on one day a week. At Islington the inspector made use of 'a disused stable kept by the Division as a lumber store, and the extent of the accommodation is a resting place for a box about 2 ft square'.[27]

Any suggestion that regulation of hackney carriages could raise revenue was bound to arouse the interest of the metropolitan local authorities, denied a service which, in the provinces, was securely in the sphere of local government control. In 1865 an unsuccessful attempt was made by the Metropolitan Board of Works to secure the horse and hackney carriage duties, but the application was firmly rejected by the Treasury.[28] Part of the problem lay in the lack of correspondence between the Metropolitan Police District and the area of jurisdiction of the Metropolitan Board of Works. As suburban London grew, more and more areas found themselves wholly or partially outside the Metropolitan Police District, and the risk of a conflict of authorities was increased by the passage of the Public Health Act of 1875. This incorporated the provisions of the Town Police Clauses Acts, 1847, in so far as they related to hackney carriages, and empowered urban authorities to license proprietors and drivers and to make by-laws to regulate stands and fix rates of hire. The metropolis was excluded, but this was defined as the City of London and the area of the Metropolitan Board of Works. However, the Metropolitan Police District extended beyond that, so immediately a potential conflict of interest arose.[29]

Sir Edmund Henderson, the Chief Commissioner, was not averse to handing his powers over to a municipal authority. In February 1879 he wrote to Adolphus Liddell, permanent under-secretary at the Home Office, that

a transfer of the jurisdiction over the Metropolitan Public Carriages from the Commissioner of Police to the Metropolitan Board of Works would relieve the Home Office and the Commissioner of Police of a great amount of labour and responsibility which is, properly speaking, not Police work at all.[30]

This view was strongly reminiscent of that of his predecessor, Richard Mayne, but while the commissioner might view the transfer of responsibilities with equanimity, the receiver did not view the transfer of revenues similarly.

Matters did not come to a head until 1884. Until then the suburban authorities had held their hand, thus avoiding conflict; but the Croydon Corporation Bill, then passing through Parliament, sought to grant exemption to that authority from Metropolitan Police control of hackney carriages. If allowed, considerable confusion would abound. A cab licensed by Croydon would still need to apply to the commissioner for a licence if it were to ply within the Metropolitan Police District, and a cab returning to Croydon from outside the borough would have to be so licensed, or return empty. The cab would have to carry two plates, and the driver two badges. If similar provisions were made by other authorities, the problem could only be compounded. Despite the reservations of the police, the Bill was passed and, using its by-law powers, in 1885 Croydon Borough Council set a lower tariff of fares than that laid down by the Home Secretary. There were some doubts as to the Home Secretary's powers to approve fares lower than those laid down in the Metropolitan Public Carriages Act of 1869 and the tariff was declared *ultra vires* in a test case before the Croydon bench in December 1885. This attempt at unilateral action by Croydon only served to demonstrate that effective regulation of cabs within the metropolis had to be a centralized function, irrespective of whether the authority was the Home Office or some central municipal body.[31]

A driving test in progress. It was not until the very end of the century that a driving test for cab drivers was instituted, the vehicles for which were contracted out to Thomas Tilling, one of London's largest jobmasters, for £250 a year. From George R. Sims, *Living London*, 1906

The setting up of the London County Council (LCC) in 1888 might have presented such an opportunity. The LCC took its first plunge into public transport in 1891 when it decided to acquire tramways in the metropolis, and three years later it made a bid for control of cabs. The problem remained that its boundaries were not conterminous with those of the police district, which contained the whole or part of nine local authorities that might equally claim such powers. Had there been the political will this problem could no doubt have been overcome, but there was none. Calculations made by the receiver purported to show that the loss of hackney carriage revenue would correspond to the loss from the force of about 270 men unless the LCC paid for them, which would defeat the object of their intentions. This proved a compelling argument, and at the end of April the Home Secretary decided that he was not prepared to consent to the change.[32]

From time to time the question continued to be raised, but there were powerful vested interests involved, and any change was likely to throw up as many problems as it solved. To do nothing must often, therefore, have appeared the least unattractive course of action. Cabs remained the responsibility of the Home Office until 1984, when the Department of Transport assumed responsibility. In 1989 that department completed a nine-month review of the law on taxis and hire cars. Legislation was planned that would have replaced laws which had been in force for a century and a half. But the proposed Bill was dropped when it was pointed out that a substantial number of cab drivers were constituents of the Prime Minister, Margaret Thatcher, and were not to be antagonized![33]

Chapter Eight

THE CAB DRIVER

From my earliest youth I was taught to regard cabmen as birds of prey. I was led to consider that their hands were against every man, and every man's hand ought to be against them in self defence. I was forbidden to attribute their husky voices to anything but unlimited indulgence in common spiritous liquors. The red noses that I saw peeping from under broad-brimmed hats, and over bee-hive-looking caped great coats, were never said in my hearing to arise from exposure to the weather. When I was sent on a solitary journey – perhaps to school – in a four-wheeled hackney-coach or cab, I always heard a stern voice bargaining with the driver before I was placed inside; and I looked upon him, through the small window in the front . . . as a dangerous ogre who might leap down and devour me at any moment.

In due time I became a married man . . . My early teaching with regard to the utter badness of all cabmen had not disappeared, and I still treated them with moderate severity. I never pampered them with bonuses over their legal fares; and I learned every distance as if I had been an Ordnance Surveyor. I still looked upon them as untamed, devouring creatures, who hung upon the skirts of society, and I was prepared to impress this view upon my children, as my guardians had impressed it upon me.

Before, however, I had an opportunity of doing this, my sentiments underwent a marked change.[1]

John Hollingshead, the author of this passage, found himself – if not on the road to Damascus – at least on a foggy journey across London in 1860. The conversion that he experienced was the discovery that cab drivers are human beings like the rest of mankind. It was an experience that spawned a distinct genre of Victorian social writing, the appreciation that behind the stereotype there lies a creature of flesh and blood. Hollingshead was not the first to write in this vein, and he was certainly not the last. James Greenwood, whose apotheosis as a social writer came with *A Night in the Workhouse*, made similar discoveries about 'that ruffianly, blackguardly, bullying race' in *The Wilds of London* in 1874. The evil reputation which the cabman suffered lingered on, however, and achieved international recognition. 'These London Cabbies are, as a general thing, the most provoking and abusive fellows in the world', was the view of the American journalist, Daniel Joseph Kirwan. Perhaps he had never been to Boston.[2]

Kirwan's writings are little known today, but Anna Sewell, whose *Black Beauty* first appeared only a few years later, in 1877, reached tens of millions of readers. It is true that she described an evil proprietor, Nicholas Skinner, whose 'mouth was as full of teeth as a bull-dog's, and his voice . . . as harsh as the grinding of cart wheels over gravel-stones'; but Jerry Barker, the owner-driver to whom the equine hero of the book is sold, is a sympathetic character, almost (but not quite) too good to be true.

In reality, the Victorian period knew not one stereotype but two, for the hansom cab driver and the driver of a four-wheeled cab were looked upon as different breeds, a distinction with which the drivers themselves willingly acquiesced. An article in *Fraser's Magazine* in 1851 catches the difference in alleged style and manner:

The 'turn-out', deportment, address, and character of the driver of a four-wheeler, are not less distinct than are his cab and its appointments from those of the driver of a Hansom's patent. A four-wheeler is usually entrusted to a little swarthy, dingy man, of many coats and no capes . . . [He is] pertinacious and apologetic: he has a broken whip, a dilapidated hat, and a cracked voice. He follows you the whole length, even of Baker Street, hugging the kerbstone with his pottering wheels, whilst he tries to inveigle a fare with all the coaxing humility of a hawker of bad sealing-wax and worse pencils. His manner is obnoxious, his eagerness obtrusive, his throat-shawl and his face equally coarse and dirty; his hair very little brushed, but full-powdered with the road dust. His importunity, moreover, is indefatigable . . . A Hansom's man is usually stouter and better built; fresh complexioned; frugal, in the worst weathers, in the number of his coats, but prodigal in his array of capes. In fine weather he sports a spruce bouquet in his buttonhole . . . He has a voluminous, gay-patterned wrapper round his neck; and is neither too proud nor too lazy to discard the cleansing ministry of soap, razor, or brushes. His flat, low hat, glazed and bottle-green, is so stuck on his head that it resembles the top of an apothecary's one-ounce phial . . . He has an air of great confidence that he shall be hired. His mode of catching a fare is at all times abrupt and offhand.[3]

As in all stereotypes there is an element of truth here, for the two vehicles tended to do very different kinds of work. The hansom was the faster and flashier vehicle, which no doubt appealed to the more 'flash' among the driving fraternity.

Part of the fascination which this raffish group exerted over the general public was the belief that within their ranks were to be found men of superior birth. Among the drivers plying the streets in 1891 were reckoned to be the son of a judge, several university men and a man who could 'remember his bright days as a captain in Her Majesty's navy, the wearer of eight medals and the *Légion d'honneur*'.[4] Most such stories were apocryphal and arose, no doubt, from the practice among cabmen of giving each other extravagant nicknames. However, there can be little doubt that cab-driving was, in many respects, a residual occupation into which men sank as a last resort. Furthermore, it was an occupation into which a man might indeed lose himself. Instead of running off to the Foreign Legion (no doubt taking a cab to catch the Dover boat-train), Beau Geste might well have been advised to jump on the box himself, for the cab driver was (and remains) the most anonymous of men. In this he differs from the bus driver, who works a regular route and can, without undue difficulty, be traced from one day to the next.

It was the anonymity of the cab driver that made him such a potentially dangerous man, for his relationship with his passenger is a fleeting one. With over 10,000 drivers licensed in the 1870s, rising to over 15,000 twenty years later, the chances that the paths of a passenger and a particular cabman would pass more than once were distinctly limited. This being so, the social and moral controls over the driver were that much weaker. Nor was the driver the only one to experience temptation, for bilking a driver of his fare, or dealing with him in a pusillanimous manner, was encouraged by the likelihood of never seeing him again. Meanness towards cab drivers was common sport, as it had been towards their predecessors. The odious Jonas Chuzzlewit set out to show his cousins, the Misses Pecksniff 'one of the best pieces of fun with which he was acquainted. This joke was of a practical kind, and its humour lay in taking a hackney-coach to the extreme limits of possibility for a shilling.'[5]

That the encounters between ephemeral cabmen and their middle class clients took place on the streets only added to the problem, for the streets provided the setting where men (and, particularly, women) from different social classes, living otherwise separate lives, came into contact with each other. As Michael Wolff and Celina Fox put it, 'In the street, the division between one's own safe familiar world and the world of the rest, the others, could never be complete.' In his *London Labour and the London Poor* (1861–2), Henry Mayhew represented the streetfolk almost as a race apart. They were marked out by the 'greater development of the animal than of the intellectual or moral nature of man . . . for their high cheekbones and protruding jaws – for their use of slang language – for their lax ideas of property – for their general improvidence – their repugnance to continuous labour – their disregard of female honour – their love of cruelty – their pugnacity – and their utter want of religion'. Mayhew specified that the race of streetfolk included pickpockets, beggars, prostitutes, streetsellers, street performers – and cabmen![6] Except for the very timid, most middle class men, especially if they lived, worked and played in London, would have confronted the street tribes without undue fear; unless they found themselves in the alien territory of the East End. But that confidence would not necessarily have been shared by the visitor from the country or from abroad; and especially not by the 'unprotected female'. 'Cabmen bully ladies dreadfully,' wrote Mayhew in 1881, but he was only voicing the common view. Whereas a male passenger might seek redress for extortion or foul language, a woman was much less likely to do so. *The Times* in 1851 described the agonies that must be endured by the lady who decided to summons a cabman for charging an excess fare:

> She must take off her glove in the presence of an indefinite number of stern policemen and perspiring spectators, and recount the history of her disasters to a matter-of-fact magistrate. Who would expose a lady to such an ordeal for the sake of five-shillings – it may be of sixpence?

Court appearances no doubt entailed agonies for the cab driver also, but of a different kind, for the cards were stacked against him. A driver told W.H. Wilkins in the 1890s:

> Wherever we are and whatever we do we are liable to be summoned . . . You can sometimes step into Marlborough Street Police Court and find about thirty cases disposed of in about half an hour. Should a cabman plead 'not guilty', we reckon it costs about 1s. a word. As an instance: I was called off the rank to St. James' Hall by a gentleman who, after hailing me, went back for a lady, and the constable would not allow me to wait for him. I was summoned for loitering, and pleaded 'not guilty', and was fined 3s. and costs, total 5s. If I had pleaded 'guilty', I should only have had to pay 6*d* and 2*s* costs. Therefore it is always better to plead guilty, as the policeman's word is always taken before the cabman's.[7]

If the cab driver was both dangerous and anonymous, the solution was (as with other trades tempted to immorality and illegality) to license him, but furthermore to make him wear a badge so that he might be more easily identified. Heavy bronze, numbered badges were issued from 1843 down to 1870, when they were replaced by lighter badges of enamelled iron. Still the men complained of their weight, and motor drivers later claimed that the badge (which was on a leather strap) could become entangled in the working parts of an engine if they were leaning over it. It still took until 1930 to get the weight down to 1½ oz. But it was the stigma, rather than the discomfort, that the men objected to. The badge, said a witness to the Royal Commission on Labour in 1892, meant that the cabman was 'looked upon by a largish section of the community as a sort of convict'.[8]

The badge which was granted with his licence was meant to be proof of the driver's good character, and enquiries were made to vouch for this. The licence was certainly no proof of a man's ability to drive. Although motor cab drivers were tested as to their vehicle handling skills from the earliest days, drivers of horse cabs were not given a driving test until June 1896. The commissioner reported after the first six months that 1,344 applicants for a licence had been examined, of whom sixty-seven had failed (though 'some few' had subsequently qualified). The small number of failures probably signifies that many men came to the cab trade with some experience of driving, but also that the test was not very demanding. There can be little doubt that, on the job, men acquired a considerable degree of driving skill, for the harsh competitiveness of the busy streets demanded it. The commissioner admitted in 1873 that 'If the drivers of unlicensed vehicles drove under the same sense of responsibility as the hackney carriage drivers . . . accidents might be diminished.[9]

In *Black Beauty*, Anna Sewell gave a horse's eye view of driving in the congested London streets:

It is always difficult to drive fast in the city in the middle of the day, when the streets are full of traffic, but we did what could be done; and when a good driver and a good horse, who understand each other, are of one mind, it is wonderful what they can do. I had a very good mouth – that is, I could be guided by the slightest touch of the rein, and that is a great thing in London, amongst carriages, omnibuses, carts, vans, trucks, cabs, and great wagons creeping along at a walking pace; some going one way, some another, some going slowly, others wanting to pass them, omnibuses stopping short every few minutes to take up a passenger, obliging the horse that is coming behind to pull up too, or to pass and get before them: perhaps you try to pass, but just then something else comes dashing in through the narrow opening, and you have to keep in behind the omnibus again; presently you think you see a chance, and manage to get to the front, going so near the wheels on each side that half an inch nearer and they would scrape . . . you have to be ready for any chance – to dash forward if there be an opening, and be as quick as a rat dog to see if there be room, and if there be time, lest you get your own wheels locked, or smashed, or the shaft of some other vehicle run into your chest or shoulder. If you want to get through London fast in the middle of the day, it wants a deal of practice.

Driving skill was given a lower priority by the Home Office and the Metropolitan Police than a knowledge of the London streets. The legendary test of 'The Knowledge' was started in May 1866 on the express orders of Sir Richard Mayne. It is very difficult to know how arduous the test was. The applicant was required, in an oral test, to demonstrate a knowledge of the principal routes across London, and the whereabouts of all manner of public buildings. Established cabmen (for whom the test represented a means of keeping out casual drivers) complained of its laxity; proprietors, who preferred a pool of surplus drivers to depress pay, and who would welcome the opportunity to tap more country and provincial men, were inclined to argue that it was too strict. The probability is that it got more difficult as the century progressed. It certainly became more structured, with sample questions being issued from 1906. Motor drivers were given a tougher test that was extended to include the suburbs, and it was said in 1910 that it took a man about six weeks to learn – a period that would seem as nothing to today's more rigorously tested taxidrivers.[10]

Knowledge of the London streets – of short cuts; of the locations of likely blockages; of places where fares were likely to be found at particular times of the day – was, of course, essential to the cab driver, who looked down with contempt upon the bus driver plying his set routes. Testing that knowledge also went some way towards protecting the passenger from overcharge, although there were other means of redress.

It would be difficult to conclude that, in the matter of fares, the law offered the cab driver equal protection with that of his passenger. Section 43 of the London Hackney Carriage Act of 1831 laid down that an agreement made with the driver for the payment of more than his proper fare was not binding, although Section 45 made an agreement to charge less than the full fare enforceable by the courts. As a driver put it to Richard Rowe in 1882, this was decidedly not a case of sauce for the goose being sauce for the gander. He went on:

> Which is goose and which is gander it ain't for me to decide; but look here, you agree to give me more than my fare, and then, when you've got to where you want to go to, you back out. If I try to keep you to your word, like a gen'leman, it's forty shillin's, or in default one calendar month for me again. But if I agree to drive you for less than my fare, and then think I've been a fool, and want to git what I've a right to, it's the old story over again for me – forty shillin's.[11]

The unfairness of this rankled with both drivers and proprietors, and the cabman's case was put vigorously to Henry Matthews, the Home Secretary, when a deputation met him in March 1892. The issue was not principally that of charging more or less than the prescribed fare, but of driving beyond the distance the cabman was bound to go (set at six miles from the place at which hired) especially in special circumstances, such as in deep snow, or on special occasions like a race day at Epsom. The 1895 Departmental Committee favoured the making of such bargains legally binding, but this was not conceded – for journeys over six miles – until 1947.[12]

Section 18 of the Fitzroy Act of 1853 empowered a hirer, in the case of dispute, to require the driver to proceed immediately to the nearest police station or magistrate's

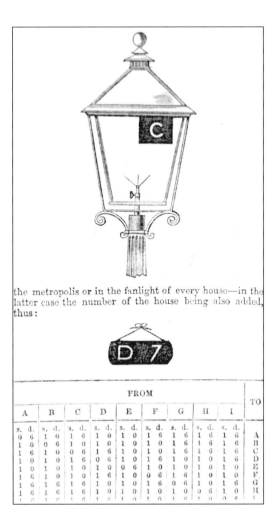

the metropolis or in the fanlight of every house—in the latter case the number of the house being also added, thus :

			FROM						TO
A	B	C	D	E	F	G	H	I	
s. d.	s. d.	s. d.	s. d.	s. d.	s. d.	s. d.	s. d.	s. d.	
0 6	1 0	1 6	1 0	1 0	1 6	1 6	1 6	1 6	A
1 0	0 6	1 0	1 0	1 0	1 0	1 6	1 6	1 6	B
1 6	1 0	0 6	1 6	1 0	1 0	1 6	1 6	1 6	C
1 0	1 0	1 6	0 6	1 0	1 6	1 0	1 0	1 6	D
1 0	1 0	1 0	1 0	0 6	1 0	1 0	1 0	1 0	E
1 6	1 0	1 0	1 6	1 0	0 6	1 6	1 0	1 0	F
1 6	1 6	1 6	1 6	1 0	1 0	1 0	0 6	1 6	G
1 6	1 6	1 6	1 6	1 0	1 0	1 0	0 6	1 0	H

Throughout the nineteenth century a number of novel methods for determining cab fares were put forward, including many different maps and fare indicators. In the late 1860s considerable attention was given to the 'course' system which was used in Paris. J.L. Haddan proposed a system of dividing the map of London into squares, each one representing a 'course' or unit of fare. He proposed marking the districts by placing perforated tin numbers in street lamps and the fanlights of houses. The system was never tried, for the apparent simplicity of the Haddan system was belied by the complexity of many actual cab journeys. From the *Journal of the Society of Arts*, 15 February 1867

court in order to have the matter settled. It did not give an equivalent power to the driver, the fear being that unscrupulous men would hold passengers to ransom, especially if they were taking them to a station and they might miss a train. A case reported in *The Times* of 29 July 1853 involved a passenger who had been obliged to pay twelve guineas to engage a special train after a wrangle with a cab driver had caused him to miss the one he had intended to catch. He refused to pay the fare demanded and, in this case, the driver summoned him. When the case came to court, the passenger declined to have the distance measured and conceded that the driver's estimate was possibly correct. No doubt the publicity which was at that time surrounding the notorious Phillips case (which had come to court only a few days earlier) took away the passenger's stomach for a fight. Experienced cabmen were familiar with distances, and J.R. Lyell, the chief clerk at Marlborough Street Magistrates' Court, gave his opinion to the 1895 Committee that in cases of dispute the driver was 'invariably right'. Perhaps not always; for in the mid 1870s, cabmen came up against a formidable opponent in the form of Mrs Giacometti Prodgers (or Mrs 'Grumbling Sloggers', as the *Cab and Omnibus News* called her.) Mrs Prodgers was to the cab trade of the mid-1870s what Mrs Whitehouse became to the media a century later – a scourge. Dickens might have invented this lady (the wife of an admiral in the Austrian Navy) but she was real enough. Armed with a formidable knowledge of cab fares and cab law, she hauled many a driver before the courts, and usually won. H.C. Moore recalled that 'After a time she became so dreaded that the warning cry of "Mother Prodgers" would send every cab within hail dashing away up side streets to escape her.' Even when he wrote, in 1902, there were 'scores of cabmen who [could not] hear her name mentioned without fuming with indignation'.[13]

If further evidence is needed that driver and passenger were afforded unequal protection by the law, it is to be found in the issue of bilking. The cabdriver as vehicular vampire is part of the stereotype, but the driver as victim is not. Yet bilking – the refusal of a passenger to pay a fare, or his (or her) disappearance without paying, was a very real problem to cabmen. Cabmen knew the likely places for a disappearing act to take place, and would be suspicious when asked to wait at places like the Burlington Arcade, Swan and Edgar's (the department store) or any place with a multiplicity of entrances and exits.

The Act of 1831 had offered some protection, for Section 41 had laid down that refusal or omission to pay the driver his legal fare was a criminal offence, rendering the offender liable to up to a month's imprisonment with hard labour. In practice, of course, the police and the courts treated the respectable classes differently from the rest, and few cabmen could afford the time to pursue their grievances through the courts. It was difficult, if not impossible, to trace offenders, and while drivers, after 1853, were required to give the passenger a ticket containing the number of his cab, passengers were not required to hand over their visiting cards – nor even to give their name and address. The 1870 Report of the Chief Commissioner of the Metropolitan Police suggested that the driver be granted the power to give into charge and custody anyone refusing to supply this information, but nothing came of the recommendation. Quite the reverse: the Summary Jurisdiction Act, 1879, removed the criminal element from bilking, and made the recovery of a fare a civil matter. This increased the hardship to cabmen, and in 1892 the Chief Magistrate at Bow Street urged the Home Office to restore the law to its previous position.[14]

The Departmental Committee of 1895 considered the matter at great length. Lyell gave evidence that not a single bilking case had come before the Marlborough Street

Court in all his eleven years there, and he, too, argued for bilking once more to be made criminal. Legislation against bilking was passed in the following year, but it was badly drafted and did not prove effective, with the result that by 1901 the offence was reported to be once again on the increase. The introduction of the taxi-cab, which resulted in larger fares being earned for single journeys, made the grievance greater than it had been, and the motor driver felt every bit as vulnerable as his horse-driving colleague.[15]

There is no evidence that women passengers were more prone to bilk cab drivers than men, but (despite the public concern for the 'unprotected female') there is ample evidence that women were among those whom cabmen least liked to carry. Women, they believed, were much more likely to offer the exact fare and, in common with casual cab users, were less familiar with the driver/passenger relationship and with the delicate but crucial matter of tipping. W.H. Wilkins observed that 'Drivers will tell one that the fare "most respected" by them is the City man. He puts the money down on the roof without a word, and he almost invariably gives sixpence over the fare.' Like many servants (either private or public), drivers were inclined to hold in contempt those who did not appreciate the niceties of protocol; unlike domestic servants, they took no pains to disguise their feelings. They had then (as they have now) a reputation for being masters of repartee, and the passenger was always likely

The passenger of a side-seat cab comes off worst in an exchange with its driver. 'I can see thief in your face fellow!' he exclaims. 'Vell s'help me,' replies the cabman, 'wot a funny old Gentleman to take my physog for a Looking-glass!'

WRITTEN & COMPOSED
JOSEPH TABRAR.

SUNG WITH THE GREATEST SUCCESS
GEORGE LEYBOURNE.

LONDON·FRANCIS BROTHERS & DAY BLENHEIM HOUSE, OXFORD ST W

'I Say Cabby!': a music hall song, first published in 1881, and sung by George Leybourne, whose speciality was the 'masher' song. 'Champagne Charlie' was one of his best known songs. All the cabmen loved a 'toff', for he was more likely to be generous with a tip

to be worsted in any exchange, having less experience of chaff, and being more inhibited by the restraints of respectable and polite behaviour.[16]

The point is that, as with many low-paid workers, tipping was vital to the cabman if he was to make a living. However, because London cab drivers were unwaged, and made what they could over and above the hiring price for their cab, it is very difficult to get precise information on actual earnings. This is especially true of the period prior to the 1890s, in which decade the income of cabmen became a subject of much enquiry, both by social investigators such as Charles Booth, and by public bodies such as the Royal Commission on Labour and the Departmental Committee on the Cab Service of the Metropolis. Writing in 1893, Wilkins reflected on the difficulty of the task, as well as on the factors which caused earnings to fluctuate:

It is well-nigh impossible to give an accurate idea of a cabman's average earnings. Speaking roughly, it may be said to average from about 15s. to 18s. a week . . . The earnings vary, and must vary, according to the season, the weather, and the value of the 'property', i.e. of the horse and cab. Doubtless something depends upon the driver, and certainly much depends upon his luck – the number of his fares, and the generosity of those who pay them. As to fares, it may be stated that if everyone only paid a cabman his strictly legal fare he would starve . . .[17]

Witness after witness before the Departmental Committee complained that earnings had fallen. John Beasley, a former general secretary of the London Cab Drivers' Trade Union, who had just left the trade in order to start up a coffee shop, argued that earnings had been in decline since 1869. Fred White, the current president of the union, who had driven continuously for sixteen years, claimed that he had been earning £2 a week when he started in the late 1870s, but that earnings were now down to about £1 a week, a figure broadly in line with that declared by William Tackley, the

A cab stand in Queen Victoria Street in the City, 1899. Cabs in the City of London thrived on business, but increasingly that was carried out by telephone by the turn of the century. The roof of Albert Buildings is festooned with wires; while at the pavement entrance stands another bane of the cabman – a messenger boy. These, and other new means of communication, made serious inroads into the trade undertaken by the hansom

driver of a four-wheeled cab. Robert Musk, who had also driven for sixteen years, and was now a hansom cab driver for the London Improved Cab Company, claimed that he had frequently earned £2, but was now earning about 30s a week. For this, however, he worked thirteen days in every fortnight, and was out of the house for sixteen hours a day. All agreed that increased competition, both within the trade and between cabs and other forms of transport, was the reason for the decline. Buses had increased in number and were now running later (until 1.00 a.m. according to White), when they took trade from cabs at a time of day when passengers had tended to be ' a little bit more liberal'. Technology had taken its toll, with the telephone impinging on their trade. White gloomily observed:

> Of course it used to be a common thing for a cab driver to take a fare into the city [sic], and when he was in the city he would sometimes get seven or eight short shilling runs from, say, Throgmorton Street, that neighbourhood, to Leadenhall Street, perhaps well within a mile; but what we call very easy shillings, sir. But now the gentlemen seems as it was hardly necessary to leave their offices; they can do the work by telephone or messenger.[18]

Booth reckoned 30s to be about the average made, a small return (considering the hours worked) when compared with omnibus drivers. From that sum would also have to be deducted the cost of meals, as well as the payments to ancillary workers. 'Yard Money' – or tips to stablemen – had been formally abolished by the settlement of 1894, but were still given by many drivers as a bribe to secure an extra smart turn-out. In addition to the stablemen and carriage washers, the drivers were dependent on 'bucks'. The function of bucks or 'buck riders' seems to have changed over the years. Originally these men, often debadged drivers who had lost their licence for some offence, were used by the regular drivers to enable them to snatch a meal break, or to afford them brief periods of rest in the course of their long day. Later they came to be used in the constant warfare between cabdrivers and police over the matter of street obstruction. Because the street traffic powers of the police were so limited, there was inevitably a temptation to come down heavily on those vehicles over which they did have some control, namely public service vehicles – and cabs especially. Congestion black spots shifted in the course of the day. In the late evening the worst area was that part of the West End in which theatres were so heavily concentrated. When the theatres closed there was an inevitable demand for cabs, which were drawn into the district as though by a magnet. In order to prevent congestion, towards the end of the century the police cordoned off the theatre district in the evening, and refused to let in empty cabs to prevent them from blocking up the streets. Taking on a buck to masquerade as a passenger, to be rewarded with some small sum, would help the cabman to run the gauntlet of the police and get into the places where genuine paying passengers were to be found.[19]

Using bucks in this manner was of course illegal, but as J.T. Dexter had said in 1862, the men were 'long tossed about as shuttlecocks by inharmonious laws and conflicting decisions, and between the public and the police, and almost compelled to be bad men to remain cabmen'.[20] It is therefore not surprising that, in an age when there was no shortage of people eager to reform the morals and manners of others, cabmen should have received special attention.

The pioneer was the Society for Promoting Christian Knowledge, which, soon after it was founded in 1698, began circulating specially written pamphlets to groups in moral jeopardy. These included the sailors of Admiral Benbow's fleet, soldiers in Marlborough's army, London innkeepers – and hackney coachmen, among whom eight hundred copies of a tract against swearing were distributed. Thus started a history of missionary effort among hackneymen and cabmen that continues to this day.

In 1835 an evangelical Glaswegian, David Nasmith, founded the London City Mission, seeing the streets of the imperial capital to be as ripe for missionary effort as any colonial territory. District missionaries were appointed, and, in around 1840, a former cabman named Adams (who had himself been converted through the efforts of the mission) was appointed as a missionary specifically to cab drivers. Finance was a perennial problem, for a second missionary, appointed in 1847, had to return to general district work because of lack of funds. A night missionary was appointed in 1861. The mission's historian wrote in 1875:

He leaves home at eleven at night, and returns at six in the morning, so that in the silence of the night watches he is reading the Scriptures under lamp posts to groups of diseased and ignorant old men. In inclement weather he stands with groups of them under arch or door ways, and frequently with three of them sits in a cab instructing and comforting with gospel truth.

So that patrons might see that their subscriptions were expended with efficiency, the work was carefully documented. Thus, in 1852, for example, it was recorded that some 14,638 visits were made to cabmen (of which 329 were to the sick and dying); 154,062 religious tracts were distributed; and the Scriptures were read 555 times.[21]

The London City Mission was not alone in addressing the spiritual needs of cabmen, and other organizations included the London Cabmen's Lord's Day Rest Association, the United Cabdrivers' Gospel Temperance Association and the London Cabmen's Mission Hall Shelter, King's Cross, which was run by the Revd John Dupee. The King's Cross Mission issued a monthly paper, the *Cabman*, and in the later 1880s opened a home of rest for former cabmen at Ventnor on the Isle of Wight.

CAB-DRIVERS' BENEVOLENT ASSOCIATION,
15, SOHO SQUARE, W.

Patron.
HIS ROYAL HIGHNESS THE PRINCE OF WALES, K.G.
President.—THE DUKE OF RICHMOND AND GORDON, K.G.
Treasurer.—THE LORD STALBRIDGE.

THE CAB-DRIVERS' BENEVOLENT ASSOCIATION
was founded in 1870;

its principal object being to make some provision for deserving aged or infirm Cab-Drivers, who are broken down in health, or are unable longer to earn their living.

There are between twelve and thirteen thousand licensed Cab-Drivers in London, of whom about eight thousand are actually employed, and of these, upwards of one thousand are members of the Association, and contribute yearly a Subscription of Five Shillings each.

A Cab-Driver's earnings are necessarily very precarious, and small in proportion to the nature and amount of his labour, for he is often with his cab from 16 to 17 hours a day, sometimes earning barely sufficient to pay for its hire. And yet the Cabmen maintain a character for honesty and probity seldom found in so numerous a body of men. Upwards of **ONE HUNDRED THOUSAND POUNDS'** worth of property left by the public in cabs during a period of **FIVE YEARS** has been deposited by the drivers at Scotland Yard, and thence restored to the original owners.

Fifty-three Annuities, of £20 a year each, are at the present time being granted by the Association to aged Cab-Drivers, who, but for this help, would probably have been reduced, after long years of honest industry, to the Workhouse.

DONATIONS or SUBSCRIPTIONS in aid of the Society's objects may be paid to the Treasurer's Account, UNION BANK, Charing Cross; or they will be thankfully received at the Office of the Association by
G. STORMONT MURPHY, Hon. Secretary.

The Cab-drivers' Benevolent Association undoubtedly kept some aged cabmen from the workhouse; but only around a thousand of the 12,000 to 13,000 London cabdrivers were members, and the union was resentful of what it regarded as the Association's patronising attitude. From Herbert Fry, *Royal Guide to the London Charities*, 1889–90

In the fiercely competitive world of charity work, the patronage of the great and the good was essential. The president of Dupee's mission was Samuel Morley, MP, the hosiery magnate who was active in all manner of philanthropic, religious and temperance movements. Lord Shaftesbury presided over the West London Cabmen's Mission set up in 1858. The Marquis of Townshend took an active part in setting up the largest of the cabmen's charities, the Cab Drivers' Benevolent Association.

Townshend seems to have been the instigator of the association, which got off the ground in March 1870 with the aid of five cabmen. By the end of June, when the membership was around four hundred, the association was already being described as 'the Marquis's Fund', a title that seemed more successful at attracting influential supporters than actual members. A series of meetings was held around London in order to drum up support, and the platform parties included many prominent men, including Lord Arthur Wriotheslay Russell; Lord George Hamilton, Member of Parliament for Middlesex; Herbert Fry, publisher of *Fry's Royal Guide to the London Charities* (one of the leading guides to charitable giving); and W.T. Charley, author of a standard text on cab law, and Member of Parliament for Salford. Eventually the list of vice-presidents came to resemble the roll call of the House of Lords on a reasonable day. Charley, taking the chair at a meeting on 25 May, observed that many similar associations had been formed, but had failed, 'owing to what are called the higher classes of society not having taken that interest in their welfare they ought to have taken'. He outlined the objects of the new association, starting with the establishment of a fund for annuities to aged and infirm drivers, and one for the relief of drivers in temporary distress. Such a provident society, with members paying an annual subscription of 5*s*, was just the type of association that appealed to the charitable classes, especially if (as was the case) there was a strong spirit against strong spirits. Temperance was never far below the surface of the new association. The third object which Charley outlined was more contentious:

> To provide for the protection of the interests of individual members of the trade (by giving legal assistance when necessary, shortening the hours of cabmen, and generally reforming the abuses which exist at the present time).

This, it might be felt, was more appropriate to the functions of a trade union, which (it was stressed at a subsequent meeting in Pentonville) this association was decidedly not. Providence and protection proved uncomfortable bedfellows and, in the course of time it was the latter that was kicked out.

A decade previously, a cabman was reported in *All the Year Round* as saying, with regard to charitable clubs,

> The 'penny bank' and the 'sick fund' may be all very well, because the member pays for all he gets, but the 'free tea' provided every Sunday afternoon always sticks in my throat. While I'm able to do my work and pay my way, I don't want anything given to me. I ain't a child . . .

The old and the infirm, of course, could not pay their way, and it seems that it was to them that the Benevolent Association principally appealed, although at annual general meetings in the early 1880s there were regular complaints of an indifference on the part of cabmen in general. *The Centaur*, the mouthpiece of the Amalgamated Cab Drivers' Society, a trade union founded in 1874, was frequently scathing in its comments on unwanted patronage, referring to the 'slavish toadyism' that was evident at meetings of the Benevolent Association. In May 1879 it carried an article on 'Charity and Philanthropy *v* Self-Help and Self-Reliance', in which it contrasted the efforts of the Benevolent Association with those of the union. By that date the Prince of Wales had become patron, and he had presided over the association's annual dinner, giving the writer the chance to comment on the miserable condition of labourers on the Prince's Duchy of Cornwall estates. The article pointed out that, on the association's own showing, it had advanced less than £600 on loan, and had given, in the previous three to four years, pensions to 'some dozen old and decayed drivers'. Yet, in less than that time the union had expended £1,700 for benevolent purposes, including £700 on sick pay and £400 on legal fees. The union's antipathy to the patronizing tone of the Benevolent Association was carried over to the Cabmen's Shelter Fund, with which, for a time, it shared offices at 15 Soho Square.[22]

Like so many innovations in the London cab trade, the initiative came from outside, principally from Birmingham, although shelters had previously been established in Edinburgh in 1859 and in Liverpool ten years later. The latter was a permanent, brick-built construction, costly to erect and presenting problems of obstruction on a busy thoroughfare. The solution of erecting a removable wooden shelter was taken up in Birmingham, the first one being opened in 1872 outside the town hall, an unconscious tribute to its architect, Joseph Hansom. Others quickly followed, and within five years there were over a dozen. The 'Birmingham Shelter' – a 'lightsome and tastefully glazed box which suddenly made its appearance one morning, like a miniature Alladin's palace, complete in every detail' – quickly received the attention of the press.[23]

The *Globe* and the *British Medical Journal* upbraided London for being slow to follow suit, although an attempt to do so was made at about the same time that the first Birmingham shelter was opened. In January 1872, Henderson, the Chief Commissioner of the Metropolitan Police, wrote to the Home Office supporting a proposal, approved by the local Board of Works, to set up a shelter at Knightsbridge. The Home Office gave its permission, and work commenced on constructing the shelter, but was halted when an influential deputation from the neighbourhood complained that it 'would become the resort of idle, loose people'. Work therefore ceased, and the contractor sought compensation for his loss. It was not just residents who complained, for tradespeople might also see shelters as a threat. A shelter at Victoria Station was moved twice; firstly when the person holding the railway refreshment contract complained of loss of business, and secondly when the St George's Vestry complained of its re-erection at Stockbridge Terrace, just outside the station.[24]

The tradespeople least likely to receive a sympathetic ear were publicans, and the provision of cab shelters was seen as an effective weapon in the war against drink. In 1875 Sir George Armstrong, proprietor and editor of the *Globe*, was instrumental in setting up the Cabmen's Shelter Fund in London, an organization which, while independent of the Cabmen's Benevolent Association, had a measure of overlap with it. The earliest shelters were rather like bathing machines, and cost around £80 to £100 to construct, but, after a number of complaints, the fund ran a competition for an

CABMEN'S SHELTER FUND.

OFFICES—185, VICTORIA STREET, S.W.

President.

HIS GRACE THE DUKE OF PORTLAND.

Hon. Treasurer.	Hon. Secretary.
CAPT. G. C. H. ARMSTRONG.	WALTER H. MACNAMARA, Esq.

THIS FUND was established in 1875 for the purpose of supplying Cabmen, when on the ranks, with a place of shelter where they can obtain good and wholesome refreshments at very moderate prices. The Shelters are supplied with papers, and small Libraries are attached to many of them. No charge is made to the driver for admission.

Forty Shelters have now been placed in various parts of the Metropolis, and are used by over 3000 Cabmen daily.

The Committee desire to extend the movement, so that eventually every cab-stand in the Metropolis of sufficient size may be provided with a place of shelter in inclement weather for those who at present are driven to the public-house for refreshment and warmth.

DONATIONS and ANNUAL SUBSCRIPTIONS in aid of this Fund will be thankfully received by the Honorary Secretary at the Office, or by the Bankers, Messrs. BARCLAY, BEVAN, TRITTON, RANSOM, BOUVERIE & Co., Pall Mall, S.W.

BRABAZON H. MORRIS, *Gen. Superintendent.*

FORM OF BEQUEST.

" I give and bequeath unto the Treasurer, for the time being, of the Charitable Institution known as the CABMEN'S SHELTER FUND, London, the sum of *   pounds, to be paid, free of Legacy Duty, out of such part of my Personal Estate as I may by law bequeath to Charitable Institutions, to be applied towards the general purposes of the said Fund, and to be payable as soon after my decease as possible."

* The sum to be expressed in words, *not* figures.

The cabman's shelter was a provincial innovation, brought to London largely through the efforts of the Cabmen's Shelter Fund. Some still survive, and at least one has been listed as a building of historical and architectural interest. From Herbert Fry, *Royal Guide to the London Charities*, 1889–90

A London cabmen's shelter, from the
Illustrated London News, 1890. This gives a
good sense of the cramped interior, although
it cannot be supposed that the cabmen ate
their meals in such apparent, trappist silence

improved design, which led to a more satisfactory shelter being introduced at a cost of
around £200. Space was always at a premium, for the Metropolitan Police insisted that
the shelters should not take up more space at a stand than that occupied by a horse and
cab. At busy stands the shelters were invariably full at meal-times, and drivers spilled
out into the street. Originally the fund appointed paid attendants and allowed them to
keep the profits from the refreshments which they provided, at a tariff set by the
committee. To meet the cost of wages, tickets were issued to drivers at not less than 1*d*
a day or more than 4*d* a week. Some 60,000 tickets were issued in the first year, but
many drivers refused to pay merely to enter a shelter, and the system was speedily
changed. By 1876 the shelters were thrown open free to cabmen, the wages of
attendants were discontinued and the fund took instead a weekly sum varying from 6*d*
to 7*s* 6*d*, depending on the location. In addition to providing tea, coffee, and bread and
butter, the attendants were allowed to charge 1*d* for cooking food brought into the
shelter by the drivers, although, by the 1890s, regular meals were being prepared and
served. Although much of this was good, plain fare, there were gourmet cabmen.
Walter Macnamara, the secretary of the fund, reported in 1894 that

In the Piccadilly shelter and Palace Yard, and one or two other shelters you get a
smart set of men, hansom cab drivers, who are extremely particular . . . about their

112

steaks and their new potatoes, and their salads, and everything of that kind. They are quite as ready to complain as members of West End clubs if things are not right.

By this time there were some forty shelters, used by 3,500 cabmen daily, and the fund prided itself on its contribution to temperance. An appeal for funds in 1896 observed that

> The warm and well-lighted Shelter, with its accompaniment of good tea, coffee, and other drinks of non-alcoholic character, is a strong incentive to sobriety; and the Committee have abundant testimony that their work has conduced to this happy result, intemperance having gradually decreased amongst the cab-driving fraternity in the most marked manner since the formation of the Fund.

Many cabmen resented this attempt to reform them. They objected to the rules of the committee, which prevented card playing in the shelters, and prohibited any publications, notices or pictures being displayed without its sanction. The committee was adamant in its refusal to open itself up to representatives of the men, and ill-feeling was aroused when union notices were forbidden in shelters during the privilege strike of 1894.[25]

Self-help (through friendly societies, co-operatives or trade unions) was felt by many cab drivers to be the only effective source of protection and to offer the only hope of a solution of their problems. Organization was particularly difficult among cabmen, however. Casual drivers were always attracted to the trade, while many cabs were driven by owner-drivers who, being self-employed, were not regular trade union material. The early labour history of the London cab trade is therefore one of small, ephemeral organizations, struggling hard to maintain their existence. Charles Booth wrote of a shortlived union formed in 1867 which was advanced for its time, but which soon collapsed. More successful was the Amalgamated Cab Drivers' Society, which was formally registered in July 1874, the leadership being taken by H.W. Rowland, a driver who had been in the trade for some five or six years. In 1879 Rowland started *The Centaur* as a weekly mouthpiece for the union, and this ran until 1885 when he disappeared in suspicious circumstances and the union broke up. By the early 1880s membership was fluctuating around the eight hundred mark (out of more than 12,500 licensed drivers), and in 1883 an attempt was made to widen membership by admitting owner-drivers with a single cab and by introducing a new membership class (with benefits limited to legal aid) at a weekly subscription of 2d, half the normal rate.[26]

The collapse of the Amalgamated Cab Drivers' Society was partially offset by the Cab Drivers' Mutual Aid and Protection Society, set up in 1888. It speedily attracted two thousand members, but they fell off to around three hundred by 1890. In the summer of that year the society was reorganized as the Metropolitan Cab Drivers' Trade Union with the help of John Burns, who had been among the leaders of the successful London Dock Strike in 1889. It fought a successful strike against the Shrewsbury and Talbot Company in 1891, but, as so often happened, membership fell off once the men's demands were met. By the time of the great strikes against the railway privilege in 1894 and 1896 the union had again been transformed, this time into the London Cab Drivers' Trade Union. The latter struggle cost the union £20,000, and, in the bitterness of defeat, membership fell from a strike-time high of seven thousand to three thousand thereafter. In order to give more power to the branches, it was restructured in 1904, but membership did not pick up. After further metamorphoses in 1911 and 1920, the union merged with the Transport and General Workers' Union in 1922.[27]

The history of cab trade unionism before the First World War is not one of success. Wilkins saw the problem clearly when he wrote in 1893:

Unfortunately the great bulk of London cabdrivers are too underpaid, too overworked, too isolated to combine, and it is just because they do not combine that they remain underpaid, overworked, and isolated.[28]

Chapter Nine

CABS AND THE RAILWAYS

A t the beginning of the railway age there were many people who predicted that the iron horse would soon bring about the demise of the horse of flesh and blood. That this would happen was not universally seen as a disaster. In 1836 Henry Fairbairn, in his *Political Economy of Railroads*, argued that, as four people could be fed from the land that produced fodder for one horse, railways would 'make room for human beings to a considerable extent'. But Fairbairn, like other less optimistic prophets, was wrong; for, while long-distance road traffic soon felt the competition of the railway, local traffic was greatly increased. Professor Michael Thompson once observed that 'Without carriages and carts the railways would have been like stranded whales, giants unable to use their strength, for these were the only means of getting people and goods right to the doors of houses, warehouses, markets and factories, where they wanted to be.'[1] To carriages and carts we may add cabs. In 1839 the mail coach magnate George Sherman cheerfully announced that 'there would be as much employ for horses as ever there was', because of the 'extraordinary quantity of omnibuses and cabs'. But even he might not have foretold that, between then and the turn of the century, the number of cabs in London would increase by well over sixfold.

The image of the railway as a stranded whale is perhaps too cosy. In their vast power and their conquest of territory they might be considered as armies, their termini like great transit camps staffed by uniformed officers subjected to almost military discipline. It should come as no surprise, therefore, that the railways attempted to exert a similar order upon their mercenaries – the cabs which brought the passengers to their gates, or who sped them on their way, either to their homes and hotels, or to connect with some rival army, half way across the metropolis. Railway directors, with their gold or silver passes, were like generals. Their numbers in Parliament often ran into three figures, making 'the railway interest' a powerful force to be reckoned with. That power can be seen in many things, including the tenacity with which the railway companies defended 'the privilege', or the right to determine which cabs might ply for hire from the stations, which remained their private property. No cab, of course, was barred from depositing a passenger at the departure side of a station, but strict controls were applied at the arrivals side. Only privileged cabs had the right to wait there, for which selected masters were obliged to pay a security of £2, together with a weekly fee of around 1*s* 6*d* or 2*s*. Having brought a passenger to the station, the unprivileged cabman was required to drive away, empty. Each company struck its own agreements, but by granting 'the privilege' to certain cab proprietors to the exclusion of others, they were in the position to distribute monopoly powers within a trade where such powers had so recently been overthrown. Even so, the practice was not abandoned until January 1908, when it was finally outlawed by Parliament.

The privilege began at Euston in 1839, not long after the opening there of the London and Birmingham Railway's terminus. An agreement was reached between the directors and a Mr Moss for the supply of twelve new four-wheeled cabs for the exclusive use of the company. Perhaps because it was so well served by omnibuses, it was not until 1845 that the Great Western Railway adopted the privilege at Paddington, but most other companies embarked upon the practice at that time, or as soon as their termini opened. The extent of railway-generated cab traffic is made clear by evidence presented to the Royal Commission on Metropolitan Termini, which showed that, between 11 March and 11 April 1846, some 3,185 cabs left Euston with passengers for the City, and 6,989 made journeys to the West End. From Euston, cabs carried over 130,000 passengers annually to and from the City, and over 308,000 to the West End, totals greatly in excess of those carried by omnibus. That much of this lucrative traffic was reserved for a few proprietors – only 1,875 out of 11,297 licensed cabs were 'privileged' in 1890 – was bound to lead to friction. This was especially so as the conditions which may have justified the practice when it was first instituted did not last long.[2]

Although we have little detailed knowledge of the privilege in its early years, there can be little doubt that it was defended on the same grounds that were cited throughout the century: that it provided a means of controlling and disciplining the drivers; that it ensured a supply of superior vehicles; and that it guaranteed an adequate supply of cabs to meet all the trains. While it may have been necessary to secure such guarantees before Metropolitan Police control of the cab trade had become effective, there was less justification afterwards, and each of the arguments was opposed by the mass of unprivileged cabmen.

The railway companies claimed that granting the privilege to selected cab proprietors enabled them to secure drivers who were smarter, more polite and more honest than the run of their brethren. Francis Bond Head explained how the system worked at Euston in 1849, but the description was true also of other stations and other times:

Close to each departure-gate there is stationed a person whose duty it is to write down in a book the number of each cabman carrying away a passenger, as well as the place to which he is conveying him, which two facts each driver is required to exclaim as he trots by; and thus any traveller desirous to complain of a cabman, or who may have left any property in a carriage from Euston Station, has only to state on what day and by what train he arrived, also whither he was conveyed, and from these data the driver's name can at any lapse of time be readily ascertained.[3]

Offending drivers were subject to a fine, amounting in 1853 to 5s for drunkenness, insolence or overcharge of fare, or 10s for retaining an article left by a passenger in the cab. A second offence rendered a man liable to dismissal. While such disciplinary powers might have been necessary when the first railway termini were opened, it is harder to justify them once all cab drivers were licensed. Drivers resented the quasi-magisterial claims of the railway companies to control them, and at times the latter were guilty of employing a circular argument. For example, in 1895, Henry Lambert, general manager of the Great Western, claimed that the company could take disciplinary action against a privileged driver who refused to take a passenger from the station which, being private property, he was legally entitled to do. But had the railway cab stands been declared public – which the companies consistently opposed – the ordinary forces of the law would have taken over. In other words, the railway companies created disciplinary problems for themselves by removing their stands from the authority of the Metropolitan Police. They argued that drivers of privileged cabs developed an attachment to them, but it has to be recognized that that attachment could be broken, at any time, by the master. He determined which men should drive his cabs, and his dismissal of a driver meant that any advantage the man might have enjoyed would be lost at a stroke. James Scott, Secretary of the London Improved Cab Company, claimed that first class drivers on the streets would consider it beneath them to become privileged drivers, though the work might appeal to what he described as, 'men who have stood the test of years.' To this extent, the privilege might have given the railways a body of docile, tractable men who preferred the regularity of station work to the greater risks (and greater rewards) of street work.[4]

It seems harder still to sustain the railway companies' view that the privilege secured them a better class of vehicle. While the practice might have spared them from the very worst vehicles, there is ample testimony that it did not secure them the best. Herbert Walker, District Superintendent of the London and North Western Railway, admitted as much in 1906. 'It is known . . . ,' he said, 'that the very smartest cabs will not do railway work if they can afford it, on account of the damage that is caused . . . by the conveyance of luggage.' At much the same time the firm of Phillips and Brickland, who held the Great Eastern privilege, produced coachbuilders' accounts which showed that the wear and tear on their station cabs was 12.5 per cent higher than for street cabs. Roofs had to be more frequently recovered because of

The Liverpool Street terminus of the Great Eastern Railway, *c.* 1905. At this time Liverpool Street had 125 privileged cabs, while Paddington, the terminus of the Great Western Railway, had 290 – more than any other station

damage by tin trunks and other heavy luggage; linings were more easily ripped; and horses, startled by trains, knocked the cabs about more. John Colam, Secretary of the Royal Society for the Prevention of Cruelty to Animals (RSPCA), singled out the London, Brighton and South Coast railway at Victoria as a 'nest of cruelty in regard to the horses' owing to collusion between the railway superintendent and the largest of the privileged owners there. RSPCA inspectors were forbidden to enter that station, and Public Carriage Office inspectors were not allowed in to inspect vehicles. There was every temptation, therefore, for privileged masters to hide away their inferior horses and vehicles in the dark interiors of railway stations, especially as departing passengers were eager to get away (perhaps having to make a connection with a train on the other side of London) and were less likely to pick and choose.[5]

The third argument employed by the railway companies to justify the privilege was that it ensured an adequate supply of cabs to meet all trains. There may have been a real problem in the beginning, for the early termini were built on the outer fringes of the built-up area where, in ordinary circumstances, cabs might not choose to ply. When the lines opened, trains were not all that frequent. In 1839, for example, between 7.00 a.m. and

11.30 p.m. there were on weekdays only fourteen trains arriving at or leaving from Euston daily, and on Sundays there were but eight.[6] Once passenger traffic built up, however, the stations generated a very large part of the traffic carried by cabs. While the privileged cabs might be able to cope with the steady traffic, at peak times, or when boat trains or trains from the race courses came in, they often proved inadequate for the task, and ordinary street cabs had to be drawn in off the stands. Cabmen had a language of their own, and such vehicles came to be known as 'Bluchers' – last onto the field of battle and given the task of mopping up. It was the hope that they might be called in (at a flat fee of 1d in the 1880s and '90s) that encouraged many cab drivers to crawl around the streets adjacent to railway stations, adding considerably to the traffic congestion. The *Builder* calculated in 1882 that, each day, seven miles of London's streets were occupied by cabs crawling as a result of the privilege. This figure tells us more about the Victorians' love of bogus statistics than anything else, but the problem was a genuine one. The vivid description of John Burns, the Labour MP, may not have been far from the truth:

If I come to Victoria Station or to Charing Cross, as I do frequently, I find that privileged cab yard unoccupied. In some cases as at Victoria, which is capable of holding seven or eight hundred cabs, I find the stand relatively empty, or with the

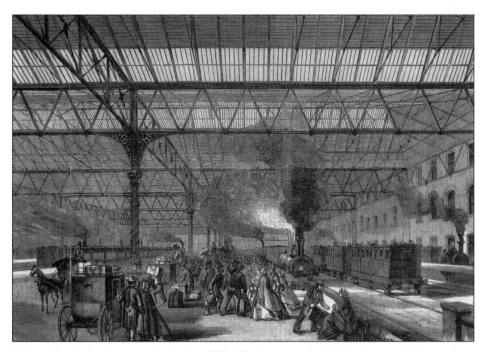

Cabs at Victoria Station, opened in October 1860. Whether or not the 'privilege' succeeded in securing a supply of superior cabs at the stations was hotly disputed. From the *Illustrated London News*, 4 May 1861

privileged cabs standing too far back, and in these days of speed and hurry, businessmen going to the City won't go to the privileged cab but walk straight on and find outside the non-privileged cabs and cabmen fighting for customers like flies round a butcher's block. They cannot get access to the station, but in trying to get the fares outside they obstruct all the narrow approaches to Victoria Station to the alarm and danger of some asthmatical old men and women who have to dodge about in front of buses or behind cabs and among the horses. There are fifty or sixty cabs outside the Victoria Station but not allowed to go in. If they were allowed, much of the crowding and obstruction outside the station would be removed.[7]

The railways' demand for cabs fluctuated seasonally. From a peak in July and August, when there was much interchange work between stations on account of the summer holidays, the demand fell until February, when the trough was reached, with just a slight rise during the Christmas period. The privileged cab season was thus slightly different from that of the street cab, with July, August and September being good months for the former, but falling months for the latter. Street cabs provided the element of flexibility in this annual cycle, being called upon principally in the summer peak, and (to a much lesser extent) at Christmas. Opponents of the privilege argued that, if street cabs were good enough to bail out passengers at peak times, it was wrong to exclude them from the 80 to 90 per cent of railway work reserved for the privileged cabs.[8]

Although isolated complaints against the privilege system were made from at least the 1840s, it was not until the end of the 1860s that the issue came to prominence. On 3 February 1868 a deputation of cab proprietors met Benjamin Disraeli, the Chancellor of the Exchequer, and requested a reduction of duties. They argued that rent and the cost of fodder had increased since fares had last been fixed in 1853, while developments in London's transport system had diminished their trade. In particular, 'The Metropolitan Railway now carried passengers at so small a price from the west-end to the City, and so expeditiously, that cabs had lost one of their principal sources of profit.' Cabs were not required as much as before, they argued, 'in consequence of the connection of the various railways'.[9] A general dullness of trade was complained of in London at this time. On 28 May *The Times* reported in its leader columns that, 'Never was there so bad a season, never was trade so dull, never was London so *triste* in the Epsom week . . .' The Queen's constant absence from London was blamed for this state of affairs, as was the aftermath of the 1866 commercial crisis. A scapegoat was sought for the cabmen's ills, and they found it, as they did at other times, in the privilege system.[10]

The driving force for change was the Amalgamated Hackney Carriage Proprietors' Association. On 5 June I.S. Crocker, the Association's secretary, wrote to the railway companies with termini in London. If the stations were opened the association offered

1*d* per entrance, and they supported their claim by observing that 'the cabs are so much superior to what they were ten or twelve years ago'.[11] Their petitions to the railway companies fell on deaf ears, only the London and North-Western Railway deigning even to meet the deputation. Proprietors and men met at the Cambridge Hall, Newman Street, on 21 July. They mulled over familiar complaints, but they drew back from strike action. The cab strike of 1853 had been only partially successful, and furthermore had led to a change in the law which rendered a proprietor liable to a fine of 20*s* a day and revocation of his licence if he kept his cab off the streets for two successive days, or two days in one week, without due cause. It was not until the end of August that non-privileged proprietors decided to withdraw their cabs, and then (to circumvent the law) it was planned to keep them off the streets until 11.00 a.m., and to take them off again after 2.00 p.m. This was designed to hit the railway companies at their points of peak travel, but they do not appear to have been greatly inconvenienced, and responded by throwing their stations open to all privileged cabs on a reciprocal basis. The cabmen were obliged to step up their campaign, and on 4 September withdrew their cabs entirely from the streets. The strike, however, came to nothing, and collapsed within five days. If anything, it actually set back the cause of the non-privileged cabmen. The privilege had not previously figured large in the eyes of the public, but now it seemed vindicated. With the public apparently on their side, the railway companies remained intransigent, and even threatened to license and run their own cabs if pushed too far.[12]

The question did not disappear from the political agenda, however. On 3 December 1868, following the Liberal victory in a general election, Gladstone formed his first ministry. Just over three weeks later, Sir Richard Mayne died at his London home. The cab trade was to find itself under a new Home Secretary, Henry Bruce, and a new Commissioner of Police, Colonel Edmund Henderson. Robert Lowe, in his first budget of April 1869, repealed the weekly duty on hackney carriages, paving the way for Bruce (who was in favour of free trade in cabs) to introduce a system whereby proprietors could, in effect, set their own fares. The privilege system did not fit easily with these *laissez-faire* principles, but a frontal attack on the railway interest was to be avoided, if at all possible. Instead, a provision was surreptitiously slipped into new hackney carriage regulations of 1870 which, if carried through to its logical conclusion, would have made the privilege unworkable. Section 9 of the regulations, which were to come into effect on 1 January 1870, ordered that

No Hackney Carriage shall be let to hire elsewhere than on an authorized public standing, nor shall any fare be recoverable in respect of any hiring unless at the time of the hiring the Carriage hired shall have been plying on an authorized public standing . . .

Great Northern Railway.

REGULATIONS

To be adopted by Owners and Drivers of Hackney Carriages, engaged to wait for the arrival of Trains at the Great Northern Railway Station, King's Cross.

1st.—That each Driver, on entering the Station, shall fall into line upon the prescribed Stand, and take his place in rotation, and there wait upon his box until specially engaged by an authorised servant of the Company, or by a Train Passenger, for whose use and the use, of the Company's Officers exclusively, such carriages are to enter the Station and to remain in waiting till required.

2nd.—That no Driver be permitted to ply for hire while in waiting within the Station, either by word, gesture, signal, or otherwise, under pain of dismissal.

3rd.—Each Driver to have in his possession a supply of small Tickets, provided by the Company showing the number of his vehicle; and he must invariably, on being called for, or taking a Job, offer to the Passenger one of those Tickets, whether it be asked for or not.

4th.—No charge may be made for a reasonable quantity of Luggage when only one passenger is conveyed. The Drivers are not entitled to ask for anything beyond the regulated fare, even though there may be three or more persons and luggage, unless the parties be informed prior to the job been taken, that such will be the case.

5th.—That on each day every Driver shall render an account, in writing, on the prescribed form, at the departure Lodge, to the Hackney Carriage Number Taker, stating the previous day's work, or jobs performed by him from the Station, with the particulars, and duly signed by him.

6th.—That the sum of Forty Shillings be deposited by the undersigned Owner of and for each and every of his carriages, with the Superintendent of the Company, as security for the due adherence to these regulations : and any fines which may be inflicted in pursuance thereof are to be taken from the deposit, unless paid by the Driver at the time. *one by a gentleman*

7th.—That the sum of Two Shillings per week for each carriage be paid by the undersigned Owner, to the Superintendent of the Company, towards the expense of the attendance of a Hackney Carriage Clerk, and other Hackney Carriage Porters or Attendants, or other person to see to the well working of the said carriages, as from time to time directed by the Company's Superintendent.

8th.—That each carriage authorised to be admitted under these Regulations shall be inspected and approved by the Superintendent of the Great Northern Railway prior to its admission ; that the body of each vehicle shall be painted blue, and the carriage and wheels white, according to pattern, and shall bear on the upper panel on each side the words "Great Northern Railway," and the Register Number in gold characters, the whole in accordance, and samples to be shown ; that each carriage shall be provided with iron rails at the edge of the roof, for the purpose of placing and securing Luggage ; and a chain to pass over the several articles placed outside each carriage ; and that the carriages shall be constantly maintained or kept in proper repair.

9th.—That every Driver, as well as the carriages and horses so employed, shall, if afterwards objected to or disapproved of by the said Superintendent, be immediately removed, and if another more efficient Driver, or a better carriage or horse (to the said Superintendent's satisfaction), be not sent within this contract to be cancelled, and the deposit money forfeited, and carried to the Provident Fund for the maintenance of the sick Servants of the Company.

10th.—That it shall be the duty of each Driver, in case any parcel, package, or other article shall be left by a passenger in his carriage, to give notice forthwith to the Hackney Carriage Clerk, and the Driver shall also deposit such parcel, package, or other article, according to law, and to the regulations made by the Stamp Officer.

11th.—That each and every Proprietor shall guilty of any or either of the following irregularities, namely,—

Drunkenness.
Insolence.
Overcharge of Fare or Luggage. *his route or destination the Station*
Refusing to give or show his number at the gate before leaving, or for not keeping his rank.
Not having a copy of the Company's Regulations in his carriage.
Keeping any parcel, package, or other article, left by a passenger in his carriage, without giving notice forthwith to the Hackney Carriage Clerk of the Great Northern Railway, at the Station, and without depositing such parcel, package, or other article, according to law, and to the regulations made by the Stamp Office.
Or for the breach of any of the Regulations in this Agreement, not in this Rule specifically referred to.

12th.—That the Hackney Carriage Owner who becomes party to this Agreement agrees to give fourteen days' previous notice, in writing, of his desire to discontinue the same, and withdraw his Carriages, or forfeit the sum deposited for each Carriage, which shall be

Signed

185

SEYMOUR CLARKE,
General Manager.

I have read over and received a Copy of the above " Regulations," as to the working of Public Vehicles in the King's Cross Station ; and I hereby undertake to send in_____ Carriages, well appointed, and in all respects according to the above " Regulations," to which I agree to abide in full : and in witness thereof I hereto set my hand, this_____ day of_____ 18__

WITNESS

A draft for revised rules for the Great Northern Railway in the 1860s. The regulations which the railway companies drew up for privileged cabs were very similar. (PRO, RAIL 236/283/7)

The effect would have been that ill-disposed people could take a cab from a station, refuse to pay the fare and leave the driver with no remedy. When the railway companies pointed out what they thought, at first, was a drafting error, the Home Office pointed out that the solution lay with the companies themselves. They should agree to make the railway stands authorized public standings, 'with the effect that all cabs which so pleased might enter, as might inspectors from the Public Carriage Office'. A Home Office minute makes it quite clear that

> The clause was expressly intended by Henderson to put a stop to the "privileged system" of the Railway Companies and to prevent the "creeping cabs" . . . [It had] been done advisedly and after great consideration by Henderson.'[13]

Once the cat was out of the bag, the press turned on the new order, pouring scorn on all its provisions, but in particular on Section 9, which *The Times* described as an 'absurd arrangement'. Bruce quickly withdrew the regulations, and soon let the vexed

A Thomas Tilling cab, outside a station of the South Eastern Railway, 1885. Tilling's, with a head office at Peckham, was one of the largest of the London firms of jobmasters, with a stud of 2,500 horses in the early 1890s. His horses served the London Fire Brigade and the Metropolitan Police, and also ran in trams. This is a posed photograph, and a badly posed one at that, for no self-respecting driver would set off with his cab so badly out of trim. The great advantage of the hansom was that the driver could maintain the cab in balance both with and without a passenger

question of the privilege drop. By 1871 he was involved in a yet more contentious matter, namely the passing of a Licensing Bill. One such problem at a time was surely enough. 'Beer and Cabs had better be left alone as far as possible', said R.A. Cross, Home Secretary in 1879. Bruce would no doubt have agreed with him.[14]

What might have proved the breakthrough came four years later when, in March 1883, H.W. Rowland, Secretary of the Amalgamated Cab Drivers' Society and publisher of *The Centaur*, announced that, as from 1 May, the South Eastern Railway would abandon the privilege, on an experimental basis, at its three termini of Charing Cross, London Bridge and Cannon Street.[15] If the opening of these stations to all cabs was to prove a success, opponents of the privilege would score a considerable victory. But, for reasons which are unclear (but which carry the taint of dirty tricks on the part of certain privileged proprietors), the experiment was a failure, and within four years had failed entirely. It seems that the company originally wanted 1½d from the driver for each entrance, but the union (not without difficulty) secured the support of proprietors to guarantee the South Eastern against loss if they were admitted for 1d. This the company accepted. It was not long, however, before there were complaints of lack of discipline at Charing Cross, which even *The Centaur* railed against: 'We find a section of the drivers running riot there and the staid men, in most instances, standing by and letting the whole thing go by the board.'[16]

In addition to problems of discipline, the company found the financial arrangements unsatisfactory and, by December 1884, seemed ready to bring the experiment to an end. In order to keep the stations open, Rowland proposed that the union should farm the tolls at the same rate that the privileged cabs had previously paid. In June 1885 the union commenced to pay the company £40 a week, and to collect the money from the drivers. Within two weeks the union was in deficit to the sum of £25, and had to raise the charge from 1d to 1½d. In the second week of October, Rowland disappeared (the *Hackney Carriage Guardian* said he *absconded*) and the union was thrown into turmoil. The company agreed to drop the weekly toll from £40 to £30, but they continued to feel that the arrangement was unsatisfactory, and in February 1887 the privilege was reintroduced.[17]

The abortive experiment at the South Eastern Railway stations helped to wreck the Amalgamated Cab Drivers' Society. In 1890 the more militant Metropolitan Cabdrivers' Trade Union was formed, which was itself reconstructed four years later as the London Cabdrivers' Trade Union. With many of the men imbued with a new spirit of militancy, there were numerous strikes between 1891 and 1896 over the questions of hiring prices and the privilege. It was also at this time, under the Liberal Government from 1892 to 1895, that the question of the privilege was most systematically investigated, principally by a Home Office Committee of Enquiry which was appointed in June 1894 and reported in the following January.[18]

Herbert Asquith became Home Secretary (his first ministerial appointment) in August 1892. He was initiated into the London cab trade in September 1893 when a strong deputation of cab drivers was received at the Home Office, introduced by Thomas Lough, MP for Islington West. Lough argued that the cab trade had been depressed for the past twenty years, but that this year was one of the most trying. He went through a familiar list of grievances but concentrated on just two: the privilege and the railway omnibuses. He claimed that, together, these milked the cabmen of £100,000 a year. He based this claim on two assumptions. The first was that the privileged proprietors charged their drivers £55,000 a year in extra hiring charges, although they paid the railways only £11,000. This he described as 'a system of sub-contracting or sweating'. Secondly, he argued that the 160 omnibuses run by the railways themselves each earned £5 a week, making over £40,000 a year lost to the cab trade.[19]

It was hard to shake the railway companies from their complacency, but the drivers now had the bit between their teeth, and a strike which broke out in May 1894 made some of the companies realize that they were a little more vulnerable than they might care to believe. At the outset they probably shared the view, expressed in *Herapath's Railway Journal*, that the railways would be but little inconvenienced. But this time things were different. The greater militancy of the union expressed itself in the picketing of stations as well as cab yards, while the contracts which the companies had with privileged masters proved of no value in securing a supply of cabs when disenchanted drivers struck against their employers. On 16 May, Sir Henry Oakley, General Manager of the Great Northern Railway, reported to the traffic committee that they had been obliged 'to scour the streets' in order to secure cabs, and when Superintendent Parish of the King's Cross traffic police made enquiries among the other companies, it was apparent that a number of them were in difficulty, although they put a brave face on it. Oakley's resolve was shaken. When the strike was over he reported to the traffic committee that 'it may be a matter for consideration, whether we shall renew the system of "privilege"'.[20]

Asquith was in the middle of the series of meetings at which he aimed to mediate between the drivers and their masters when, on 9 June, he set up a Departmental Committee with a very wide brief to consider the metropolitan cab service, including 'the relations of cab-owners and drivers with the railway companies'. The chairman was G.W.E. Russell, MP, Under Secretary of State at the Home Office, and he was joined by Henry Cunynghame, who had recently been appointed legal assistant under secretary in the department. From the Board of Trade, which was playing an increasingly important role in industrial relations, came Francis Hopwood. The remaining four members were Members of Parliament. Thomas Lough and John Burns represented the interests of the men. E.H. Bayley (Liberal, North Camberwell), chairman of the London Improved Cab Company, took the employers' side, as in large part did C.A. Whitmore (Conservative, Chelsea), trustee of the Temiscouata Railroad, Canada, and former assistant private secretary to Henry Matthews, the previous Home Secretary. The committee held eighteen meetings and took evidence from nearly fifty witnesses.

When the report of the Departmental Committee was published in January 1895, the majority of the members were in favour of the abolition of the privilege. They were strongly influenced by the irritation which the privilege caused within the trade, and they believed that the increased strictness of vehicle inspection and examination of drivers, which they recommended elsewhere in the report, would provide sufficient guarantees to the railway companies in respect of both cabs and drivers. They fell short of proposing that railway stations be declared public places, but recommended that companies be required to draw up regulations to admit all cabs on payment of a penny toll.

Before any action could be taken, however, the government went out of office. After a general election in July the Conservatives returned to power, with Sir Matthew White Ridley as Home Secretary. Ridley, a director of both the North Eastern and Forth Bridge Railways, was more sympathetic to the railways' position. Faced with their implacable opposition, and unwilling to introduce legislation that would have forced them to end the privilege, he had decided by the beginning of September to let the whole matter drop. *Herapath's Railway Journal* was triumphant: 'The Home Office has no power to interfere with anything inside the gates of a railway yard, and parliament, we feel sure, would not countenance legislation subversive of the rights of property where such rights are clearly exercised in the public interest.' The Home Office kept up a pretence of seeking a negotiated settlement, but the effect was simply to allow the railway companies to make plans to counter the inevitable industrial action of the non-privileged cabmen. When strike action was taken in September 1896, the companies were ready for it. All their available private omnibuses were put into operation; licences were secured for their own employees to drive cabs provided by sympathetic cabmasters (the Great Western had plans to bring in cabs from the provinces); and arrangements were made for the forwarding of passengers' luggage by parcels van, at the rate of 3*d* per package. This simple expedient, which was subsequently made permanent, had a serious impact on the demand for cabs, for heavy luggage had previously been the impediment to many passengers who otherwise would have used omnibuses or the underground railway.[21]

Faced with the superior organization and combined strength of the railway companies, on 26 October a general strike was declared against all yards which refused to carry the union's anti-privilege label. Three days later the union played its final card, refusing to set down any passenger on railway property, insisting instead that they be dropped in the street. This proved a fatal move. The magistrates quickly declared this to be illegal (a decision which was upheld by the High Court) and public

Cabs at Victoria Station. The hansom on the right is a privileged cab of the London & North-Western Railway, at Euston. In 1896, in an attempt to break an anti-privilege cabstrike, the railway companies instituted a reciprocal arrangement whereby cabs privileged by one company might also ply at the stations of another

opinion was alienated. By the first week of November the strike had virtually collapsed, with the men, once more, having made no progress towards their goal.[22]

It was to take a change of government (a new Home Secretary, Herbert Gladstone) and yet another enquiry (this time a Select Committee of the House of Commons in 1906) before the privilege eventually came to an end. The Select Committee was highly critical of the indecisiveness of the Home Office:

We observe that the questions referred to us under [the] head [of horsed vehicles] have mostly either (1) been previously reported upon by Committees or officials, whose recommendations have hitherto remained without effect; or (2) are regarded as so difficult that the Department of State concerned is careful to avoid the expression of any opinion upon their solution.

It was in the public interest, the Select Committee concluded, that the large questions affecting the cab trade should be settled without delay, and without continuing 'the search for an ideal solution'. They therefore reiterated the recommendation that the privilege be abolished for a trial period of one year. It would not be lost to members of the trade, they concluded, that a railway company which failed to secure an adequate supply of cabs would be under a great inducement to start cabs of its own - and these were likely to be motor cabs.[23]

The rapid rise of the motor cab, from 96 vehicles licensed in 1906 to 723 licensed in 1907, heralded a dramatic change in the cab trade, and Herbert Gladstone seized upon this as a pretext for action. Whatever they might feel about privileged cabs, he argued that all would agree that something had to be done to ease the drivers' hardships. Opponents of his Bill, however, were able to argue that it was essentially a measure to facilitate the fixing of taximeters in cabs, and that the clause to abolish the privilege had been 'pitchforked' into it (and, by implication, could just as easily be pitchforked out again). Gladstone was determined to succeed, however. It was he who had secured the electoral pact with Ramsay MacDonald and the Labour Party in 1903, and his years at the Home Office from 1905 to 1910 were marked by a number of measures favourable to labour, not least the Workmen's Compensation Act of 1906.[24]

The London Cab and Stage Carriage Act received the royal assent in August 1907. On 1 January 1908 all the main line termini were thrown open for an experimental period of two years. Ironically, abolition came just at the moment when it became impossible to tell whether the fears and hopes which such a move inspired were justified. Although it was not until 1910 that the motor cabs of London came to outnumber the horse cabs, 1908 perhaps marks the year when this outcome truly became inevitable. Whether the motor cab companies would have annexed the privilege, had it still existed, we shall never know. As it happened, the motor cabs were kept from entering the stations until 1910, allegedly because of insurance problems. Nor is it likely that the non-privileged drivers received much benefit from abolition, although the situation might have been different in 1895 or 1869 had the change come then.[25]

Why the railway companies clung to the privilege system with such passion is not easy to explain. It was clearly not for the financial gain, which was trifling. Nor is there much in the argument that the railways saw the privilege as the best way of providing a cab service for their passengers. Motives were probably mixed, but the dominant one would seem to have been a fierce attachment to the rights of private property, coupled with the fear that the loss of control over cabs, and the full assumption of that control by the Metropolitan Police, might set the precedent for a diminution of their authority in other, more crucial areas.

Chapter Ten

FROM HORSE TO MOTOR

The abolition of the privilege in 1907 came at a time when the cab trade was undergoing the most fundamental change of its history – the transition from horse to mechanical power. Although the change-over was not complete by 1914, by that date the battle had been won, and there were more than five times as many motor cabs on the streets of London as there were horse cabs. The transformation was very rapid. The Home Office departmental committee of 1894 did

The design of the Bersey electric cab owed much to the London growler. 'Humming Birds' is what the horse cab drivers came to call them. From H.C. Moore, *Omnibuses and Cabs*, 1902

not once consider mechanical traction, although an electric cab had been running on the streets of Brighton a decade before. The first electric cabs in London were introduced in 1897. The earliest internal combustion engined cab received its licence in 1898, and from 1903 onwards motor cabs were a permanent feature of the streets. Until 1907 fewer than 100 cabs were in operation, but in that year the number leapt to 723, and by 1910 the number of motor cabs had overtaken that of horse cabs (Appendix 4). [1]

When the London Electrical Cab Company placed eighteen cabs on the road in 1897, the Metropolitan Police were enthusiastic about the prospects:

[The] vehicles are roomy, the interiors well-fitted and the mechanism is well under the control of the driver. Experiments are, however, being made with a view to reduce their weight, &c.

Should electric carriages come generally into use, the effect on the traffic of the Metropolis will be marked, as such vehicles occupy but a little over one-half the space of that of a similar vehicle drawn by a horse. From a sanitary point of view also, a diminution in the number of horses in the streets is a desideratum. [2]

Electric cabs did not, however, come into general use, and the chief commissioner had correctly foreseen one of the principal problems, namely excessive weight. Writing in 1900, the engineer, W. Worby Beaumont, claimed that the London Electrical Cab Company's vehicles were subjected to much strain from the movement of the heavy batteries. One electric charge was sufficient for only 25 to 30 miles, and the company made the unwise choice of initially installing alternating current generators using costly electricity supplied from the power station at Deptford. Power was not the only problem, however, for the heavy vehicles were also plagued with tyre troubles. All of the cabs had been withdrawn by 1899, whereupon Worby Beaumont assessed this pioneering venture thus:

They were practical cabs but not commercial cabs . . . They were under-powered, and were too slow for people accustomed to London hansoms. After the novelty had worn off, public patronage fell off, and adverse criticism as to the rumble of the machinery and the jerking when stopping, starting, and slowing was very common. [3]

It was inevitable that the early days of the motor cab would witness false starts and technical dead-ends. This presented the police with a problem, for they had to regulate the construction of cabs with public comfort and safety in mind, while at the same time taking care not to stifle innovation. As motor manufacturers brought out new models, many of which had a potential use as cabs, the police had to establish that

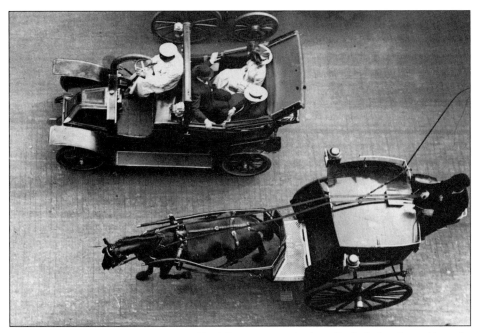

A Renault motor cab overtakes a hansom, 1907. It is easy to see why the police looked so favourably on the motor cab, for it took up much less road space. In 1906 fifteen feet were allowed for a four-wheeled horse cab on a rank, while a motor cab was reckoned to need only nine. The horse cab was also considered to be less 'environmentally friendly', contributing as it did to the total of around three million tons of manure that English towns have been estimated to have faced annually at the turn of the century

they were fitted to the task. This 'type approval' was intended to be rigorous, for, once it had been granted, a proprietor presenting a cab for licensing merely had to present a certificate that his vehicle was of an approved type and that no modifications had been made. It was then road tested, with particular attention being paid to brakes and steering. Thereafter the cab would be inspected annually for roadworthiness and condition, in the same manner as a horse cab and, like its predecessor, was subject to random checks.

The examination of motor vehicles was estimated to take three times as long as that of horse vehicles, and was more frequent. Barring accidents, a horse cab might not come under police notice for several months, whereas motor cabs frequently developed defects which required police examination. There was the additional problem that the burden of work in particular police divisions could fluctuate dramatically. For example the opening of the W. & G Du Cros Cab Company's garage at Acton necessitated the erection of a temporary building at Shepherd's Bush police station in 1910, in order to eliminate the hardship experienced by the company in having to send its cabs 4½ miles to the nearest police inspecting station.[4]

The first regulations for the construction of motor cabs were issued, in a provisional form, in March 1906. They were drawn up in consultation with the motor trade, and with the advice of a technical expert, W. Worby Beaumont, whom Lord Montague described to the Home Secretary as 'a very good man though between ourselves a trifle cranky'. Worby Beaumont was Editor of *Engineer*; Vice-president of the Society of Engineers, Vice-chairman of the Roads Improvement Association and Consulting Engineer to the Automobile Club. If, at a type inspection, the police rejected a motor cab, the manufacturer might appeal, in which event Worby Beaumont's opinion was taken, but his role as adviser both to the trade and to the police gave rise to a potential conflict of interest, which was objected to by the Select Committee on Motor Traffic in 1913.[5]

Giving evidence to the Select Committee on Cabs and Omnibuses in 1906, James Sturmey, Manager of the Duryea Motor Company and a spokesman for the Society of Motor Manufacturers and Traders, set out the manufacturers' view:

[We] hope no more restrictions will be put upon us than are absolutely necessary at the present time, because the construction of motor vehicles designed for the purposes of cab work is so entirely new that we have had very little experience in that direction. At present practically all the vehicles which are being used as cabs are merely the ordinary pleasure car chassis with a different body, and it is quite possible, as time goes on, very considerable modifications may be found desirable to suit the vehicles for this particular class of work, and if we make restrictive rules with regard to the construction, based upon our present knowledge only, we may be very likely preventing development along lines which may be very much to the benefit of the public in the end.[6]

Before the First World War many manufacturers dabbled in the cab market, but the modifications required by the police might dissuade a manufacturer from diverting resources in that direction if there was a large private demand to be satisfied. The 1919 Beardmore Mark 1 is regarded as the first London cab designed specifically to meet the requirements of the trade, and the history of the London cab since the First World War has been one where a very small number of manufacturers have dominated the trade. The police regulations regarding construction have been one of the principal causes of this.[7]

The coming of the motor cab provided an unprecedented opportunity for the introduction of the taximeter. Such a device had been offered to the authorities at least as early as 1829 and, although none was both practical and acceptable to the trade, they appeared at regular intervals throughout the century.[8] The first extended discussion of the taximeter was before the Home Office Departmental Committee of

A cab fitted with Von Uster's Patent Mile-index. An engraving from the *Illustrated London News*, 6 February 1847. There was a whole succession of such inventions from at least the 1820s, when one had been demonstrated to the Hackney Coach Commissioners

1894, when machines were demonstrated by Messrs Bruhn, Westendorp, Junge and Max of the Taxameter Manufactory, Hamburg and Berlin, and by Messrs Ridge and Hupton, who were British manufacturers. Over seven hundred cabs in Hamburg were already using the German taximeter, and meters were compulsory on first class cabs in that city. The trade witnesses, whether drivers or proprietors, gave the machines a very muted response, on account of their unreliability and their proneness to being tampered with. Neither Assistant Commissioner Alexander Bruce of the Metropolitan Police nor Edwin Ware from the Public Carriage Office felt that the taximeter could readily be adapted to the needs of the metropolis. The Home Office expressed no objection of principle if a machine could be devised that would satisfy all the requirements, though it was observed that legislation would be necessary if taximeters were to be introduced generally. Despite this lack of enthusiasm, the committee took the view that 'the advantages that would be attained by an instrument on which reliance could be placed appear . . . undeniable', and it suggested that the Commissioner should invite the submission of machines to be examined by a practical committee to include representatives of both proprietors and drivers. This, however, was not made one of the committee's formal recommendations, with the result that the Home Office and the Metropolitan Police were able quietly to ignore the whole question.[9]

It was not long before the taximeter attracted the interest of speculators, among whom was Frederick Simms, a key figure in the development of the British motor

The Taxameter Syndicate, incorporated in 1898, experimented with meters imported from Germany, which the drivers characterized as 'German toys'. They were never compulsory on horse-drawn cabs, and were a rarity on such vehicles

industry. Simms, a fluent German speaker, had been born in Hamburg, knew Gottfried Daimler well and acquired from him the British rights to his patents in 1893. He was later to work in collaboration with Bosch on the development of the magneto, and was an associate of Harry J. Lawson in the formation of the British Motor Syndicate and the Great Horseless Carriage Company. In December 1897 Simms entered into an agreement with the Berliner Taxameter Gesellschaft to form a company to purchase the British and American patent rights to the taximeter, and on 26 February the Taxameter Syndicate was incorporated. The syndicate acquired preferential rights to a thousand taximeters to be hired out, as well as a two-and-a-half-year option to purchase both the British and the American rights, and was required to introduce the meters into London and at least one large provincial town in England. In May 1898 Simms wrote to the Chief Commissioner with a request that he should demonstrate the device, but the police were diffident. A report from the Public Carriage Office held that there were 'two fatal faults' to the meter: starting the machine was dependent on the driver, who could not be legally compelled to do so; and in cases of dispute the evidence of the machine would not be accepted by a court of law. The syndicate continued to press the Commissioner, and at the end of June secured a statement that he had no objection to the meter being introduced, provided that the existing tariff was used.[10]

The syndicate introduced six hansom cabs fitted with taximeters on 16 March 1899, running them from the Hotel Cecil in the Strand for three months. The syndicate attempted to increase the number of its taximeter cabs by making arrangements with proprietors to hire their vehicles at a rate higher than the Asquith Award. However, the union picketed the yards, with the result that the syndicate was obliged to pay 16s a day rent on over forty cabs for which they had great difficulty getting drivers. No union member would work them, and the syndicate was able to find only unsatisfactory blackleg labour. Part of the problem was the altered relationship between proprietor and driver which the taximeter necessitated. Drivers were paid £2 a day, but were contractually bound to bring in a specified daily minimum sum, with no allowance being made for 'shorts'. Drivers had no incentive to earn more than the minimum, and the syndicate was therefore obliged to supplement the wage with a small commission. Fred Simmons, one of the union leaders, claimed that the annual rent of the meter (£9 2s 6d) was an extra burden which the trade could not afford, a view which seems to have been shared by many proprietors. The experiment proved a failure, as did the attempt by the Taxameter Syndicate to sell its patent rights.[11]

Speculative interest did not diminish, especially as the replacement of horse cabs by motors seemed to offer fresh opportunities to introduce the taximeter. Charles Mascart was a French inventor, and Managing Director of the Société Générale des Compteurs de Voitures (Taximètres) of Paris. An attempt by the city authorities of Paris to make the taximeter compulsory was overruled by the French supreme court in 1895, but taximeters were re-introduced in August 1904, and by May of 1906 some 8,500 of the city's 12,000 cabs had been fitted, many of them with Mascart's machine. It was from France that the great majority of investors came when, in December 1905, the Metropolitan Fare Register Company was incorporated, with the aim of exploiting Mascart's inventions in Britain. He gave evidence to the 1906 Select Committee on Cabs and Omnibuses, and his account of the Parisian experience weighed heavily with committee members, despite the fact that three witnesses from the Hackney Carriage Mutual Benefit Society, representing small masters, opposed meters on the ground of the additional expense to which proprietors would be put, as well as to the inaccuracy of the devices.[12]

Chief Inspector Bassom gave evidence for the police, who felt that none of the meters currently in existence would meet the needs of the London trade. Four had been tested by

Scotland Yard, but none could be relied upon, and all were liable to be tampered with. A further problem was the existing fare tariff, and all but one of the manufacturers had suggested that the tariff be made to fit the taximeter, rather than *vice versa*.[13]

The misgivings felt by Bassom were dismissed by the committee. Tampering with the mechanism would be easily detected, they claimed, and would be largely self-defeating as the bulk of any gains would pass to the proprietor rather than the driver (although they seem to have forgotten that, in the case of the owner-driver, they were one and the same person). The committee was greatly influenced by the apparent success of the taximeters in Berlin, Hamburg and Paris, and felt that the problems of the London fare structure could be easily overcome. They therefore proposed a new tariff, working in stages of one-sixth of a mile, that raised fares slightly over certain distances, but compensated for this by reducing the tariff for short distances. While the taximeter should be permissive for the horse cab, the committee felt that it should be compulsory for motor cabs, recommending a slightly higher tariff by distance and a more substantial rise by time.[14]

In no way was the evidence that had been heard overwhelmingly in favour of the introduction of the taximeter, and it is not surprising, therefore, that the committee's enthusiastic response should have been open to question. In particular, attention focused on the role of the committee's joint chairman, Henry Norman, especially as he became a director of two of the largest cab companies only a few months after the committee reported. In January and February 1907 there was discussion in the trade and financial press of the links between British and French taximeter and motor cab syndicates. Charles Mascart, for example, in addition to being Managing Director of the Société Générale des Compteurs de Voitures (Taximètres), was also a director of the Compagnie Française des Automobiles de Place (the leading taxi-cab company in Paris). But he was also a director of the General Motor Cab and United Motor Cab Companies, of whose boards Henry Norman was also a member. Commenting on these interconnections, *Motor Finance* observed at the beginning of January 1907 that

> [If] the parties interested could get matters so arranged between the Scotland Yard officials and the Home Office, that taximeters became compulsory adjuncts to all cabs, horse-drawn or motor propelled, working in London, and, further, that *their* taximeter was to be the chosen article, a valuable monopoly – some would call it a trust – would be established for their own exclusive benefit.

Motor Finance described the prospects of such a monopoly as 'not roseate', correctly observing that Scotland Yard could not see its way to advising the Home Office to make meters compulsory because of continuing difficulties with the fare structure, and also pointing out that there were several models on the market, none of which could be considered to enjoy a master patent. The tendency of the Home Office towards inaction was countered by the pressure coming from below. The earliest motor cabs had not been equipped with meters, but the General Motor Cab Company, incorporated in May 1906, proposed to place five hundred Renault cabs fitted with taximeters onto the streets, and there was a flurry of cab company incorporations in 1907.[15]

In order to introduce meters, two administrative problems had to be overcome. Firstly, the tariff had to be determined; secondly, the accuracy of the meters themselves had to be tested. On 22 January 1907 an unsigned draft Order of the Secretary of State was published, making taximeters optional for horse cabs from 1 March, but compulsory for motor cabs from 1 July. Setting 1 March as the date upon which horse cabs might introduce the taximeter presented problems, for it would seem that the suppliers were concentrating on the large orders from cab companies and that horse proprietors (who now saw that the public were attracted to the new device) found difficulty in getting hold of meters once they decided to fit them. There were also doubts as to the legality of the fares under the Secretary of States's Order, for Section 9(3) of the Metropolitan Public Carriage Act of 1869 prohibited the Home Secretary from fixing compulsory fares lower than those prevailing at the time the Act was passed. That level was set at 1s for journeys up to 2 miles. Gladstone retained this tariff for horse cabs not fitted with taximeters; but where a taximeter was fitted he proposed one of 6d for the first mile (or twelve minutes), with 3d for each half mile of six minutes thereafter. It was this lower tariff which posed legal difficulties. In March, therefore, a revised order was issued, which omitted a tariff for horse cabs fitted with taximeters, though it left a loophole by means of which proprietors could voluntarily adopt the lower tariff. However, the Home Office was finding itself completely wrong-footed over the whole issue. On 7 May a motor cab driver was summoned at Bow Street for demanding more than the legal fare as set out in the new order. The hirer had undertaken a journey of half a mile, for which the meter showed 8d but the driver had demanded 1s. His defence was that the order was *ultra vires*. The question was not settled, however, because the magistrates dismissed the summons on the grounds that the meter, though approved by the police, was unsealed. Gladstone had to admit in the House of Commons that none of the 140 taxicabs then in service had their meters sealed, as the police had yet to decide what tests should be undertaken.[16]

The introduction of taximeters added enormously to the administrative burdens on the Public Carriage Office. Between April and December 1908 some 12,979 meters were tested by Public Carriage Office staff, each test involving a drive of between 3 and 6 miles (which took twenty minutes or so), accompanied by a fifteen minute time test. Initially, as many as 30 per cent of meters failed, although the proportion was down to 10 per cent by the end of the year. In addition there was a considerable clerical burden keeping track of meters as they failed, were replaced, retested and refitted.[17]

It was not merely the technical aspects of the transition from the horse cab to the motor taxicab which demanded fresh procedures from the authorities. Like the licensing of vehicles, the licensing of motor cab drivers, while able to draw on previous experience, required some fresh thinking from the police. Between 1907 and 1910 there was a shortage of motor drivers, a problem quite unfamiliar to horse cab proprietors, who always managed to maintain a surplus of drivers. The nadir was reached in 1908, when there were only about seven drivers for every ten cabs. It remains possible that the ratio of drivers to vehicles was lower for motor cabs than for horse cabs for purely technical reasons. For example, it could be that the early motor cabs were so mechanically unreliable that they spent more time in the garage, thus reducing the demand for drivers. This does not seem to have been the case, however, for the motor companies complained of a shortage of drivers, and argued that cabs were lying idle because of this. The conclusion that has to be drawn, therefore, is that, at the height of company promotion, motor cabs were introduced by cab companies in excess of their ability to find drivers for them.[18]

The most obvious source of motor cab drivers was from among the ranks of horse cab drivers. They possessed experience of street traffic, as well as the all-important 'knowledge' of London. Having already passed their 'knowledge' test, their redeployment depended principally on the acquisition of motor-driving skills, while those from outside the trade had the double hurdle of the knowledge test as well as the driving test. A large proportion of motor cab drivers did consist of men making the transition from the horse cab. The Departmental Committee on Taxi-cab Fares reported in 1911 that 67 per cent were old horse cab drivers. The Public Carriage Office claimed that it gave every facility to horsemen to become motor drivers by allowing four free motor driving tests as against the two allowed to others. Moreover they were prepared to reduce from five years to three the ban on men whose licences had been revoked for drunkenness – a concession that seems quite inappropriate by modern standards.[19]

We can only guess at the origin of those motor drivers who did not transfer from horse cabs, with the exception of the years 1911 to 1914, for which a return produced by the Public Carriage Office is extant. The list is of men who applied to take the 'knowledge' of London test, and therefore excludes horse cab drivers, although sixteen cab proprietors are included. Altogether there were some 3,878 applicants, drawn from 175 occupations. The leading five, each of which supplied over two hundred applicants, were (in order): coachmen, conductors, carmen, porters, and bus and tram drivers. Of the coachmen, 74 per cent passed the 'knowledge' test, whereas only 58 per cent of bus and tram drivers were successful, their knowledge of London perhaps being confined to specific routes. Comparatively few of the entrants into the motor cab trade had previous driving experience, although 151 of the applicants for licences between 1911 and 1914 were chauffeurs, placing that occupation seventh in rank order. It was necessary for most men to be given driving instruction before they could obtain their licence, a burden which frequently fell on the companies themselves.[20]

From 1906 onwards the Public Carriage Office published lists of specimen questions for the 'knowledge' test so that candidates could prepare themselves. If a man did reasonably well at his first attempt he was granted a permit to learn to drive, but had subsequently to re-present himself until he eventually passed the whole of the test. This two-stage process was designed to protect proprietors, for a man who had got as far as receiving the permit was worth training to drive. The most systematic attempt at training men for the 'knowledge' was made by the British Motor Cab Company, which operated five schools under the supervision of a former examiner at the Public Carriage Office. In addition to instructing men with the aid of maps, they had a number of wagonettes in which trainees were driven around the streets. Tuition was estimated to take about seven months, and the whole exercise cost the company around £700 to £800 a month in 1915. The company attempted to retain the services of men they had trained by means of an agreement binding a man to remain with them for twelve months after receiving his licence. However, in 1914, in an action before the High Court, the company failed to enforce such agreements.[21]

After he had passed the 'knowledge' test the candidate had to take a driving test, to which horse cab drivers could proceed directly. The driving test for horse-drawn cabs had only been instituted in 1895, so there was less weight of bureaucratic inertia when it came to devising a motor driving test. The absence of a general driving test (not introduced until 1935) was a matter of contention for cab drivers, who argued that street accidents – for which they were frequently blamed – would be lessened if all drivers had to be tested. In 1910, for example, one of the members of a cab drivers' deputation to the Home Office claimed that a blind man applied for, and received, a London County Council driving licence every year (for a 5s fee), in order to demonstrate the inadequacy of the 1903 Motor Car Act.[22]

New procedures were necessary, for whereas a man found competent to drive one type of horse cab might be presumed to be equally competent to drive any other, this could not be assumed in the case of motor cabs, where the arrangement of gears, clutch and brakes was quite different. The mechanical competence of most drivers was extremely limited, and it was therefore decided, in December 1904, that a driver had to be tested for each make of cab that he might wish to drive. The licence was endorsed for each vehicle that the driver was qualified to drive, but in order that this might be done he was required to withdraw his licence from his employer. The drivers

The original caption to this picture, which appeared in *Motor Traction* on 19 January 1907 was as follows: 'The above photograph is of an old London cabby who has learned to drive an Argyll motor cab. Members of the slow-growing London Cab Drivers' Union should follow his example and join the motor school which Messrs. Argylls, London, Ltd., has inaugurated.' In fact, the union was prepared to give its members driving instruction, using a vehicle and instructor financed by the London Motor Cab Comapny

were strongly opposed to this, for it immediately made it evident to the master that a man was contemplating a move to a different yard. The police made this rule explicitly in the interests of the proprietors, for it was claimed that men obtained clandestine instruction on different types of cab 'to the detriment of the vehicle and the danger of the public', and the withdrawal of the licence was the sole hint of what was taking place.[23]

The older horse cab driver had much greater difficulty in changing over to the motor cab, for employers found it difficult to secure insurance cover for them. In 1910 the union complained of the large number of men in their fifties and sixties who could not get a motor cab and who were 'gradually being squeezed out into the workhouse'. For such men, charitable aid was often the only resort. The Benevolent Society placed a small number of ex-horse cabmen into uniform as newspaper salesmen, while The Horses' and Drivers' Aid Committee, set up in 1912, took over some cabs which they operated on a jobbing basis.[24]

What of the driver who was also the owner of a horse cab? We know that in 1893 there were 2,038 owners of a single cab, and they constituted 13.6 per cent of all drivers at that date. How easy and how attractive was it for the owner-driver or the small proprietor of horse cabs to adopt the motor cab? The Chief Commissioner of the Metropolitan Police reported in 1907 that 'The old horse masters do not seem disposed to embark upon motor vehicles, but are leaving the developments to the new companies.' Change was not without its difficulties, of course. The capital embarked on a single hansom or growler would only go half way towards that necessary to acquire a motor cab. The 1911 Select Committee on Taxi-cab Fares estimated the cost of a horse cab, with its pair of horses, its harness and its rest horse, to be about £175, while a motor taxi-cab, ready for the road, would not amount to much less than £350. That the earning capacity of a motor cab was more than twice that of the horse cab was small comfort. The value of horse cab stock was greatly diminished by the rise of the motor cab. In July 1909 *Motor Traction* noted that eight hundred cab horses and two hundred cabs had been disposed of at the Barbican Repository in the previous six months, and that, while horses had fetched anything between £10 and £40, some cabs had fetched as little as £1 each.[25]

There were two means by which the horse cab owner-driver, or the driver with aspirations towards independence, could finance the purchase of a motor cab: through a hire-purchase agreement made direct with a supplier, or by owning shares in a 'mutual' cab company or co-operative society. There was nothing new about the hire purchase of cabs, for as early as 1887 the *Hackney Carriage Guardian* was blaming increased credit facilities for overstocking the trade, and by 1895 between four thousand and five thousand London horse cabs were subject to hire-purchase agreements.[26]

One of the earliest firms to involve itself with the hire purchase of motor cabs was Mann and Overton Ltd, which was incorporated in 1901. The company acquired the agency for the French Unic cabs, which they were supplying in 1908 at £100 down. Apart from Mann & Overton (who went on to take the Austin cab agency, and continue trading to this day), the most successful cab supply company was the Chesham Automobile Supply Company, which was incorporated in January 1908. The principal promoters were two engineers, Walter E. and Peter C. Middleton, who, in November 1907, had obtained an option from Mann and Overton for the purchase of motor cabs. In the following month the Middletons set up the Eccleston Motor Cab Company, which, by 1911, was running twenty-one Unic cabs. The option with Mann and Overton was sold on to the Chesham Automobile Supply Company in February 1908. Mann and Overton's agency with Unic ran out in 1909, for in November of that year Unic Automobile & Marine Motors Ltd was formed, to operate the sole agency (acquired by Peter Middleton) for Unic cars in Great Britain, Ireland, and the British colonies and dependencies. Originally the French manufacturing company held 50 per cent of the shares in its English distributor, but by 1920 the Chesham Supply Company had acquired 14,950 of the 15,000 shares in Unic Motors and the two companies were merged.[27]

One outlet for cab manufacturers was to enter into agreements with 'mutuals', either subsidiaries of the company or independent. Peter Middleton, for example, was a director of the Mutual Taxi-cab Supply Company, formed in September 1909, with £100 nominal capital divided into five hundred shares of 4s each. Every share carried

The Unic Delivery Van
gained
GOLD MEDAL
Royal Automobile Club
Commercial Vehicle Trials.
1907.

UNIC DELIVERY VAN. £325.

The cheapest van to run.
We used less petrol than any other petrol van competing in the trials. Average 22¼ miles per gallon (carrying 15 cwt).

UNIC

The finest cab for real hard work.
Guarantee given with every cab. Over 1,000 in daily use.
Supplied on extended payment if desired.

UNIC CABS are used by the
City & Suburban Cab Co., Ltd.
United Motor Cab Co., Ltd.
West End Motor Co.
Chesham Automobile Supply Co.
Eccleston Motor Cab Co.
The Motor Cab Garage, Brighton.
Eastbourne Motor Cab Co.
La Cie Generale des Voitures Automobiles, Paris.
La Cie des Services Automobiles Meteor, Paris.
La Ste Franco Argentine Buenos-Ayres.
The Auto Garage and Auto Cabs Co., Cairo.
Cie des Taximetres, Monte Carlo.
Cie des Taximetres, Nantes.

UNIC CAB.
10-12 h.p. 2 cyl. and 12-14 h.p. 4 cyl.
MANN & OVERTONS, Ltd., 7a. LOWER BELGRAVE ST., S.W.

The firm of Mann & Overton, formed in 1901, has enjoyed a distinguished career in the motor cab trade. It acquired the English rights to the French Unic cab, which was one of the most popular models before the First World War

an obligation to pay 2*s* 6*d* a week to the company, of which 3*d* went towards management costs, while the rest was credited to the shareholder. Cabs, supplied by the Chesham Supply Company, were balloted for as they were acquired, at the rate of three per fortnight in the first year, rising to four a week after the second year. Once he had been allotted a cab, the shareholder was required to pay the company £16 a month until the purchase price had been fully paid. Alternatively the winner of the ballot could put his option up for sale by inviting sealed bids – by which means he might obtain £30 or £40. This, at any rate, was the theory, but in practice the arrangement worked very differently. The directorate and staff of the Mutual and the Chesham companies were the same, and most of the shares in the Mutual were held by the Chesham Company itself. That company therefore received most of the allotments in the draw, and was able to sell them again at a profit. In addition, the hire-purchase agreement bound the purchaser to have repairs undertaken as the vendor required (generally executing the work themselves) and to have the cab insured by an insurance company which was also an offshoot of the vendor company. The Commissioner of Police concluded, therefore, that the Mutual and Chesham companies 'stood in every case to gain, but could under no circumstances lose'. The cards were stacked heavily against the would-be purchaser, who was required to pay £495 for a cab or £100 in excess of the actual value.[28]

Facilities for hire purchase no doubt account in large part for the steady increase in the proportion of cabs owned by owner-drivers and small proprietors. In 1908 small proprietors, owning between one and five motor cabs, represented over 80 per cent of cab owners, although they owned only 4 per cent of the licensed motor cabs. They steadily improved on this position, and the Owner Drivers' Association, which had sixty full members (owning eighty-one cabs) in 1911, had five hundred cabs registered by 1913. Figures produced by the London Traffic Branch of the Board of Trade show that just prior to the outbreak of war in 1914 some 53.7 per cent of cabs were owned by individuals, compared with 46.2 per cent owned by companies.[29]

The survival of the owner-driver was in the face of the determined efforts of motor cab companies to control the new trade. There was great activity in the decade before the First World War, and especially in the years 1907–9, when at least thirty-six companies were incorporated, eighteen of them in 1908 alone. Cab company promotion formed part of the general investment boom in motor vehicles, which began in November 1895 with the flotation of the British Motor Syndicate by Harry J. Lawson, a leading figure in the cycle industry. Lawson's aim was to secure a patent monopoly with motor cars, to achieve which, in January 1896, he purchased the British rights to the Daimler motor car from F.R. Simms, vesting them in the Great Horseless Carriage Company, which would construct vehicle bodies for the British Motor Syndicate while Daimler supplied the engines.[30]

One of the directors of the British Motor Syndicate was Herbert H. Mulliner, a member of the coachbuilding dynasty with branches in Birmingham, Northampton and Liverpool. His forebear, Henry Mulliner, had been involved with the promotion of the Birmingham Cab Company, and had also supplied cabs to the Victoria Hansom Cab Company. The Mulliner family, in its various branches, represents the most successful attempt to transfer skills and resources from the coachbuilding and carriage trades to the motor trade, a transition which the equally active Forder family signally failed to make.[31]

In April 1895 Mulliner converted his business into a limited company, acting in concert with Arthur Du Cros, a key figure in the development of the Dunlop Rubber Company. A year later, Mulliner, Harvey Du Cros (Chairman of the Dunlop Pneumatic Tyre Company, and financial backer of Herbert Austin) and Martin Rucker (Harry J. Lawson's closest associate) came together, when the Coupé and Dunlop Brougham Company was incorporated, to purchase the jobmaster businesses carried on by the Coupé Company and the Dunlop Brougham Company, which had been formed to fit pneumatic tyres to horse cabs. The Coupé and Dunlop Brougham Company was basically a horse cab business, but in 1908 it was acquired by the Motor Cab Company of Great Britain. The new company, soon renamed the Coupé and Motor Cab

A group of horse cab veterans, 1920s. They are led by a man who claimed to have driven the Prince of Wales from Waterloo Station to Marlborough House in 1868

Company of Great Britain, had on its first board (in addition to Harvey and George Du Cros) Montague Napier and S.F. Edge, with whom the company had an agreement to be supplied with Napier chassis, the bodies to be built by W. & G. Du Cros of Acton.[32]

In November 1896 Mulliner was one of the motivating forces behind the Traffic Syndicate, formed 'to promote . . . the placing of cabs and all kinds of vehicles electrically or mechanically propelled on the common roads and streets'. The Traffic Syndicate immediately promoted the London Electrical Cab Company but, as has already been noted, the attempt to introduce electric cabs to the streets of London was not a commercial success.[33]

By December 1898 the largest shareholder in the London Electrical Cab Company was Dalziel News Ltd, a news agency owned by Davison Alexander Dalziel, the doyen of London motor cab promoters and the man who, more than others, was responsible for the Anglo-French flavour of taxi-cab development before the First World War. From 1895 until 1901 Dalziel was a founding director of a promotion company, Southern Development Ltd (which paid a dividend of 25 per cent on £250,000 in its first year of operation), and in 1902 he set up the United Investment Corporation. It was this company, of which Dalziel personally held over 78 per cent of the shares, that was used in May 1906 to promote the General Motor Cab Company, by means of which Dalziel planned to dominate the London cab trade.[34]

Dalziel turned this time to Paris for the bulk of his finance. At the first issue of shares, made shortly after incorporation, 230,000 preferred ordinary shares were offered to the public and were allotted mainly to applicants on the Continent, fewer than 35,000 shares being taken up by British investors. The General Motor Cab Company linked the Dalziel interests with those of the Paris-based Société Générale des Compteurs de Voitures (Taximètres) and the Compagnie Française des Automobiles de Place. In 1905 the latter company had placed orders for 250 cab chassis with Renault, and the small, two-cylinder, 8/9 hp taxi-cab became that company's best seller. The Compagnie Française subsequently acquired more cabs for its own use, and also secured them for the General Motor Cab Company, which obtained the right to their exclusive use in London until October 1907.[35]

It was not until December 1906 that the company managed to get a single cab onto London streets. Undeterred by this it decided to increase its capital to £500,000, the nominal reason being to purchase an additional five hundred Renault cabs together with fifty 'de luxe' cabs manufactured by Charron – yet another of Dalziel's enterprises. *Motor Finance* was quite scathing about the scheme, implying that the real aim was for the promoters to secure lucrative underwriting commissions. The promotion of cab companies offered great speculative profits, and, between the decision to raise the capital of the General Motor Cab Company in December and the issue of the prospectus in February, Dalziel had launched yet another cab company onto the public. In January 1907 he floated the United Motor Cab Company with the aim of taking over the City and Suburban and its small fleet of twenty-five vehicles. He also entered into agreements with Darracq for the purchase of a further 250 cabs; with Unic for 200; and with Charron for 50.[36]

By April 1907 British investors had taken up only 5,000 shares, while 86,000 had been subscribed for in France. The largest single holding was that of £30,000, allotted to the General Motor Cab Company, a transaction of doubtful propriety which, it was alleged, was intended to relieve the promoters and underwriters and help to enhance their profits. The General Motor Cab Company and the United Motor Cab Company had an interlocking directorate, and, although initially the two companies were nominally independent, between them they dominated the cab trade.[37]

It will be seem from Appendix 6 that in October 1907 the General Cab Company alone possessed almost seventy per cent of the motor cabs in operation, and that, when combined with the United, it accounted for just under 80 per cent. It was not to be expected that this near monopoly would last, and through much of 1907–8 the price of motor cab shares was kept in check by nervousness at the prospect of the influx of competitors.[38]

Despite such activity actual profits continued to be purely hypothetical, and *Motor Traction* forecast that until some clear evidence of profitability was produced the public would naturally fight shy. What it regarded as a 'reassuring statement' came in

September 1907, when the General Motor Cab Company announced that, since it had commenced running with taximeters in May, profits had been higher than forecast in the prospectus. The company currently had 375 cabs on the road, and anticipated 1,000 by the end of the year. If expansion was that rapid, it claimed, revenue would exceed £240,000 a year, or 50 per cent of issued capital. But, as *Motor Traction* correctly observed, that was a big 'if', for the three months on which such a rosy estimate was based were the best months of the year. Not only that, but these were new cabs which had yet to face expensive repair bills.[39]

The whole question of depreciation was one which company promoters treated in a cavalier manner. The experience of horse cabs was of little direct relevance, not that many managers possessed it, in any case. Furthermore, motor vehicles were themselves a novelty and knowledge of wear and tear had yet to be built up. Many company prospectuses paid not the slightest attention to depreciation, but in those that did the estimates generally ranged from four years (the Victoria Motor Cab Company) to six years (the Dalziel group and the Landaulette Motor Cab Company). Some claimed that there was no need to make any allowance for depreciation at all as the Scotland Yard requirements were so severe that cabs were thoroughly overhauled annually. The ABC Cab Company, for example, claimed that 'It may occur that practically every part of each cab will be renewed in the course of five years, so that it is in as good condition at the end of that period as when first built . . .' However, this attitude ignored the fact that obsolescence was of greater significance than mechanical deterioration. W. Worby Beaumont made this point in 1912:

A cab can be kept on the road by efficient maintenance for six years, or under private ownership and driving perhaps as much as seven years, where competition is small, but antiquation and fashion, and public preference, and growing fastidiousness, and knowledge of different types (and thereby, in ordinary weather, selection) by the public reduces this term of years to five or less.

It is clear that motor cab companies before the First World War underestimated the extent of depreciation, and this caught up with many of them from 1912 on, when the fleets introduced in large blocks from 1907 reached the end of their working lives.[40]

A Home Office Departmental Committee on Taxi-cab Fares in 1911 makes it clear how narrow were the profit margins on which cab companies were working at that time. Nowhere is this more clearly shown than in the vexed question of 'extras'. Superintendent Bassom of the Public Carriage Office explained how the extra payment for passengers and luggage became such a contentious issue. In March 1907, at the time when the Home Secretary's order setting taxi-cab fares was adopted, the General Motor Cab Company was taking delivery of its first Renault cabs. The

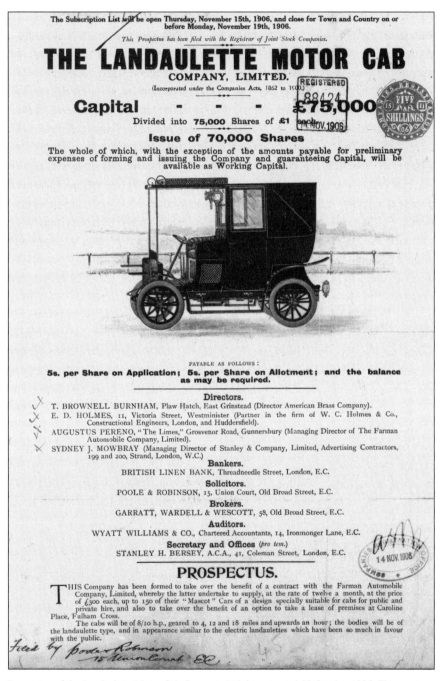

The Subscription List will be open **Thursday, November 15th, 1906**, and close for Town and Country on or before **Monday, November 19th, 1906**.

This Prospectus has been filed with the Registrar of Joint Stock Companies.

THE LANDAULETTE MOTOR CAB
COMPANY, LIMITED.
(Incorporated under the Companies Acts, 1862 to 1900.)

Capital - - - £75,000
Divided into **75,000** Shares of **£1** each.

Issue of 70,000 Shares

The whole of which, with the exception of the amounts payable for preliminary expenses of forming and issuing the Company and guaranteeing Capital, will be available as Working Capital.

PAYABLE AS FOLLOWS :

5s. per Share on Application; 5s. per Share on Allotment; and the balance as may be required.

Directors.

T. BROWNELL BURNHAM, Plaw Hatch, East Grinstead (Director American Brass Company).

E. D. HOLMES, 11, Victoria Street, Westminister (Partner in the firm of W. C. Holmes & Co., Constructional Engineers, London, and Huddersfield).

AUGUSTUS PERENO, "The Limes," Grosvenor Road, Gunnersbury (Managing Director of The Farman Automobile Company, Limited).

SYDNEY J. MOWBRAY (Managing Director of Stanley & Company, Limited, Advertising Contractors, 199 and 200, Strand, London, W.C.)

Bankers.
BRITISH LINEN BANK, Threadneedle Street, London, E.C.

Solicitors.
POOLE & ROBINSON, 15, Union Court, Old Broad Street, E.C.

Brokers.
GARRATT, WARDELL & WESCOTT, 58, Old Broad Street, E.C.

Auditors.
WYATT WILLIAMS & CO., Chartered Accountants, 14, Ironmonger Lane, E.C.

Secretary and Offices (*pro tem.*)
STANLEY H. BERSEY, A.C.A., 41, Coleman Street, London, E.C.

PROSCPECTUS.

THIS Company has been formed to take over the benefit of a contract with the Farman Automobile Company, Limited, whereby the latter undertake to supply, at the rate of twelve a month, at the price of £300 each, up to 150 of their "Mascot" Cars of a design specially suitable for cabs for public and private hire, and also to take over the benefit of an option to take a lease of premises at Caroline Place, Fulham Cross.

The cabs will be of 8/10 h.p., geared to 4, 12 and 18 miles and upwards an hour ; the bodies will be of the landaulette type, and in appearance similar to the electric landaulettes which have been so much in favour with the public.

Prospectus of the Landaulette Motor Cab Company Ltd, incorporated 29 October 1906. The company was formed to set up a hundred 'Mascot' cabs to ply for hire, and fifty for use as private hire vehicles. Not one seems to have found its way onto the streets, for like many early motor cab companies the flimsy capital was swallowed up in promotion expenses. The company had been wound up by 1909. (PRO, BT11701/90597)

manufacturers faced problems with the construction regulations of the Metropolitan Police, and doubted their capacity to make a vehicle that would meet both the space requirement for four passengers and the maximum turning circle of 25 feet. In consequence, the cabs were licensed for two persons only. Folding seats were allowed inside, which could be used for such purposes as supporting luggage. Inevitably, passengers did sometimes use them, although the driver had no legal power to charge for their use. These cabs were modified touring cars, with the further consequence that they were fitted with a front bench seat, which enabled a passenger to sit beside the driver. The police came to object to this on two grounds: horse cab drivers were incensed at what seemed like overloading of motor cabs, and several serious accidents were allegedly caused by passengers on the front seat. The Home Secretary at first refused to ban them, on the grounds that having a passenger on the front seat was common practice in private cars, and in an emergency might prove valuable. Bassom was insistent, however. The passenger was likely to attract the driver's attention by talking, or might hamper his movements. He continued:

> Further, it must be remembered that cabs are not like private motors where the owner knows the class of person he has beside the driver, but public carriages are frequently used by persons who are more hilarious than wise and one can easily imagine a party of students, young men about town or others leaving a place of entertainment, getting beside the driver and interfering with the mechanism, throttle lever, switch, brake or clutch pedal, or lubricators so as to be a source of danger both to themselves and others using the roads. Further, the petrol tank is invariably placed just under the front seat, and an unthinking person might throw down a match after lighting a cigar, and cause the whole to burst into flame in a very short while.

Such an alarming prospect convinced the Home Secretary, and the ban was forthwith imposed.[41]

As the extra charge for a third or fourth passenger could not legally be made in the case of a cab licensed as a two-seater, the proprietors did not bother to collect it, or the charge for luggage. But the drivers did collect the extras – and pocketed them. The companies acquiesced as they were initially prosperous, and because they wished to attract drivers, who were in short supply. However, from the commencement of motor cabs there had been a tariff for extra passengers and luggage (as there had been in horse cab days), and this was continued as the authorities desired to encourage the development of the 'general utility' cab (like the old growler), rather than the less flexible two-seater. The policy worked, and newcomers to the trade frequently introduced four-seater cabs to which the extra charges legally applied. The competition which this posed for the General Motor Cab Company's now dated two-seaters forced the company to convert the bodies, at a cost of £25 to £30 a cab. But by this time the drivers had come to regard extras as their perquisites, and no amount of effort by the companies could wrest these sums from them. If drivers failed to clock up the extras on the taximeter, the proprietors had no way of knowing how much they were losing; but by 1911 they estimated the sum to be in the region of 2s 6d a day – enough to make a real difference to the balance between earnings and operating expenses.[42]

A Home Office committee of enquiry drew the conclusion in 1911 that 'The whole system is unfortunate, as it leads an otherwise honourable class of men to appropriate under a claim of perquisite that to which they know they are not entitled, and which they pay over only when detected.' The committee did not, however, think that the owners' loss was as great as they made out. Calculating from a series of observations made by the police, they estimated that extras amounted to between 1s 3d and 1s 6d in the pound. The committee decided against abolishing extras, partly on the grounds that the absence of such a charge would probably denude the railway stations of taxi-cabs, for the carrying of luggage was so remunerative. They recommended that the drivers be given an express right to extras, but should be required to record them on the meter in order to protect the fare, and 'for statistical purposes'. However, in exchange for this right the committee proposed an amendment to the terms normally arranged between owners and drivers. In future, they suggested, the driver should receive 20 per cent (as against 25 per cent) on the first £1 earned, and 25 per cent of subsequent earnings. In effect, this loss of 1s on the first £1 earned gave the owners a sum equivalent to two-thirds or more of the extras. The committee further suggested that if such an arrangement was arrived at, the owners should in future sell petrol to their drivers at 8d per gallon, independent of market fluctuations within 20 per cent of that price, up or down. They rejected any increase in fares, or any limitation on the number of cabs or drivers licensed.[43]

The response of the London Motor Cab Proprietors' Association was predictable. It claimed that the recommendation that extras should belong to the drivers had 'caused incalculable damage to the prestige and authority of the proprietors by its subordination of their legal claims to the demands and fraudulent proclivity of their dishonest drivers'. Furthermore, the suggestion that petrol should be sold to men at a pegged price was 'utterly impossible'.[44]

Despite a lock-out in November 1911, and the intervention of the Board of Trade (which set up a Court of Arbitration under Viscount St Aldwyn), the Home Office held firm on the matter of fares, although C.F.G. Masterman, the Junior Minister, acknowledged the dilemma:

This is an extremely difficult question. If the Companies are really going to ruin, I suppose the fares must be raised: but it is a swindle on the public that, after driving horse cabs off the streets by a rates [sic] which they suggested and accepted, they should now want those rates to be raised.[45]

The refusal of the Home Secretary to increase fares was a major blow to overextended cab companies. The General Motor Cab Company found itself in serious trouble, and a receiver was appointed in April 1912. The company was suffering from the effects of having established such a large fleet of small cabs, which had been overtaken by more powerful models. In the year ending 31 July 1912 a loss of nearly £165,000 was made on the sale of 698 cabs, leaving the company with a total loss in that year of almost £149,000. It was bailed out by the New Motor Cab Company, a front for the Paris bankers, Hirschler & Co, who owned the entire share capital of £612,000. With this, a loan of £600,000 was made to the General Motor Cab Company, carrying interest at 7 per cent, plus 35 per cent of trading profit before providing for depreciation. In 1913 both the General and the New Motor Cab companies were absorbed by the British Motor Cab Company, which, despite its name, was effectively French-owned. Five of the first seven directors were French, and virtually all of the £400,000 share capital was raised in Paris. The promoter was the Société Française d'Études et d'Entreprises, which secured agreement with Louis Renault for the supply of a thousand cabs. All of these had been delivered by April 1911, although the company found it impossible to secure enough drivers. It made a profit of £23,826 in the year ending 31 March 1912, which leapt to £58,314 in 1914, after the takeover of the General Motor Cab Company. The First World War saw its profits diminish, and they were down to £4,963 in 1917. One of the problems at that time was securing spare parts for French cabs, and, although they had the workshop capacity to manufacture spares themselves, 95 per cent was commandeered for munitions work. In 1918 a loss of £69,635 was made, and in February of that year the company closed down. It subsequently reconditioned its cabs, which were sold to owner-drivers on the hire-purchase system, the purchasers being required to garage their cabs with the company during the period of the agreement.[46]

A two-month strike at the beginning of 1913, caused by an attempt by the London Motor Cab Proprietors' Association to pass on to drivers an increase in the price of petrol, marked a further step in the shifting balance away from cab companies towards owner-drivers. *Motor Traction* alleged that the public were apathetic towards this strike, and reported that 'the general impression [is] to the effect that even with the strike in progress there are quite enough cabs on the streets for ordinary purposes'.[47]

By 1914 the cab trade was described as 'the least flourishing of the London transport industries'. The number of cabs licensed at the end of 1914 was over a

Motor cabs, many of them Renaults, 'ranking it' in Bishopsgate, 9.45 a.m. on Monday 15 April 1912. It is unusual to be able to date and time a photograph with such precision

thousand fewer than at the end of the previous year. This partly reflects the commencement of the First World War, with some cabs being converted to ambulances or for other war use, and others being withdrawn because of the absence of habitual users at the front. However, it is also indicative of a malaise which had been apparent since at least 1910.[48]

Motor cabs had been a permanent feature of the London streets for little more than a decade when the First World War started. In that time the horse cab had been ousted, the number falling from its peak in 1898, when 11,519 were licensed, to a mere 1,391 in 1914 . All but 232 of these were four-wheelers, still just able to compete with motor cabs for heavy station work. The triumph of the motor cab was overwhelmingly due to market forces, for there is no real evidence that the rapid running-down of the London horse cab trade was ever official policy – unlike Berlin, where horse cabs were banned by official decree in April 1912. If the police made things more difficult for horse cab proprietors it was only by making it easier for horse cab drivers to desert to the motor cab, and that was done by extending to them certain privileges which were not shared by applicants for motor cab driving licences from other occupations.

Another remarkable fact is the speed with which the Home Office and the police reacted to the new vehicle. The Home Office was hardly renowned for rapid response to changes in the cab trade, but when motor cabs first came in the authorities showed an immediate awareness of the need to secure early control before the initiative was lost. This was reflected in prompt attention being paid to the new requirements of driver licensing and type-approval of motor cabs, but was accompanied by an appreciation of the fluidity of the situation, and an awareness that an unwise use of patronage powers might stifle technical innovation.

The rapid rise and fall of the early motor cab companies echoed the disappointing performance of most horse cab companies of earlier times. Company promoters, right back to the time of the Safety Cabriolet and Two-wheel Carriage Company, had dreamed of a monopoly of the cab trade based on the possession of key patents. This had never proved a practical reality with the horse cab, and it was to be no more capable of realization with the motor cab. The greatest efforts were put into the patenting of taximeters, but these proved a weak foundation for commercial supremacy, as there existed no master patent that could be defended, while the Public Carriage Office steadfastly refused to endorse particular models. The same was true of the motor cab itself.

However, most motor cab companies laboured under difficulties of their own creation. They tended to be overcapitalized, and were weighed down by heavy promotion expenses and management charges. Previous experience of the cab trade (or of public transport generally) was a rarity, while the short time which had elapsed since the birth of the motor car itself meant that there was only a limited body of knowledge on such questions as the depreciation of motor vehicles.

An exception to the trend was the London Improved Cab Company which, on the basis of its confidential financial returns, was described in 1911 as being carefully and skilfully worked. It is noticeable that its fleet was small – only fifty in that year – and that it did not rush into the new form of transportation, but introduced motor cabs slowly. One or two experimental cabs were introduced in 1906–7; thirteen were put on the streets in 1909; and thirty-seven in 1910. The London Improved Cab Company had experience as a successful horse cab company on which to draw, and it also benefited from not being the first onto the field.[49]

Too rapid expansion of cab fleets could lead to problems. Large numbers of vehicles came up for renewal at the same time, placing strain on company finances, especially if (as was often the case) inadequate provision had been made for depreciation. It was difficult to find drivers for over-large fleets, which were also more vulnerable to obsolescence during a period of rapid technological change. Finally, it is hard to escape the conclusion that the trade was overstocked. By 1910 it was claimed that 'A man has now to go and look for his work . . . He is driving about all the time. He is coming back to the old horse power system of mouching round the streets in order to get a job.'[50] None of the big company fleets survived the war. As in the old horse cab days, the future lay with the more modest operator.

Postscript

SUBURBAN AND PROVINCIAL CABS

W hen Hackney Coach Commissioners for London were established in 1694 and 1710, the area of their jurisdiction was defined as the Bills of Mortality and the suburbs; and it was as the suburbs grew that the hackney carriages working at the centre came to differ from those on the periphery, both in their type and in their organization. The attempt to define a metropolitan area proved an enormously difficult problem that dogged the reform of local government throughout the century. In 1831 London hackney carriages were defined as those within a 5 mile radius of the General Post Office, in the City. This circle was extended to ten miles in 1838. Such a rule, while having the merit of simplicity when drawn on a map, bore no relationship whatsoever to the actual growth of London on the ground, where development was very uneven. Some built-up areas found themselves outside the circle, while others, as yet free from bricks and mortar, found themselves within. The defining area was pushed further out in 1843, when the Metropolitan Police District, together with the City of London, became the administrative district. In places, this stretches 18 miles or so from the centre of London, and included districts that remain rural to this day. By the middle of the nineteenth century, therefore, vehicles defined as London hackney carriages, and legally administered as such, included cabs on the streets of the largest and busiest city in the world, cabs in the suburbs, cabs in small market towns that still maintained an independent existence, and cabs in the heart of the country.

It was inevitable that cabs in the central district and cabs in the outer areas should go their separate ways. In the first place the work which they did was different. In the heart of London cabs were used largely for business purposes by day, and for leisure purposes in the evenings and at night, with a considerable trade in linking together the railway termini. In the suburbs the bulk of the work was conveying passengers to and from the railway stations, and for leisure and excursion purposes. Cabs were more likely to form part of the stock of a general jobmaster, and were often lighter, open carriages, such as victorias or 'flies'. Drivers were not the bailees of the cab proprietors, but were generally waged (as was the general, but not invariable, practice in the provinces) and received a fixed sum each week, which was supplemented by tips, and sometimes by commission. In south-east London in the early 1890s, for

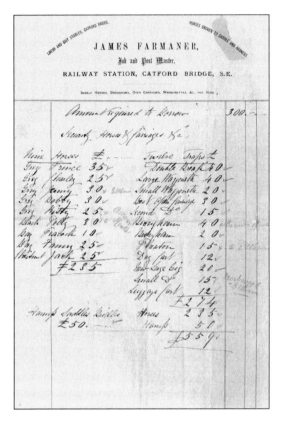

James Farmaner was a Catford jobmaster and postmaster, with horses and carriages for hire. He was of the class of men who might well have a cab or two licensed to ply for hire on the streets, although there is no evidence that he actually did. Like many such men he seems to have encountered financial difficulties, which he tried in vain to solve by borrowing money on the security of his stock. Unable to make the repayments, his horses and carriages, as well as his household furniture and other items, were put up for sale in 1873. This document lists his nine horses, ranging in value from 'Prince' at £35 down to 'Peacock' at £10. His twelve vehicles included two open carriages and two broughams

example, one of the largest jobmasters, Thomas Tilling, allowed 3s a day, plus the charges for luggage, and the men worked a twelve-hour day for six days a week. The driver was still required to pass the 'knowledge', but it was alleged that he could do so more easily if he carried a letter from a suburban proprietor expressing a willingness to employ him.[1]

The London Hackney Carriage Act of 1831 compelled a cabman to drive anywhere within the 5 mile radius, and up to 5 miles from the place hired, distances raised to 6 miles in 1853. The great fear of the inner London cab driver was to be drawn further and further away from the busy, central streets, and out into the periphery where fares were harder to find. It was to address the problem of cabs returning empty from jobs that had taken them to outlying parts that back-fare was introduced. The 1831 Act allowed a driver, if driven 4 miles or more beyond the 5 mile radius, to demand back-fare of 6d a mile, as far as the limits; and at night, full fare might be charged back to the limits, for any journey beyond them. If the journey had been both started and finished beyond the limits, the driver could demand back-fare to the standing from which he had been hired. Back-fare illustrated well some of the problems of a radius, which would cover a very different area depending on the centre from which the circle was drawn. Five miles from the General Post Office missed the very busy Great Western Railway terminus at Paddington by about a quarter of a mile, allowing cab drivers to demand back-fare, something which they could not have done had the radius been centred on Charing Cross. There were other anomalies. The driver of a cab taken from a stand beyond the limits and driven towards London could, if still discharged beyond the limits, charge back-fare to the original standing even though the journey had been taking him 'into business' or towards the more profitable districts. To avoid this extra payment, some parsimonious passengers would require the driver to carry a servant back within the limits, leaving the maid or footman to walk back home. Back-fare, as one complainant put it, was also 'based upon the supposition either that all the cabmen in the metropolis sleep in the General Post Office, or that all cab mews are located in St. Martin's-le-Grand', whereas many of them were on the outskirts of the metropolitan area.[2]

In the early 1850s there were complaints that back-fare threw an unnecessary burden on passengers, and it was abolished by the Fitzroy Act of 1853. However, later in that year (which was such a turbulent one for the cab trade) back-fare was replaced by a fare structure which distinguished between the central and outlying areas. A radius of 4 miles was drawn, not from the General Post Office but from Charing Cross, thus shifting the balance a mile or so to the west. Beyond the radius a driver was entitled to charge 1s a mile or part of a mile, or approximately double the ordinary rate. This fare structure reinforced the distinction between central and suburban cabs. Jobs were fewer in the suburbs, and the pace of work slower, but the suburban cab operators were rewarded by a higher fare, which helped them resist any temptation to ply for hire in the already crowded London streets. Their lower fares were no hardship to the central men, for, as suburban railways and tramways developed, they rarely ventured beyond the radius, but could charge accordingly when they did.

As the balance of population shifted, however, a number of local authorities on the suburban fringes questioned a system which subjected their inhabitants to higher cab fares, and from the 1880s onwards there were repeated demands to extend the radius, thus bringing more and more districts into the area of cheaper cabs. The Home Office Departmental Committee which sat in 1894 recommended that the radius be extended to cover the whole of the London County Council area, with the exception of Plumstead, but both the Home Office and the Metropolitan Police dragged their feet, their fear being that men on the fringes of the proposed district would either move further out, in order to gain the higher rates of fare, or would be tempted further in, in order to take advantage of the greater traffic. Either way, they feared that the fringe area would be denuded of cabs, while the central area would become even more congested. As the drivers themselves were not anxious for change, and as the larger grievance of 'the privilege' had yet to be settled, the authorities decided not to rock the boat. In the end the advent of the taximeter and of the motor cab made the issue of the radius irrelevant. Taximeters could not cope with a fare scale that might change in the middle of a journey, and the question was quietly allowed to drop when the Secretary of State issued new scales of fares in his order of 1907. Horse cabs not fitted with taximeters were allowed to maintain the distinction, and it was in the suburbs that these cabs lingered longest, so that even in 1913 the Chief Commissioner could speak of the supremacy of the motor cab in the suburbs as a thing of the future.[3]

Whether they were suburban cabs or inner city cabs, London's hackney cabs were unique (and to this day remain unique) in that their ultimate control was in the hands of a member of the national government. Elsewhere in the kingdom hackney carriages were the responsibility of local authorities. A measure of uniformity was introduced

Aylesbury Station, photographed in 1856 by John Charles May, painter, grainer and photographic artist. This neatly posed photograph illustrates well the kind of horse traffic generated by the railway. The vehicle on the right is the type of light victoria much used by jobmasters outside London for use as a cab, and appears to have a licence plate just below the driver's seat. There were four jobmasters and livery stable keepers in Aylesbury at this time, including Charles William Long, whose premises were at the station. The coach in the centre, despite its appearance, is probably not a gentleman's carriage but a mail coach, of which one ran to Thame and another to High Wycombe. This vehicle, like the victoria, appears to have a licence plate, just in front of the door. The dishevelled dress of the driver also suggests a public, rather than a private, vehicle. The private omnibus drawn up behind it appears to have 'Risborough' painted on its side, which suggests that this, too, is a conveyance used for making a connection with a neighbouring town

by the Town Police Clauses Act, 1847, which set out the parameters for by-laws, although some towns regulated their hackney carriages through by-laws drawn up under a Local Act. For example, the Liverpool Improvement Act of 1842 and the Manchester Borough Police Act of 1844 provided the authority for those two cities. All by-laws had to be confirmed by the Secretary of State, those for hackney carriages being the responsibility of the Home Secretary until 1884 when the Local Government Board took over. When Sir Richard Mayne was Chief Commissioner of the Metropolitan Police, draft by-laws were sent by the Home Office for his consideration, a practice which appears to have continued under his successors.[4]

However, despite these general unifying tendencies, cab services varied from place to place, reflecting the different business which they undertook, and the variety of their urban transport networks of buses and trams. In major urban centres, such as Manchester, Birmingham and Glasgow, the scene was much like that of London, only on a reduced scale. In such places cabs met the needs of business and pleasure, and serviced the railway stations. After the passenger terminals opened at Glasgow, the number of cab stands increased fivefold in two decades, and half of these were either at or outside the stations. As in London, large operators competed for the railway 'privilege'. In the mid-1860s, for example, John Walker of Glasgow kept 366 horses, and paid £500 for the privilege at the Buchanan and Queen Street stations, to and from which his cabs probably made between 70,000 and 90,000 journeys a year.[5] The basic similarity between London's cab trade and that of the great provincial cities was matched by the similarity between the trade of the outer London suburbs and towns within the Metropolitan Police District, such as Uxbridge and Croyden, and the small towns of the provinces.

There were, of course, some towns in which the cabs serviced peculiar needs, and these included seaside towns and other watering places. Here there were holiday-makers, invalids and convalescents to attend to, and the hackney carriage authorities might have to oversee wheelchairmen as well as hackneymen. Hastings sought powers to license hand-chairmen in 1870, and in Brighton (where there were 1,055 cab drivers) there were 274 wheelchair drawers in 1890. The cabmen of Brighton constituted an important occupational grouping. In 1879 they were the first provincial cabmen to form a branch of the London-based Amalgamated Cab Drivers' Society. Although it boasted no shelters, Brighton hosted its own Cabmen's Mission ('The Brighton Mission to Wheelchairmen, Cabmen, 'Busmen, Tramcarmen and Others Similarly Occupied') and, for a short while, produced an evangelical Christian magazine, the *Cabmen's Messenger*.[6]

The bulk of Brighton's cabs were landaus, open chaises and victorias, which suited their mainly recreational use; and it was alleged that there were no hansoms in the town on account of its hilly nature. It seems, however, to have been a fairly general characteristic that hansoms were less dominant in the provinces, which the *Hackney Carriage Guardian* explained in 1885 as due to London life being lived at a faster pace. If the two-wheeled hansom was slower to appear, the two-horse cab was slower to disappear – at least in some places. Newcastle still had nearly as many two-horse cabs in 1884 as single-horse ones, although in London the single horse had distinguished the cab from the hackney coach as early as 1815.[7] It is difficult, if not impossible, to compare the quality of cabs between once place and another. Comparing provincial cabs with those in London, Henry Cole observed in 1867 that

> His own experience was that the cabs were better in Birmingham and Liverpool, and very much better in Edinburgh. He was told that one reason for that in the latter city was that gentlemen did not usually keep their own carriages because of the hills, and they found it better to hire public vehicles.[8]

Any superiority of vehicles could not have been due to a limitation of the number of cabs, which was an expedient that some had vainly argued for in London. In 1894 the Metropolitan Police circularized sixty-two provincial cab authorities, and found that the number of cabs was limited by only seven, of which Leeds was the largest. Leeds imposed no limitation on the number of cab drivers, but licensed a maximum of only 159 cabs, to serve a population of around 367,000. This worked out at one cab for every 2,300 people, as against a ration of 1: 500 in London. Only about fifty of the cabs were hansoms.[9]

Unlike London, a number of provincial cab authorities licensed cabs to ply from particular standings only. Leeds, however, pursued a curious practice of its own. The city was divided into three districts, and the cab licences were similarly divided into three groups. On a day-by-day basis the groups of cabs rotated between one district and another. This, it was argued, had the effect of allowing the men equal access to the busier and more profitable parts of the town, as well as equal access to the stations, for in that city the railway privilege did not operate.[10]

Manchester had an 'open system' in 1894, but only because of intense pressure that had been applied in the previous decade. In 1880 Manchester had 113 cab proprietors, operating 361 four-wheeled cabs and 100 hansoms. Each cab was licensed to a particular stand, and a by-law required the proprietor to give up the licence if he sold or ceased to use a cab. The right which the licence carried to ply from a particular standing was then offered to a long established proprietor at an inferior stand, who had perhaps waited a long time for this chance to improve his prospects. By this means it was intended that newcomers to the trade could gradually work themselves up to the stands where the richest pickings were to be

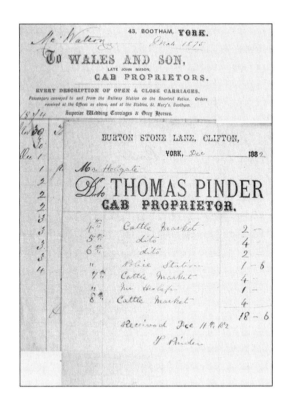

Ephemeral evidence of cab proprietors is sometimes to be found. These billheads of 1875 and 1882 record work done during cattle shows at York – a temporary, but valuable, boon to cabmen and jobmasters alike

found. But it was alleged that the reality was very different, and that 'stands' were sold with cabs, sometimes for large sums. It was claimed in July 1880, for example, that two cabs licensed to ply from the Piccadilly stand had been sold for £270 and £235 respectively, sums greatly in excess of the actual value of the stock. As much as £300 had been given for a vehicle and its number on a choice stand, and there were charges of corruption in the allocation of licences. In June 1882 the council passed a resolution to throw the stands open, but the Hackney Coach Committee dragged its feet when it came to implementing the new rule, and the councillors who were members of the committee secured a return to the closed system early in 1883. Not until new by-laws were introduced in 1888 were the stands successfully thrown open – and this in the very home of Free Trade![11]

As was the case in London, the dream of creating a cab monopoly was an appealing one to provincial speculators. The mid-1880s witnessed a number of attempts to create large-scale cab companies, either by buying out existing proprietors or by attempting to exploit patents for particular improved cabs. In 1886 at least three such attempts were made – in Brighton, Bristol and Birmingham. Brighton, at that time, had some 800 cabs owned by 200 proprietors, of whom some 180 were one-number or two-number men. The Brighton and Hove Cab and Carriage Company, formed in that year, aimed to take over these small concerns and to run, instead, Forder-built victoria hansoms. To keep them at bay, the owners banded together and formed the Cab Owners' Protection Association, and nothing came of the scheme.[12]

A similar fate befell the Bristol Cab Company, formed with a nominal capital of £25,000 in July 1886 by men chiefly associated with the Bristol Tramway Company. The venture started confidently enough by taking over a number of cab yards and livery stables, including a jobmaster with a lucrative funeral trade worth between £4,000 and £5,000 a year; but again the mass of proprietors fought them off, and in less than two years the company was wound up.[13]

The most interesting example, however, was in Birmingham, where the 'Birmingham Gang' or the 'Wolverhampton Ring' as they became known in the trade and financial press, attempted to button up that city prior to moving on to London. In September 1885 the Birmingham Cab Company was incorporated with a nominal capital of £100,000, of which £75,000 was immediately offered for subscription. The prospectus – the vital document in persuading the public to take up shares – listed the directors as Councillor Thomas J. Moore, Chairman of the Birmingham Central Tramways Company; Edward Pritchard, Chairman of the Birmingham and Aston Tramways Company; Thomas Startin, carriage builder; and Frederick Forder. The real promoter, however, appears to have been the mysterious Alfred Humpage, the developer of financially unsuccessful property in central Birmingham and promoter of the equally unsuccessful Tivoli Restaurant in London's Strand. He had been declared bankrupt in 1882, and when shareholders took the Birmingham Cab Company to court in 1891 it was declared that the merest hint that Humpage had been associated with the promotion would have aroused the suspicions of the investors.

Great play was made in the prospectus of the involvement of Forder:

Mr. Forder's experience of running cabs, both in London and the provinces, is probably greater than that of any other man in the kingdom, and extends to upwards of thirty years. He has been the trusted adviser of most of the large cab proprietors in London, who have in every case ensured marked success, when following out his recommendations. He has worked out elaborate and careful estimates of the probable financial results of the Company's business, *based upon his past experience*, which show that a profit of nearly 30 per cent may be made, after providing ample reserves for depreciation, &c., and his estimates are borne out by the opinions of a number of other experts who have been consulted on the point. The Board, therefore, feel that the Shareholders may safely look for dividends of at least 10 per cent per annum.[14]

This, of course, was poppycock. Forder's experience (which was less than thirty years) was in cab building, not in cab running, and it is quite implausible that any proprietor made anything approaching a 30 per cent profit.

The Birmingham Cab Company is chiefly of interest in that it was seen as a trial run for a similar undertaking to be launched in London. Indeed, a company with this end in view was promoted in 1886 – the New London Cab Company, with E.H. Bayley (of the London Improved Cab Company), Frederick Carkeet Bryant (of Bryant and May, match manufacturers), Thomas Moore, and George Kynoch (the Birmingham ammunition manufacturer) among its subscribers. Moore, who was Chairman of the Birmingham Cab Company, Kynoch and Sir John Astley, the aristocratic cabman, were among the first directors. The company never got off the ground and was dissolved in 1891, some six months after the final collapse of the Birmingham company. No more successful was the New London Victoria-Hansom Cab Company, of which Moore, together with J.C. Robinson, Manager of the Birmingham Cab Company, was a promoter.

The aim of the Birmingham Cab Company was to create a monopoly over the entire cab trade of that city. This was to be achieved by the purchase of existing businesses at sums to be valued, it seems, by Frederick Forder and Henry Mulliner. The prospectus claimed that 'most of the cab proprietors [had] . . . entered into provisional agreements to sell, if the Company call upon them to do so'. This was later challenged, and it was held that only thirty-two such agreements had been made (all, apparently, by Humpage), and mostly with the smallest proprietors. The brief life of the company was tempestuous throughout. The company seems to have expanded too fast, paid inflated sums for the stock and goodwill of the cab businesses it bought out, and made inadequate legal provisions to prevent those proprietors re-entering the trade in direct competition. In 1887 a committee of investigation was set up, which reported that all of the capital was expended, that there was a bank overdraft of £14,000 and that the business was losing considerably every week. By that time the auditor, a member of a prominent Birmingham family, had committed suicide, troubled, it was said, at having been taken in by the company.[15]

Provincial speculators were later involved in attempts to bring motor cabs to their towns, including W.J. Kershaw, a Birmingham accountant, who was one of the promoters of the Birmingham Cab Company, and later a principal shareholder of the Motor Cab Company, incorporated in 1896, but dissolved nine years later having engaged in little, if any, actual business.[16]

One of the most active companies was the Provincial Motor Cab Company, spawned by Davison Dalziel's United Investment Corporation in 1908, with Dalziel, Lazare Weiller and Godfrey Isaacs on the board of directors. The aim, according to the prospectus, was to establish motor cabs in a number of provincial towns, including

Manchester, Liverpool, Glasgow, Birmingham, Sheffield, Newcastle and Dublin – starting with Brighton, where one of the first electric cabs in the country had been running in the 1880s. *Motor Finance*, a journal particularly concerned with company promotion in the car industry, was consistently critical of this company, which it characterized as a venture principally designed to line the pockets of the promoters. The company's confessed aim was to exploit contracts for Darracq, Charron and Siddeley cabs, but at a price which *Motor Finance* regarded as excessive, and greatly above the cost of cabs which were already experiencing difficulty in making a profit on the streets of the metropolis.

What,' asked that journal, 'is likely to be the return on high powered £500 vehicles waiting to pounce upon a few commercial travellers and visitors in provincial towns, where the population as a whole are not addicted to the cab habit, and prefer the cheaper transportation afforded by their local tramway services?

The answer was, of course, 'Very little'. Part of the problem was the refusal of watch committees to grant licences. The company had planned to make a big impact on seaside resorts, but Folkestone refused to grant any licences, and Eastbourne granted only four of the twenty requested. The directors reported in November 1909 that cabs had been started in eighteen provincial towns, but the company faced severe competition, and suffered from a failure of its insurance companies, which led to the costly settlement of accident claims. By March 1911 a loss of over £11,000 was reported, and in 1913 steps were taken by a number of creditors, including the General Motor Cab Company (itself in liquidation), to appoint a receiver.[17]

Motor cabs were very slow to gain a hold in provincial towns. Figures produced by the Select Committee on Motor Traffic in 1913 reveal the dominance of London so far as cabs in general, and motor cabs in particular, were concerned (Appendix 7). In 1910 London possessed more than seven times the number of cabs that were on the streets of Dublin, its nearest rival, and more than sixteen times the number in Edinburgh, which ranked third. Bristol and Liverpool showed the greatest concentration of motor cabs, although their total numbers were minute when compared with the capital's. In Belfast the motor cab had hardly made an appearance.

From the Irish adventurers, Fitzgerald and Staples in the 1820s, through the Midlands innovators, Hansom and Chapman in the 1830s, and Forder, the Wolverhampton coachbuilder of the 1870s, the provinces had given much to London by way of developments in the horse cab. But with the motor taxi London led the way from the start.

APPENDICES

Appendix 1: Changes in the maximum number of hackney carriages authorized, 1662–1815

Year	Authority	Total
1662	3 & 4 Charles 2.c.2	400
1694	5 & 6 Wil. & Mary c.22	700
1710	9 Ann c.23	800
1771	11 Geo.3 c.24	1,000
1802	42 Geo.3 c.24	1,100
1813	Treasury Minute, 19 January	900
1814	54 Geo.3 c.147	1,100
	Commissioners empowered to license up to 200 chariots. Total of	
	chariots and coaches not to exceed 1,100	
1815	55 Geo.3 c.147	1,100
	Maximum number of chariots raised to 400, with authorization	
	for an unlimited number of two-wheeled vehicles.	

Appendix 2: Twenty largest hackney coach and cab proprietors, March 1827

Number of Proprietors	Number of Licences	Type of Vehicle
1	24	all cab
1	18	all cab
1	15	all coach
1	14	all coach
1	10	all coach
2	9	includes one with 7 coaches and 2 cabs
6	8	all coach
2	7	includes one with 4 coaches and 3 cabs
4	6	three, all coach; one, all cab
1	5	All coach
—	—	
20	190	Total

Source: PP 1826–7 Vol. XX, p. 341

Appendix 3: Seventeen largest hackney coach proprietors, March 1827

Name	Earliest licence held	Latest licence held	Total number of licences	Listed in directories*	
				PA	PC
Blazdell, John	1813	1826	15	no	no
Holloway, Wm	1784	1809	14	glass coach prop.	no
Giles, J.H.†	1808	1817	10	funeral carriage proprietor	
Bardell, James	1799	1808	9	horse dealer	
Russell, John	1811	1826	7 coach 2 cab	no	no
Fay, Richard	1808	1824	8	no	no
Norris, John	1813	1825	8	no	no
Young, Martha††	1815	1815	8	cart & van hirer	no
Smith, John	1799	1816	8	funeral carriage proprietor	
Rigden, William	1808	1820	8	no	no
Nichols, Wm	1806	1826	8	horse dealer	no
Law, William	1807	1827	7	no	no
Taplin, Thomas	1823	1826	4 3 cab	coach livery stable keeper	
Bignall, Wm	1794	1807	6	hac. car. & funeral carriage proprietor	no
Hattersley, James	1810	1820	6	livery stable keeper	
Pearson, Thomas	1811	1827	6	no	no
Wharram, William	1795	1809	5	funeral carriage proprietor	

Source: PP 1826–7 Vol. XX, p. 341

* The directories used were *Pigot's Alphabetical Directory*, of 1827 (PA) and *Pigot's Commercial Directory*, of 1826–7 (PC). None of the proprietors is listed in the *Post Office Directory* of 1827.

† J.H. Giles was also the proprietor of a hackney carriage stage coach from Bow to Leadenhall Street.

†† Martha Young was a widow, one of whose licences can be traced to an issue to her husband, Joseph, in 1798.

Appendix 4: Number of horse cabs licensed, 1869–1914

Year	Two-wheeled Cabs	Four-wheeled cabs	Total
1869	–	–	5782
1870	–	–	7431
1871	–	–	7818
1872	–	–	8160
1873	4408	5247	9655
1876*	–	–	8262

Year	Two-wheeled Cabs	Four-wheeled cabs	Total
1877	4535	3994	8529
1878	4877	4014	8891
1879	5065	4145	9210
1881*	5800	3847	9647
1882	6369	3713	9983
1883	6579	3802	10381
1884	6832	3737	10569
1885	6877	3873	10750
1886	7020	3997	11017
1887	7219	4027	11246
1888	7396	4013	11409
1889	7409	3966	11375
1890	7376	3921	11297
1891	7320	3809	11129
1892	7133	3679	10812
1893	7193	3613	10806
1894	7268	3629	10897
1895	7425	3536	10961
1896	7585	3449	11034
1897	7925	3565	11490
1898	7899	3620	11519
1899	7559	3634	11193
1900	7531	3721	11252
1901	7454	3719	11173
1902	7577	3805	11382
1903	7499	3905	11404
1904	7137	3920	11057
1905	6996	3935	10931
1906	6648	3844	10492
1907	5952	3866	9818
1908	4826	3649	8475
1909	3299	3263	6562
1910	2003	2721	4724
1911	1054	2293	3347
1912	567	1818	2385
1913	386	1547	1933
1914	232	1159	1391

Source: PP Annual Reports of the Commissioner of Police of the Metropolis, *1869–1914*

* Separate figures for horse cabs are not available for 1874–5 and 1880.

Appendix 5: Number of motor cabs and horse cabs, 1897–1914

Year	Motor cabs	Horse cabs
1897	18	11490
1898	28	11519
1899	–	11193
1900	–	11252
1901	–	11173
1902	–	11382
1903	1	11404
1904	2	11057
1905	19	10931
1906	96	10492
1907	723	9818
1908	2805	8475
1909	3956	6562
1910	6397	4724
1911	7626	3347
1912	7969	2385
1913	8287	1933
1914	7260	1391

Source: PP Annual Reports of the Commissioner of Police of the Metropolis, *1897–1914*

Appendix 6: Size of motor cab fleets, October 1907

Owner	Cabs	Make	Origin
General Motor Cab Co	506	Renault	France
United Motor Cab Co	67	Unic	France
Express Motor Cab Co	14	Ballot	France
London Motor Cab Co	8	Rational	Britain
British Motor Cab Co	4	Argyll	France
Carlton Garage Ltd	3	Simplex	France
London Improved Cab Co	2	Marples	Britain
other	119 *	various	various

Source: Cab Trade Record, *December 1907*

* The figure of 119 for other owners is an approximation, based on the Metropolitan Police total of 723 cabs licensed at 31 December. Little is known of the Carlton Garage, which was incorporated in 1906 with a capital of £2,000 and was formally dissolved in June 1912 (PRO BT31/88859).

Appendix 7: Horse and Motor Cabs in London and Provincial Cities, 1910–12

City	1910		1911		1912	
	Motor	Horse	Motor	Horse	Motor	Horse
London	6397	4724	7626	3347	7969	2385
Belfast	6	410	8	383	14	351
Birmingham	52	267	80	310	91	256
Bristol	155	56	175	47	167	30
Dublin	58	1439	72	1421	118	1333
Edinburgh	75	591	98	536	112	481
Glasgow	109	307	96	304	82	239
Leeds	24	149	32	137	42	130
Liverpool	158	315	210	265	239	193
Manchester	130	506	199	392	236	315
Sheffield	46	181	76	129	63	95

Based on Appendix C,62 of the Report of the Select Committee on Motor Traffic, *1913*

NOTES

Abbreviations

BL   British Library
BLSRL   British Library: Science Reference Library
CON   *Cab and Omnibus News*
CTR   *Cab Trade Record*
DCTF   PP 1911 Vol. XLI *Report of the Depart-mental Committee on Taxi-cab Fares*
HCC   Hackney Coach Commissioners
HCG   *Hackney Carriage Guardian*
HOC   PP 1895 Vol. XXXV *Report of the Home Office Committee of Enquiry into the Cab Service of the Metropolis*
IOL   India Office Library
PP   Parliamentary Papers
PRO   Public Record Office
RCL   *Report of the Royal Commission on Labour: Minutes of Evidence: Group B*
RCPM   Annual *Reports of the Commissioner of Police of the Metropolis*
SCCOM PP 1906 Vol. VII *Report of the Select Committee on Cabs and Omnibuses (Metropolis) Bill*
SCHCO PP 1830 Vol. X *Report from the Select Committee on the Hackney Coach Office*

Preface

1. D.L. Munby and A.H. Watson, *Inland Transport Statistics of Great Britain: 1900–1970*, Vol. 1, 1978, pp. 480, 650. Figures for 1898–1914 calculated from the annual *Reports of the Commissioner of Police of the Metropolis*.
2. J.T. Dexter, 'The cabmen of London', *Social Science Review*, 2 May 1865, p. 401.

Chapter One

1. 25 Henry VIII, c8 quoted in W.T. Jackman, *The Development of Transportation in Modern England*, 1916 (new edn 1962) p. 36.
2. PP 1854 Vol. XXVI *Report of the Royal Commission on the Corporation of the City of London*, p. 12.

3. G.A. Sekon, *Locomotion in Victorian London*, 1938, p. 9; Max Schlesinger, *Saunterings in and about London*, 1853, p. 156.
4. For an expanded account of the early history of hackney coaches in London see H.C. Moore, *Omnibuses and Cabs*, 1902, pp. 181–93 and W.T. Jackman, *The Development of Transportation in Modern England*, 1916, pp. 109–18.
5. 2 Geo.3, c28, section 1. For changes to the Bills of Mortality see PP 1863 Vol. LIII *General Report. Census of England and Wales for the Year 1861*, p. 13.
6. PRO T1/878, HCC to Treasury, 9 April 1802; PRO T1/1297, HCC to Treasury, 8 January 1813; PRO T29/121, 19 January 1813. For an example of hackneymen petitioning to leave the trade see PRO T1/1910, 'Petition on behalf of the Whole Body of Hackney Coach Proprietors,' December 1819.
7. PP 1797 First Series Vol. XIII, *Eleventh Report from the Select Committee on Finance*, pp. 4, 16; PRO IR51/1, 24 March 1797; PP 1830 Vol. X *SCHCO*, pp. 331, 394.
8. The two minute books at the PRO are classed respectively IR51/1 and IR51/2. For the loss of the early records see IR51/1, 11 August 1801 and 19 May 1809.
9. B.R. Mitchell and Phyllis Deane, *Abstract of British Historical Statistics*, 1962, pp. 488–9.
10. John Jervis, *The Traveller's Oracle*, 1827 (second edition, revised by William Kitchiner), p. 309. Jervis argued that there were also good and bad days – Wednesdays and Thursdays, when dinner parties were held, being the best.
11. *SCHCO* 1830, p. 325.
12. *SCHCO* 1830, p. 329. See also the evidence of Commissioner Thomas Marrable to the same committee. He imagined that many recent applications 'had been made in great ignorance of the real state of the business' *SHCO*, 1830, p. 340.
13. *The Times*, 14 January 1830.
14. PP 1826–7 Vol. XX, p. 341; PRO T1/1032, HCC to Treasury, 7 April 1808. In April 1828 it was alleged that, including owners and drivers and their families, 7,000 persons were dependent on the

hackney coach trade, see *Journal of the House of Commons*, 7 April 1828.

15. 1 Geo.1 cx57, sections 3–4.

16. PRO T1/2725, Petition from Hackney Coach and Chariot Proprietors, n.d. but registered 30 September 1830. There were only nineteen signatories in all. The poor coverage of the directories will be noticed. Only half of the proprietors appear in *Pigot's Alphabetical Directory*, while none appear in the *Post Office Directory*.

17. *SCHCO* 1830, pp. 311–4, 322, 324–5, 335; Henry Mayhew, *London Labour and the London Poor*, Vol. III, 1861, p. 348; *The Times*, 9 July 1831.

18. *SCHCO* p. 334, Evidence of Henry Clement; John Jervis, *The Traveller's Oracle*, 1827, p. 305. The registration fee is itemized in PRO IR51/3, 31 August 1827. It included a standard charge of 1*s* 4*d* to the Registrar 'for extra trouble in checking the respectability of the applicant'.

19. *SCHCO* 1830, pp. 314, 335; John Jervis, *The Traveller's Oracle,* 1827, p. 305.

20. PRO T1/1297, HCC to Treasury, 8 January 1813; IR51/3, Report of the HCC on a petition of proprietors, 14 January 1820; *SCHCO* 1830, pp. 334–6. Horse mortality was also high in the winter of 1828–9, when 'a great number of horses . . . perished . . . from standing on the streets without work, and when the spring of the year came, they fell off', *SCHCO* 1830, p. 325.

21. *SCHCO* 1830, pp. 333–4, 343, 346 349–50.

22. *SCHCO* 1830, pp. 343–4.

23. *SCHCO* 1830, pp. 319, 336.

24. PRO T1/1411, Board of Stamps to Treasury, 3 August 1814; T1/1415, Petition of Hackney Coach Owners, registered 15 August 1814; *SCHCO* 1830, p. 340.

25. PRO IR51/3, 14 June 1823; 14 December 1827; 2 February, 31 March, 9 May and 13 June 1828; *Dictionary of National Biography*, Vol. 8, pp. 851–2.

26. For the important question of the competition which hackney coaches faced from job coaches and short stagecoaches see T.F. May, *The Administration and Organisation of the London Cab Trade from the Late Eighteenth Century to the First World War*, unpublished Ph.D. thesis, University of London, 1991, pp. 36–46.

Chapter Two

1. *The Times*, 24 April 1823.

2. For biographical details see T.F. May, *The Administration and Organisation of the London Cab Trade from the Late Eighteenth Century to the First World War*, 1991, p. 48n. Moore was responsible for another error regarding the first cab

proprietors. He claimed that the two men obtained nine licences for cabs in 1805 on condition that they never entered within the Bills of Mortality. How he came by this story is impossible to tell. The Hackney Coach Commissioners had no power to license vehicles operating wholly outside the Bills; they had no power to license cabs before 1815; and even if they had, they would certainly not have licensed Rotch, then aged eleven, H.C. Moore, *Omnibuses and Cabs*, 1902, pp. 205–6.

3. *Morning Herald*, 13 May 1823; *Bell's Life in London*, 15 June 1823. See also the speech of the Lord Mayor, Alderman William Thompson, to the House of Commons, reported in the *Mirror of Parliament*, 6 April 1829.

4. William Bridges Adams, *English Pleasure Carriages*, 1837, p. 240.

5. PRO IR51/3, 2 and 13 December 1822; 21 February and 5 March 1823; T29/219, Treasury Minutes, 11 March 1823.

6. PRO IR51/3, 21 and 27 November 1823; 6 July 1827.

7. PRO IR51/4 HCO List of the Twenty Largest Coach and Cab Proprietors, 19 March 1827.

8. *SCHCO* 1830, pp. 357–8. *Robson's Directory* of 1820 lists 'Boulnois and Clark', wine merchants; and the *Post Office Directory* of 1821 has a William Boulnois listed as a sugar refiner, as well as William Boulnois Jr. (who was the cab proprietor) listed as a wine merchant.

9. *Votes and Proceedings*, 22 May 1828, Petition of Thomas Henman to the House of Commons; PRO T1/2726.

10. PRO T1/2721; IR51/3, Treasury to HCC, 28 September 1827.

11. Harriet Martineau quoted in J.F. Rippy, *British Investments in Latin America, 1822–1949*, Minneapolis, 1959, p. 18; H.S. Ferns, *Britain and Argentina in the Nineteenth Century*, 1960, pp. 67n, 83, 91; J. R. McCulloch, *A Dictionary of Commerce*, 1837, p. 801. The above paragraphs are based on a variety of sources, including Foreign Office and Treasury papers. For full references see T.F. May, *The Administration and Organisation of the London Cab Trade from the Late Eighteenth Century to the First World War*, 1991, pp. 52–4.

12. PRO IR51/4, R.P. Staples to Treasury, 19 February 1828; HCC to Treasury, 29 February 1828; T22/21, Treasury to HCC, 19 March 1828; T1/2721, Gerss to Treasury, 18 April 1828; Gerss to T. Hyde Villiers, 2 May 1828.

13. PRO T1/2721, Undated letter from A.J. O'Neill to George Dawson.

14. PRO T29/281, Treasury Minutes, 6 May 1828. .

15. PRO IR51/1, 1 and 9 December 1828, 6 and 13

September 1830; T1/2721, HCC to Treasury, 6 September 1830.

16. PRO IR51/4, 13 and 16 December 1828; 27 January 1829; T22/21, 26 December 1828, 11 February 1829.

17. PRO T22/21, Treasury to HCC, 15 October 1828; T1/2617, Memorial of Thomas Henman, Clerk to the Committee of Hackney Coach and Chariot Owners, n.d., but registered 3 December 1828; T29/288, Treasury Minutes, 9 December 1828; *Clarke's New Law List*, 1826.

18. PRO T1/2616, Memorial of Proprietors of Public Cabriolets Relative to Complaints of Hackney Coach Owners, 1 January 1829.

19. PRO IR51/4, HCC to Treasury, 17 March, 14 December 1827, 27 May 1831; *SCHCO* 1830, p. 332.

20. See, for example, the speech of Joseph Hume in the House of Commons on 22 May 1828, reported in the *Mirror of Parliament*; and a letter from 'X' in *The Times* of 16 January 1830.

21. These paragraphs are based on evidence before the Select Committee on the Hackney Coach Office, 1830; John Jervis, *The Traveller's Oracle*, 1827, p. 317; *The Times*, 25 January 1830.

22. PRO IR51/4, Memorial of William Walker to the Treasury, 9 May 1828; T1/2616, Memorial of Proprietors of Public Cabriolets Relative to Complaints of Hackney Coach Owners, 1 January 1829; *SCHCO* 1830, pp. 356, 359.

23. *Mirror of Parliament*, 6 April 1829; *SCHCO* 1830, pp. 331, 352 .

Chapter Three

1. PP 1797 First Series Vol. XIII, *Eleventh Report of the Select Committee on Finance*, pp. 3–4.

2. PRO IR51/1, Treasury to HCC, 2 October 1797; T1/795, Memorial of Hackney Coach Masters, 15 December 1797; IR51/1, HCC to Treasury, 9 October 1797.

3. PP 1810 Vol. IV, *Twenty-eighth Report from the Select Committee on Finance*, 26 June 1798 (ordered to be reprinted 7 June 1810) pp. 377–8, 421–5. See also Sir Leon Radzinowicz, *A History of English Criminal Law and its Administration from 1750*, Vol. 3, 1956, pp. 66–7, 115–6, 270–3, 305–12.

4. PRO IR51/1, HCC to Treasury, 20 April 1801; T1/996, HCC to Treasury, 17 March 1807; 31 January and 10 March 1828 ; Sir John Sinclair, *The History of the Public Revenue of the British Empire*, 1805, Vol. 2, pp. 403–4.

5. PRO T1/1457, Edward Jesse to Treasury, 20 March 1815; *SCHCO* 1830, pp. 328–34 *passim*.

6. PRO IR51/4, Treasury to HCC, 5 August 1831; Dr Granville to HCC, 18 September 1831; undated letter

from Shillibeer to the Treasury, registered September 1833; T1/2607, Shillibeer to George Dawson, 24 June 1828, Shillibeer to J. Stewart, 24 July 1828, Shillibeer to Treasury, 20 November 1828; T1/2789, Edward Jesse to Charles Arbuthnot, 23 September 1831.

7. PRO IR51/5, Copy of Treasury Minute of 20 March 1832.

8. *SCHCO* 1830, pp. 349, 368. Evidence of George Green and James Quaife; PRO T22/21, Treasury to HCC, 7 July 1831.

9. Printed notice, 19 January 1832, PRO T1/2815.

10. PRO T1/2814, Cabriolet Union to Treasury, 30 January 1832; T1/2815, J.H. Reynolds to Treasury, 7 January 1832; IR13/36, Treasury to Commissioners of Stamps, 17 January 1832; IR51/6, Board of Stamps to J.H. Reynolds, 18 May 1833. A more urgent letter was sent on 8 July 1833. This episode may explain one of the gaps in the public records.

11. *The Times*, 20 November 1832; *London Gazette*, 23 October 1832, p. 2351; PRO IR51/6, Letters of 11 October, 12 November 1832; 26 and 29 September, 5 October 1833; T1/2932, Memorial of Robert and Peter Fitzgerald to Treasury, 5 September 1833.

12. PRO IR51/6, Information requested by a Committee of Aldermen in relation to the Police of the City of London, 29 January 1834; T1/2976, Petition of Hackney Coach Proprietors, n.d., but registered by the Treasury on 14 April 1834; *The Times*, 17 November 1834.

13. *Chambers' Edinburgh Journal*, 28 June 1845, p. 409.

14. *Chambers' Edinburgh Journal*, 28 June 1845, p. 409; *Penny Magazine*, 31 March 1837, p. 120; *The Times*, 24 December 1834.

15. T.C. Barker and M. Robbins, *A History of London Transport*, Vol. I, p. 37; *Seventh Report of the Select Committee on Public Petitions*, 1833, appendix, p. 208; *Twenty-third Report of the Select Committee on Public Petitions*, 1833, appendix, p. 333; *Thirty-fourth Report of the Select Committee on Public Petitions*, 1833, appendix, p. 1303; *Albion*, 24 September, 1834.

16. T.P. Thompson, 'Cab and omnibus nuisance', *Westminster Review*, Vol. 21, 1834, p. 395. For an analysis of the available statistics see T.F. May, *The Administration and Organisation of the London Cab Trade from the Late Eighteenth Century to the First World War*, 1991, pp. 79–81.

17. *Morning Chronicle*, 28 March 1835. It was argued that if the City aldermen wanted business, they should turn their attention to street widening and the number of omnibuses should be left to market forces.

18. R.G. Thorne (ed.), *The House of Commons 1790–1820*, vol. 5, 1986, p. 647.

19. *Mirror of Parliament*, 11 August 1835, p. 2401.

For a fuller consideration of the attempts to draft fresh legislation between 1834 and 1838 see T.F. May, *The Administration and Organisation of the London Cab Trade from the Late Eighteenth Century to the First World War*, 1991, pp. 84–91.

20. *The Times*, 6 and 16 November 1832; PRO IR51/6, Board of Stamps to Treasury, 20 November, 17 December 1832 and 13 February 1833; IR13/37, Treasury to Board of Stamps, 19 January 1833. See also T1/2888.

Chapter Four

1. Figures calculated from the annual *RCPM*.
2. W.A. Young and A.A. Gomme, 'The Chapman papers: a note on the hansom cab', in *Transactions of the Newcomen Society*, Vol. 24, 1945, pp. 65–72. A more accurate account is J.W. Chapman, *Philosopher John*, Cartmel, 1983. The claim on behalf of Edward Bird was made in the *Morning Post*, 9 November 1932.
3. *Birmingham Daily Post*, 1 July 1882; *Builder*, 8 July 1882. Hansom has as yet no biographer.
4. C.J. Kirkby Fenton, 'The birthplace of the hansom cab', *Illustrated Sporting and Dramatic News*, 14 August 1894; H.C. Moore, *Omnibuses and Cabs*, 1902, p. 217; William Bridges Adams, *English Pleasure Carriages*, 1837, p. 277–8.
5. Frederick Boase, *Modern English Biography*, Vol. I, 1892, p. 419; *Dictionary of National Biography*, Vol. 24, 1890, pp. 1193–4; BL, Add. Mss. 40583, f.165, J.S. Needham to Sir Robert Peel, 26 January 1846.
6. *Victoria County History of Warwickshire*, Vol. VII, 1964, p. 289; Vol. VIII, 1969, p. 233; James Langford, *A Century of Birmingham Life*, 1878, Vol. 2, pp. 427, 436.
7. J.W. Chapman, *Philosopher John*, 1983, pp. 1–10.
8. IOL, Chapman Papers, Mss. Eur E 234, File 7, John to Mary Chapman, 1 May, 16 May, 18 August 1835; Iorwerth Prothero, *Artisans and Politics*, 1979, Ch. 10 *passim*.
9. IOL, Chapman Papers, Mss. Eur E 234, File 7, John to Mary Chapman, 18 August 1835.
10. IOL, Chapman Papers, Mss. Eur E 234, File 7, John to Mary Chapman, 27 September 1835.
11. Draft prospectuses for the company are to be found among the Chapman Papers at BLSRL. See also *Builder*, 8 July 1882, p. 44, and H.C. Moore, *Omnibuses and Cabs*, 1902, p. 218.
12. See, for example, Chapman's letter to Horace Twiss, 22 April 1837, among the Chapman Papers at BLSRL.
13. BLSRL, Chapman Papers, Report of the Safety Cabriolet and Two-wheel Carriage Company, 2 May

1836; John Chapman, 'Narrative of events connected with the patent taken out by Mr Gillett and J. Chapman.'
14. This paragraph is based on various documents among the Chapman Papers. For full references and a more detailed account see T.F. May, *The Administration and Organisation of the London Cab Trade from the Late Eighteenth Century to the First World War*, 1991, Ch. 3.
15. BLSRL, Chapman Papers, Undated draft of a letter (c. summer of 1837) from Chapman to directors.
16. J.W. Chapman, *Philosopher John*, 1983, p. 45.
17. BLSRL, Chapman Papers, Undated paper titled 'Principles and Advantages of Gillett and Chapman's Patent for Improvements in Cabs'.
18. IOL, Chapman Papers. Mss. Eur E 234, File 91, Memorandum dated 15 August 1842; BLSRL, John Chapman, 'Narrative of Events . . .'
19. BLSRL, Chapman Papers, Draft letter from Chapman to Joseph Hansom, n.d., c. last week of December 1836.
20. IOL, Chapman Papers, Mss. Eur E 234, File 91, Mr Carpmael's Report, 26 August 1836.
21. BLSRL, Chapman Papers, Report by John Chapman on renewal of cabs, 21 December 1839; IOL, Chapman Papers, Mss. Eur E 234, File 91, 'Memorandum of Conversation with Welby [sic] and Newcomb', 1 February 1840.
22. For a fuller account of the misfortunes of the Patent Safety Carriage Company see T.F. May, *The Administration and Organisation of the London Cab Trade from the Late Eighteenth Century to the First World War*, 1991, Ch. 3.
23. *Builder*, 8 July 1882. Chapman's later career is narrated in J.W. Chapman, *Philosopher John*, pp. 21ff.
24. IOL, Chapman Papers, Mss. Eur E 234, File 91, 'Memorandum of a meeting with Messrs Wilby and Newcomb', 1 February 1840.

Chapter Five

1. PRO IR51/6, Information requested by the Committee of Aldermen in relation to the Police of the City of London, 29 January 1834; HO45/728, Wedgwood to Sir James Graham, 13 September 1844; PP 1852–3, Vol. LXXVIII, *Number of Standings for Hackney Carriages in Metropolitan Police Districts*; PP 1861, Vol. VIII, *Report on the Select Committee on Metropolis Local Taxation*, Appendix 16, p. 242.
2. PP 1911, Vol. XLI, *Report of the Departmental Committee on Taxi-cab Fares*, Minutes of Evidence, qq.3, 718–25, Evidence of Superintendent Bassom.
3. Gareth Stedman Jones, *Outcast London*, 1984, Harmondsworth, p. 374; PP 1861, Vol. VIII, *Report of the Select Committee on Metropolis Local Taxation*, p.

242; PP 1895, Vol. XXV, *Report of the Home Office Committee of Enquiry into the Cab Service of the Metropolis*, p. 300.

4. PRO HO45/A55943B, Transcript of a meeting on the metropolitan cab strike, 7 June 1894; PP 1895 Vol. XXXV, *HOC* pp. 168–176; Companies House, Registered file of the London General Cab Co. Ltd (Ref: 446749); *HCG* August 1891.

5. *All The Year Round*, 18 July 1863, p. 486.

6. *HCG* 3 December 1887; John Garwood, *The Million-peopled City; or, One Half of the People of London Made Known to the Other Half*, 1853, p. 180; Henry Mayhew, *London Labour and the London Poor*, Vol. III, 1861, p. 353.

7. PP 1866 Vol. XXVI, *Tenth Report of the Commissioners of Inland Revenue*, p. 15.

8. *The Times*, 27 January 1853; Henry Mayhew, *London Labour and the London Poor*, 1861, p. 351; J.T. Dexter, 'The cabmen of London', *Social Science Review*, 2 May 1864, p. 404; *The Centaur*, 8 July 1882; Morley Roberts, 'Cabs and cabmen', *Murray's Magazine*, 1889–90, p. 379; PRO. HO/45 A55943B. Scott's remark was made at a meeting at the Home Office on 7 July 1894, when masters and men joined with the Home Secretary, Herbert Asquith, in attempting to hammer out agreed hiring prices, a problem made more difficult by the different quality of cabs.

9. J.T. Dexter, 'The Cabmen of London', 1864, p. 404; *Working Man*, 17 February 1866, p. 99. For a discussion by proprietors and drivers in 1894 on wear and tear and on the working life of a cab see PRO HO45/A55943B, Transcript of meeting on the metropolitan cabs strike, 7 June 1894.

10. *RCL* 1892 Vol. XXXVI(2), p. 368, q.16,616.

11. J.T. Dexter, 'The Cabmen of London', 1864, pp. 405–6; *The Centaur*, 1 January 1881; *RCL* 1892. Vol. XXXVI(2), p. 431, Appendix CXV.

12. PP 1839 Vol. IX *Report of the Select Committee on Turnpike Trusts*, Minutes of Evidence, p. 12, q.196ff; PP 1873, Vol. XIV, *Report of the Select Committee of the House of Lords on the Supply of Horses*, p. 229, qq.2,911–4; *The Centaur*, 16 October 1875, 8 July 1882; PRO HO45/A55943 B, Transcript of meeting on the metropolitan cab strike, 7 June 1894. See also F.M.L. Thompson (ed.), *Horses in European Economic History: a Preliminary Canter*, 1983, Reading, p. 52.

13. J.T. Dexter, 'The Cabmen of London', 1864, pp. 405–6; W.J. Gordon, *The Horse-world of London*, 1893, p. 34; PRO HO45/A55943B, Transcript of meeting on the metropolitan cab strike, 7 June 1894; *The Times*, 4 October 1875; *All the Year Round*, 18 July 1863, p. 486; PP 1873 Vol. XIV, *Report of the Select Committee of the House of Lords on the Supply of Horses*, p. 228, qq.2, 900–1.

14. A.T. Camden Pratt, *Unknown London*, n.d. pp. 194–6.

15. T.C. Barker and Michael Robbins, *A History of London Transport*, Vol. I, 1963, pp. 84, 176, 243–4; PRO HO45/A55943B, Transcript of a meeting on the metropolitan cab strike, 7 June, 1894. For an account of the remarkably mechanized and scientific feeding of horses by the leading Parisian cab company see Ghislaine Bouchet, 'La traction hippomobile dans les transports publics parisiens, 1855–1914', *Revue Historique*, Vol. CCLXXI/1, January–March 1984, pp. 125–134.

16. *SCHC0* 1830, p. 58; *Amalgamated Society of Carpenters' and Joiners' Monthly Report*, December 1868; 'An Ex-cabby', *London Cabs and Cabmen's Grievances*, 1871, p. 7; *The Centaur*, 12 July 1879; *HOC* 1895, p. 104, qq.3,770–79; *HCG* August and November 1894.

17. *SCHCO* 1830, p. 31; *The Times*, 25 and 26 January 1853; *All the year Round*, 25 February 1860; Henry Mayhew, *London Labour and the London Poor*, 1861, p. 351; *RCL* 1892, p. 38, q.17,567.

18. *HCG* 6 August 1887; PRO HO45/A55943B, Transcript of a meeting on the metropolitan cab strike, 7 June 1894; W.J. Gordon, *The Horse-world of London*, 1893, p. 44.

19. *The Times*, 4 June 1851; *Punch*, 26 April 1862; 'An Ex-Cabby', *The Horse-world of London*, 1871, p. 8; PP 1876, Vol. XXXIV; *Annual RCPM for the Year 1875*, p. 5; PRO HO45/54518, Cab Drivers' Grievances: Deputation to the Secretary of State, 1 September 1893; *The Centaur*, 8 January 1881; *HCG* January 1884; 29 April 1885; 2 January 1896; 4 June 1897.

20. PRO HO45/A55943D, Undated Board of Trade memoranda headed 'London Cab Strike' and 'Cab Strike'.

21. *All The Year Round*, 25 February 1860, p. 415; J.T. Dexter, 'The Cabmen of London', 1864, pp. 404–6; *CON* 4 June, 20 August 1870, 18 September 1875; *The Centaur*, 18 March, 1882; PP 1892 Vol. XXXVI(2) *Royal Commission on Labour*, qq.16, 609, 19, 272–6; PRO HO45/53518; *CTR* July 1898, November 1899, March 1900, July and August 1904.

22. *CTR* November 1903. For a fuller discussion of the Asquith Award see T.F. May, *The Administration and Organisation of the London Cab Trade from the Late Eighteenth Century to the First World War*, 1991, pp. 207–12.

Chapter Six

1. PP 1874 Vol. XXVIII, *RCPM for the Year 1873*, p. 4; *HCG* April 1884; *Daily Telegraph*, 19 April 1884.

2. H.I. Dutton, *The Patent System and Inventive*

Activity During the Industrial Revolution, 1750–1852, 1984, Manchester, p. 206.

3. H.C. Moore, *Omnibuses and Cabs*, 1902, pp. 228–30; *Illustrated London News*, 14 October 1848; *Punch*, 4 November 1848.

4. *The Times*, 15, 18 January 1887; *HCG* 12 February 1887.

5. The construction and use regulations were reprinted as Appendix 32 of PP 1871 Vol. XXVIII, *RCPM for 1870*.

6. *The Times*, 14 August 1874.

7. *The Times*, 14 January 1870; Prospectus of Six Days Cab Company in *Practical Mechanic's Journal*, Glasgow, 1 July 1853.

8. *HCG* 7 June 1890.

9. *Wolverhampton and South Staffordshire Illustrated*, 1898, London, p. 140; *The Times*, 4 October 1875; *CON* 2 October 1875; *The Times*, 4 October 1875.

10. PRO BT31/9884, Statement of capital and shares to 13 August 1880; PP 1878 Vol. XL, *RCPM for 1877*, p. 6; PRO BT31/9884, PRO Rail 236/356/1. Letter from Lt.-Col. G. Elliot, Director of the London General Cab Co. to Francis Cockshott, Superintendent of the Line, Great Northern Railway, 15 February 1884.

11. PRO BT31/16935.

12. PRO BT31/16069; *HCG* January 1884.

13. Frederic Boase, *Modern English Biography*, Vol. II, 1897, column 716; Vol. IV, 1908, columns 188–9; *The Centaur*, 5 June 1880, 28 January 1882; Douglas Sutherland, *The Yellow Earl: the Life of Hugh Lowther, Fifth Earl of Lonsdale*, 1965, pp. 1–3, 63, 93; Douglas Sutherland, *The Mad Hatters*, 1987, pp. 79–92, 130ff; Sir John Dugdale Astley, *Fifty Years of My Life*, Vol. II, 1894, pp. 166–7.

14. For the Pelican Club see Douglas Sutherland, *The Mad Hatters*, 1987, Ch. 11.

15. *Vanity Fair*, 7 April 1888; The Earl of Cardigan, *The Wardens of Savernake Forest*, 1949, pp. 311, 316.

16. *The Centaur*, 19 January 1884; *Daily Telegraph*, 19 April 1884.

17. *HCG* December 1884.

18. *Who Was Who, 1916–1928*, 1967, (4th edn), p. 958; *Vanity Fair*, 10 July 1886; Douglas Sutherland, *The Mad Hatters*, 1965, pp. 11–12.

19. *Midland Evening News*, Wolverhampton, 7 July 1888; *The Centaur*, 5 January 1884; PRO BT31/18001, Memorandum of association of the Noiseless Tyre Co. Ltd, registered 7 March 1883; *HCG* 5 May 1888; PRO H045/55943B, Transcript of a meeting on the metropolitan cab strike, 7 June 1894.

20. *The Centaur*, 21 June, 23 August 1884; *HCG* September 1884, 1 May 1886; PRO BT31/22059 and BT31/26910.

21. W. Outram Tristram, 'Cabs and their drivers', *English Illustrated Magazine*, 1891, p. 312; PRO. BT31/27593.

22. PRO BT31/26910, BT 31/67592; *HCG* 19 October 1889, 19 July 1890, 4,11 April 1891, February 1893, July 1895; *The Lighthouse*, 20 October 1888, 7 July 1890, 3 October 1891.

23. *The Lighthouse*, 8 September 1888; *HCG* 8 December 1888.

Chapter Seven

1. For biographical information on D.W. Harvey see the *Dictionary of National Biography*, Vol. 25, p. 79; Charlotte Fell Smith, 'Daniel Whittle Harvey 1786–1863', *Essex Review*, 1915, Vol. XXIV; PP 1839 Vol. XXX, *Extracts from Letters from D.W. Harvey, Esq., to Home Secretary Relative to the Office of Registrar of Hackney Carriages*. For Hensleigh Wedgwood see *Dictionary of National Biography*, Vol. 60, p. 140.

2. PRO HO39/12, D.W. Harvey to Lord John Russell, 4 January 1839.

3. PRO HO39/12, Hensleigh Wedgwood to Lord John Russell, 1 March 1839. The authority to appoint standings within the City was given to the Court of Mayor and Aldermen by Section 54 of the London Hackney Carriage Act, 1831.

4. PRO Mepo 1/56, Richard Mayne to Sir James Clark, 5 February 1851. For the legal issues see T.F. May, *The Administration and Organisation of the London Cab Trade from the Late Eighteenth Century to the First World War*, 1991, pp. 129–132.

5. PRO T1/5577A, Board of Inland Revenue to Treasury, 7 June 1850; PRO T1/5460A.

6. PRO Mepo 2/18, Memorial from Richard Mayne on the duties of the Registrar of Public Carriages, 24 February 1851.

7. T.C. Barker and Michael Robbins, *A History of London Transport*, Vol. 1, 1963, p. 61; *The Times*, 10, 19 April, 18 July 1851.

8. T.C. Barker and Michael Robbins, *A History of London Transport*, 1963, pp. 61–3; *The Times*, 15, 26 November 1851.

9. *Illustrated London News*, 18 June 1853.

10. *The Times*, 20, 21, 23 July, 20 August 1853; PRO HO45/4625, Phillips to Treasury, 25 July 1853; Phillips to Lord Palmerston, 1 August 1853; *The Times*, 20 August 1853. That public sympathy was strongly on the side of Phillips is apparent from a letter from Henry to the Home Office, dated 11 August, complaining that *he* was now being victimized; and from Bond, on 15 August, where he tried to clear himself of some of the odium which had been cast upon him, HO45/ 4625.

11. *The Times*, 28, 29 July, 3 August 1853.

12. PRO HO45/4625, Sir Richard Mayne to Horatio Waddington, Home Office, 9 July 1853.

13. *The Times*, 19 April 1851; Robert Reiner, *The Politics of the Police*, 1985, p. 22.

14. PRO HO69/19, Henry Fitzroy to Sir Richard Mayne, 6 March 1854; Waddington to Mayne, 27 April 1854; HO45/5710, Mayne to Waddington, 25 September 1854; HO45/6151, Mayne to Fitzroy, 1 March 1855.

15. PRO HO45/4625, Memorandum of Sir Richard Mayne on staffing requirements for public carriage work, 7 July 1853; HO45/4625, Sir Richard Mayne to Horatio Waddington, 9 July 1853; HO45/6151, Sir Richard Mayne to Henry Fitzroy, 1 March 1855; Mepo 2/18, Undated draft of letter from Mayne to Fitzroy.

16. PRO Mepo 7/19, Metropolitan Police General Orders, 3 May, 23 June 1858. For an early example of a *Notice to Proprietors*, see *The Times*, 14 August 1874.

17. PRO Mepo 7/19, 19 May 1858; PP 1866 Vol. XII, *Special Report from the Select Committee on the London (City) Traffic Regulation Bill*, Evidence of Sir Richard Mayne, qq.246–7, 255; PP 1882. Vol. 33, *RCPM for the Year 1881*, p. 6; *HOC* 1895, qq1580–2, 1603, 1740, 1759–61.

18. PRO HO45/A55585, E.L. Pemberton, Home Office, to Sir Charles Warren,11 May 1887; Mepo 2/481. Report of 10 May, 1900. For a fuller discussion of the staffing problems of the Public Carriage Office see T.F. May, *The Administration and Organisation of the London Cab Trade from the Late Eighteenth Century to the First World War*, 1991, pp. 134–157.

19. *HOC* 1895, qq.5977–9, Evidence of A.R. Pennefather, Receiver of the Metropolitan Police.

20. PRO Mepo 5/735, Observations of the Receiver on the 1895 committee report, 13 March 1895.

21. Quoted in John R. Kellett, *Railways and Victorian Cities*, 1969, p. 316.

22. For pressures on the police at this time see J.F. Moylan, *Scotland Yard and the Metropolitan Police*, 1929, pp. 38–40, and *The Times*, 30 January 1868.

23. See, for example, *HCG*, 15 April 1885.

24. PRO Mepo 5/735, Observations of the Receiver on the 1895 committee report, 13 March 1895.

25. PRO Mepo 1/57, Henderson to Augustus Liddell , permanent under-secretary, Home Office, 10 July 1869, 1 January 1870.

26. *HOC* 1895, Report, p. 4; PRO Mepo 5/735, Minute of 13 March 1895.

27. PRO Mepo 2/777. For the hackney carriage revenue question and the Metropolitan Police see T.F. May, *The Administration and Organisation of the London Cab Trade from the Late Eighteenth Century to the First World War*, 1991, pp. 158–172.

28. David Owen, *The Government of Victorian London, 1855–1889*, 1982, p. 164.

29. PRO Mepo 2/333, Edward Monckton, Chairman of East Molesey Local Board, to Chief Commissioner, 29 November 1875.

30. PRO HO45/17886, Sir Edmund Henderson to Adolphus Liddell, 1 February 1879.

31. PRO Mepo 2/333, Reports from Edward Ware, Public Carriage Office, 18, 27 March 1884; Letter from Town Clerk of Croydon to Chief Clerk, Metropolitan Police, 29 July 1885; *HCG* 12 December 1885.

32. The above paragraph is based on correspondence and memoranda in the following files: PRO HO45/A55667; Mepo 2/333; Mepo 5/33.

33. *Sunday Times*, 19 March 1989. See also the reply of Michael Portillo, MP, Minister of Public Transport, *Hansard*, Sixth Series, Vol. 152, Column 486, 11 May 1989. Proposals to transfer London cabs to municipal control are discussed in more detail in T.F. May, *The Administration and Organisation of the London Cab Trade from the Late Eighteenth Century to the First World War*, 1991, pp. 172–186.

Chapter Eight

1. *All The Year Round*, 25 February 1860, p. 414. This article, by John Hollingshead, was reprinted in *Odd Journeys*, 1862.

2. James Greenwood, *The Wilds of London*, 1874, p. 110 ; Daniel Joseph Kirwan, *Palace and Hovel, or Phases of London Life*, 1870 (1963 edn edited by A. Allan) p. 206.

3. *Fraser's Magazine*, March 1851, p. 309.

4. *Westminster Review*, 1891, Vol. 136, p. 547.

5. See the article by Thomas Smith in *The Centaur*, 2 October 1880. The best account of this relationship remains Fred Davis, 'The cabdriver and his fare: facets of a fleeting relationship', *American Journal of Sociology*, 1959, Vol. 65.

6. H.J. Dyos and Michael Wolff (eds), *The Victorian City*, Vol. 2, 1973, pp. 570–1, 711–12.

7. *The Times*, 19 May 1851; W.H. Wilkins, 'Hansoms and their drivers,' *The Nineteenth Century*, March 1893, p. 478.

8. PP 1892 Vol. XXVI, Report of the Royal Commission on Labour, qq.16630, 17518–23; PRO Mepo1/57, 19 November 1870; Mepo 5/468; Anthony Armstrong, *Taxi*, 1930, p. 189.

9. PP 1873 Vol XXXI, Report of the Commissioner of Police of the Metropolis for the Year 1872, p. 3; PP 1897 Vol. XXXIX, Report for 1896, p. 9.

10. PRO HO45/17886; HO45/157860; Mepo2/843; PP 1911 Vol. XLI, Report of the Departmental Committee on Taxicab Fares, Q402 ff; *Motor Traction*, 15 October 1910.

11. Richard Rowe, *How Our Working People Live*, c. 1882, p. 221.

12. PRO HO45/53518; Maurice Levinson, *Taxi!*, 1963, p. 68.

13. *HOC* 1895, q.2026; H.C. Moore, *Omnibuses and Cabs*, 1902, pp. 237–8.

14. PP 1872 Vol. XXX, *RCPM for the Year 1871*, p. 60; PRO HO45/54518, John Bridge, Chief Magistrate, Bow Street to Home Office, 14 September 1893.

15. *Cab Trade Record*, November 1901; PRO HO45/198845.

16. W.H. Wilkins, op.cit., 1893, p. 476.

17. W.H. Wilkins, op. cit., 1893, pp. 475–6.

18. *HOC* 1895, qq.3671–3, 4624–39, 5028–38, 5188–94, 5352–62.

19. Charles Booth, *Life and Labour of the People in London*, Vol. VII, 1896, pp. 293–4; Henry Mayhew, *London Labour and the London Poor*, Vol. III, 1861, pp. 352–3; W.H. Wilkins, op.cit., 1893, p. 476; PRO HO45/X73494.

20. J.T. Dexter, 'The cabmen of London', 1864, p. 416.

21. Victor E. Neuburg, *Popular Literature: a History and Guide*, 1977, pp. 14, 251. For the London City Mission see John Matthias Weylland, *Round the Tower; or, the Story of the London City Mission*, n.d. (c. 1875) and *These Fifty Years*, 1885; together with John Garwood, *The Million-Peopled City*, 1853.

22. *Cab and Omnibus News*, 28 May, 2 July 1870; *The Centaur*, 10 May, 1879, 8 July 1882, 11 August 1883, 12 April 1884; *All the Year Round*, 25 February, 1860, p. 416.

23. *Congregationalist*, Vol. 6, 1877, pp. 223–5.

24. PRO Mepo 1/57, Henderson to Home Office, 16 January, 27 August 1872; *The Centaur*, 21 August, 23 October 1880.

25. *HOC* 1895, evidence of Walter Macnamara; Printed Circular of the Cabmen's Shelter Fund in John Johnson collection, Bodleian Library, University of Oxford.

26. Charles Booth, op. cit., 1896, p. 302; *The Centaur*, 18 August 1883, 19 January 1884, 24,31 October 1885.

27. A brief history of trade unionism among London cabdrivers will be found in an article by A. J. Corfield in *Transport and General Workers Record*, February 1963. Further information can be found in *HCG* and *CTR*.

28. W.H. Wilkins, op.cit., 1893, pp. 478–9.

Chapter Nine

1. F.M.L. Thompson, *Victorian England: the Horse-drawn Society*, 1970, p. 13.

2. PP 1906 Vol. VII, *SCCOM*, p. 22, q.337; PP 1846 Vol. XVII, *Report of the Royal Commission on Metropolitan Termini*, q.501–3, Evidence of Benjamin Horne; Appendix 29, p. 291; PRO HO45A 54518/2.

3. Sir Francis Bond Head, *Stokers and Pokers*, 1849, p. 43.

4. John Garwood, *The Million-peopled City; or, One-half of the People of London Made Known to the Other Half*, 1853, p. 180; *HOC* 1895, qq.2731–2735, 7980–7983.

5. *HOC* 1895, qq.8598–8641; PP 1906 Vol. VII, *SCCOM*, q.353; PRO HO45/55943B.

6. Timetable of May 1839, reproduced in *Old Euston*, 1938, p. 70.

7. *Builder*, quoted in *The Centaur*, 4 February 1882; PRO HO45/54518, Cab Drivers' Grievances : Deputation to Secretary of State, 1 September 1893.

8. PRO HO45/A55943D; *HOC* 1895, q.7978. For a breakdown of the figures relating to the Paddington terminus of the Great Western Railway, 1893-6, see T.F. May, *The Administration and Organisation of the London Cab Trade from the Late Eighteenth Century to the First World War*, 1991, pp. 771–3.

9. *The Times*, 5 February 1868.

10. *The Times*, 7 May, 28 May, 29 August 1868.

11. PRO Rail 236/300/2, Petition of the Amalgamated Hackney Carriage Proprietors' Association to the Directors of the Great Northern Railway, 5 June 1868.

12. *The Times*, 2–12 September 1868 *passim*.

13. PRO HO45/17886, Seymour Clark, General Manager of the Great Northern Railway, to Adolphus Liddell, Home Office, 5 January 1870.

14. *The Times*, 31 January, 1870; PRO HO45/17886, Minute of R.A. Cross on letter addressed to him by Sir James Ingham, 18 February 1879.

15. *The Centaur*, 10 March 1883.

16. *The Centaur*, 13 October 1883.

17. *HOC* 1895, p. 180. q.6993. *The Centaur* (which was the union's mouthpiece, and was published by Rowland) ceased publication with its issue of 21 November 1885.

18. Charles Booth, *Life and Labour of the People in London*, Vol. VIII, 1896, pp. 302–3. *The Times*, 9 February 1892.

19. PRO HO45/54518, Cab Drivers' Grievances: Deputation to the Secretary of State, 1 September 1893.

20. *Herapath's Railway Journal*, 1 May 1894; PRO HO45/A55943; Rail236/376/8. Great Northern Railway file on the 1894 cab strike.

21. PRO HO45/A55943; *Herapath's Railway Journal*, 28 August 1896.

22. *The Times*, 26 September, 23, 24, 30 October, 2 November 1896; PRO Rail 236/379/14,Report of Sir Henry Oakley to traffic committee of Great Northern Railway, 4 November 1896.

23. PP 1906 Vol. VII, *SCCOM*, pp. iii, iv, ix. It has

been argued that 'frequent inability to bring about desirable change', was one of the particular characteristics of the Home Office in the late nineteenth century, Judith Pellew, *The Home Office, 1848–1914*, 1982, p. 63.

24. *Hansard*, Vol. 180, 7 August 1907, Vol. 181, 21 August 1907.

25. Philip Warren and Malcolm Linskey, *Taxicabs: a Photographic History*, 1976, p. 36; *Motor Traction*, 17 July 1909. Initially motor cabs were too light to compete with the four-wheeled horse cabs for the carrying of heavy luggage, although they soon overcame this disability, *Motor Traction*, 11 July 1908.

Chapter Ten

1. Theo Barker (ed.), *The Economic and Social Effects of the Spread of Motor Vehicles*, 1987, p.10; PRO BT31/50104; PP 1898 Vol. XLVI, *RCPM for 1897*, pp. 7–8; *CTR*, July 1898.
2. PP 1898 Vol. XLVI, *RCPM for 1897*, p. 8.
3. W. Worby Beaumont, *Motor Vehicles and Motors: their Design, Construction and Working by Steam, Oil and Electricity*, 1900, Vol. I, pp. 401–2, 414; Anthony Armstrong, *Taxi!*, 1930, p. 21; PP 1900, Vol. XL, *RCPM for 1899*, p. 11.
4. *SCCOM* 1906, p. 121; PRO Mepo2/999; Mepo2/1536; HO45/150381.
5. PRO HO45/110360, Lord Montague to Herbert Gladstone, 19 December 1905; PP 1913, Vol. VIII, *SCCOM* qq.17348–67, 17439–51.
6. *SCCOM* 1906, q.2873. For similar views, though more specifically in the context of buses, see the evidence of James Critchley, qq.2505–7; Alan Swinton, q.2609–10, and Sidney Straker, q.2802.
7. Philip Warren and Malcolm Linskey, *Taxicabs: a Photographic History*, 1976, p. 45; PP 1919 Vol. VII, *SCCOM*, qq.7638, 7660–2, Evidence of Herbert Bundy.
8. PRO HO61/1, J.W. Lee to Sir Robert Peel, 29 January 1829.
9. *HOC* 1894, Report, p. 8; Evidence, qq.674–9, 754, 1049–56, 2749, 3558, 6325, 7288, 9218–20, and Appendix viii, p. 322. In the early days the spelling 'taxameter' was often used, rather than 'taximeter'. The latter spelling is used here, except in the case of proper nouns.
10. Kenneth Richardson, *The British Motor Industry, 1896–1939*, 1977, p. 14ff; G.N. Georgano, *A History of the London Taxicab*, 1972, Newton Abbot, p. 56; PRO BT31/56247, The Taxameter Syndicate, memorandum of association; Mepo2/443; University of London Library, F.R. Simms Papers, 30/8.
11. G.N. Georgano, *A History of the London Taxicab*, pp. 56–7; *SCCOM*, 1906, q.1256, Evidence of Fred

Simmons; Evidence of C. Harrington Moore, qq.1797–1848; *CTR* April 1899; PRO BT31/56247, BT31/67759.
12. James M. Laux, *Into First Gear: the French Automobile Industry to 1914*, 1976, Liverpool, p. 141; PRO BT31/86870; *SCCOM* 1906 qq.570–2, 1607–9, 1324–5, 1340.
13. *SCCOM* 1906 qq.2157–79.
14. *SCCOM* 1906 Report, pp. xviii–xxi.
15. *Motor Finance*, 9 January 1907; *CTR* February, March 1907.
16. *CTR* June 1907; *Hansard*, Vol. 174, 24 May 1907, columns 1231–2; *The Times*, 3 July 1907; PRO Mepo2/1163.
17. PRO HO45/150381; Mepo2/1272.
18. See, for example, *DCTF* 1911 qq.393ff, q.1869.
19. *DCTF* 1911 Report, p. 5; PRO Mepo2/4817, Report from Public Carriage Office, 25 March 1910.
20. PRO HO45/157860.
21. PRO HO45/157860. See also *LVTR*, 27 May, 8 July 1914.
22. PRO HO45/195971, Notes of deputation to the Home Secretary, 19 October 1910.
23. PRO Mepo 2/1533; HO45/183647.
24. PRO HO45/195971; Mepo2/1504. Charles Reinhardt, *Old Friends in Hard Times*, n.d. (c. 1912).
25. *HOC* 1895, p. 300; PP 1908 Vol. LI, *RCPM for the Year 1907*, p. 9; *DCTF* 1911, Report, p. 5; *Motor Traction*, 17 July 1909.
26. *HCG* 1 October 1887, November 1895.
27. PRO BT31/70200, BT31/86684, BT31/96215; H045/195971; *DCTF* 1911, qq.2585–2598, Evidence of J.W. Braine; *Motor Traction*, 2 May 1908; James. M. Laux, op. cit., 1976, Liverpool, p. 146–9, 152.
28. PRO BT31/10523; HO45/210614, Sir Edward Henry to Under Secretary, Home Office, 1 September 1911. For Home Office and Metropolitan Police attitudes to hire purchase of cabs see T.F. May, *The Administration and Organisation of the London Taxi Cab Trade from the Late Eighteenth Century to the First World War*, 1991, pp. 323–6.
29. *DCTF* 1911 qq.104–5; PP 1913 Vol. VIII, *Report of the Select Committee on Motor Traffic*, q.11276; PP 1914–16 Vol. XXVI, *Seventh Report of the London Traffic Branch of the Board of Trade*, p. 20.
30. A.E. Harrison, 'Joint-stock company flotation in the cycle, motor-vehicle and related industries, 1882–1914', *Business History*, 1981, Vol. 23, The prospectuses of the Great Horseless Carriage Company and the British Motor Syndicate will be found in *Autocar*, 12 May, 28 November 1896, respectively.
31. *HCG* 25 June 1887; Kenneth Richardson, *The British Motor Industry, 1896–1939*, 1977, pp. 42–5.
32. *HCG* December 1894; PRO BT31/43913, BT31/47670.

33. PR0 BT31/50004; BT31/50104; G.N. Georgano, *A History of the London Taxicab*, 1971, p. 41; University of London Library, Simms Papers, 5/51 and 5/21/31, Arthur Mulliner to F.R. Simms, 26 May and 1 June 1896. The second of these letters, both of which are applications for the post of works manager at the Great Horseless Carriage Company, contains interesting biographical information on Mulliner. See also R.C. Michie, 'Options, concession, syndicates, and the provision of venture capital,1880–1913', *Business History*, 1981, Vol. 23.

34. PRO BT31/74635, BT31/86678; BT31/86684; *Motor Finance*, 13 February 1907; T.C. Barker and Michael Robbins, *A History of London Transport*, Vol. 2, 1974, p. 127. For the biography of Dalziel see the entry in Vol. II of David Jeremy (ed.), *Dictionary of Business Biography*, 1984, pp. 5–11.

35. *Motor Finance*, 30 January 1907; *The Times*, 1–2 July 1907; PRO BT31/88760; James M. Laux, op. cit., 1976, pp. 140–1.

36. PRO BT31/91610; *Motor Finance*, 6, 20 February 1907; *Motor Traction*, 2 February 1907. For a critical view of this promotion, particularly the question of deferred shares, see *The Economist*, 2 February 1907.

37. *Motor Finance*, 10 April 1907.

38. See, for example, *Motor Traction*, 17 August, 7 December 1907, 15 February, 11 July 1908.

39. *Motor Traction, 7, 21 September 1907.*

40. PP 1913 Vol. VIII, *Report of the Select Committee on Motor Traffic*, q.3601; PRO BT31/97990, BT31/90597,BT31/98666,BT31/99605, HO45/195971/71, Mepo 2/1448.

41. *DCTF* 1911 q.3502; PRO Mepo 2/1116.

42. *DCTF* 1911 qq.129, 346–8, 3505–3512; PRO Mepo 2/1116; Mepo 2/1448; HO45/195971.

43. PRO HO45/195971, London Motor Cab Proprietors' Association to E. Elliot Home Office, 14 March 1911; *DCTF* 199, Report, pp. 9, 13.

44. PRO HO45/195971/57.

45. PP 1912–3 Vol. XXXI, *Fifth Report of the London Traffic Branch of the Board of Trade*, p. 19; *Motor Traction*, 16 March 1912; PRO HO45/195971/80, Minute of 22 July 1912.

46. PRO BT31/88760, BT31/103868, BT31/120294; *Motor Traction,* 21 December 1912; *Licensed Vehicle Trades Record,* 13 August 1913; PP 1911 Vol. VII, *Report from the Select Committee on Transport (Metropolitan Area)*, qq.6952, 6981–9.

47. G.N. Georgano, op. cit., 1972, pp. 85–6; *Motor Traction*, 22 March 1913.

48. PP 1914 Vol. XII, *Sixth Report of the London Traffic Branch of the Board of Trade*, p. 22; PP 1916 Vol. XIV, *RCPM for the Year 1914*, p. 34.

49. *DCTF* 1911 qq.2293–6, Evidence of James Scott.

50. PRO HO45/195971, Notes of deputation of drivers to the Home Secretary, 19 October 1910.

Postscript

1. PP 1893 Vol. 3, Royal Commission on Labour, Group B, pp. 138–9. *HCG*, 24 September 1887. For an account of the cab trade on the suburban fringes of London see T.F. May, ' Road passenger transport in Harrow in the nineteenth and early twentieth centuries', *Journal of Transport History*, February 1971.

2. *The Times*, 20 November 1851, 25 January, 25 April 1853.

3. PRO HO45/53518; HO45/55943; Mepo 2/1536.

4. See, for example, PRO HO65/19, 25 April and 3 July 1854.

5. John R. Kellett, *Railways and Victorian Cities*, 1969, p. 315.

6. PRO HO45/8385; *The Centaur*, 4 October 1879; *Cabmen's Messenger*, May 1890, Brighton. For an evocative, fictional account of the cab trade of Hastings at the turn of the century see T. H. White, *Farewell Victoria*, 1933.

7. *Cabmen's Messenger*, May 1890; *The Centaur*, 22 November 1884.

8. *Journal of the Society of Arts*, 8 February 1867, p. 176.

9. *HOC* 1895, Evidence of Frederick Webb, Chief Constable of Leeds. The returns from the 62 provincial licensing authorities will be found in Appendix 3.

10. *HOC* 1895, Evidence of Frederick Webb.

11. *The Centaur*, 24 July, 20, 27 November 1880, 11 February 1882, 3 March 1883; PRO HO45/B993A.

12. *The Centaur*, 31 July, 21 August 1886.

13. *The Centaur* 10, 17 July 1886; *HCG* 12 June 1886; PRO BT31/22794, Bristol Cab Company Ltd.

14. *HCG* 21, 28 March 1891; Birmingham City Library, Prospectus of the Birmingham Cab Company Ltd, n.d.

15. PRO BT31/22788, New London Cab Company Ltd; BT 31/23239, New London Victoria-Hansom Cab Company Ltd; BT31/21577, Birmingham Cab Company Ltd, notebook presumed to have been the property of Alfred Humpage. *HCG* 21, 28 May 1887, 21, 28 March 1891. For a fuller discussion of the Birmingham Cab Company, and of other attempts to exploit the Forder patents, see T.F. May, *The Administration and Organisation of the London Cab Trade from the Late Eighteenth Century to the First World War*, 1991, pp. 226–234.

16. PRO BT31/47469.

17. PRO BT31/97055; *Motor Finance*, 12, 26 February, 22 April 1908.

BIBLIOGRAPHY

The principal sources upon which this book is based consist of manuscripts in various record offices; Parliamentary Papers and other official reports; and London and trade newspapers. These are referred to in the footnotes, while a full list will be found in my doctoral thesis, *The Administration and Organisation of the London Cab Trade from the Late Eighteenth Century to the First World War.* (University of London, 1991) The following list is therefore confined to books and articles.

Books published before 1914

Adams, William Bridges. *English Pleasure Carriages*, 1837

Astley, Sir John Dugdale. *Fifty Years of My Life*, 1894

Beaumont, W. Worby. *Motor Vehicles and Motors: their Design, Construction and Working by Steam, Oil and Electricity*, 1900

Booth, Charles. *Life and Labour of the People in London*, 1889–97

Cohen, Herman. *The Law of Cabs in London*, 1899

Cole, Henry. 'On the existing legal regulations in reference to the cab-fares in the metropolis', *Journal of the Society of Arts*, 8 February 1867

Dexter, J.T. 'The cabmen of London', *Social Science Review*, 2 May 1864

An ex-cabby. *London Cabs and Cabmen's Grievances*, 1871

Firth, J.F.B. *Municipal London*, 1876

Garwood, John. *The Million-Peopled City; or, One Half of the People of London Made Known to the Other Half*, 1853

Gilbey, Sir Walter. *Modern Carriages*, 1905

Gordon, W.J. *The Horse World of London*, 1893

Head, Sir Francis Bond. *Stokers and Pokers or, the London and North-western Railway*, 1849

Holden's Annual List of Coaches, Wagons, Carts, Vessels, etc., 1802

Jervis, John. *The Traveller's Oracle*, (2nd edn, revised by William Kitchiner), 1827

James A. Langford. *A Century of Birmingham Life*, Birmingham, 1878

Maxwell, John Irving. *Hints for Protecting the Public Against Extortion and Insolence of Hackney Coachmen*, 1815

Mayhew, Henry. *London Labour and the London Poor*, 1861

McCulloch, J.R. *A Dictionary of Commerce*, 1832

Moore, H.C. *Omnibuses and Cabs*, 1902

Norman, Henry. 'The public, the motorists and the Royal Commission', *Fortnightly Review*, April 1906

Pryor, F.R. (ed.). *Memoirs of Samuel Hoare by his Daughter Sarah and his Wife Hannah*, 1911

Reinhardt, Charles. *Old Friends in Hard Times*, n.d. (c. 1912)

Roberts, J. *Abstract of Laws Relating to Proprietors, Drivers and Conductors of Public Carriages*, 1910

Roberts, Morley. 'Cabs and cabmen', *Murray's Magazine*, Vol. 7, 1889–90

Rowe, Richard. *How Our Working People Live*, n.d. (c. 1882)

Sinclair, Sir John. *The History of the Public Revenue of the British Empire*, 1805

Thompson, T.P. 'Cab and omnibus nuisance', *Westminster Review*, Vol. 21, 1834

Warren, Charles. 'The police of the metropolis', *Murray's Magazine*, November 1888

Weyland, John Matthias. *Round the Tower, or the Story of the London City Mission*, n.d. (c. 1875)

Wilson, A.J. *Practical Hints to Investors*, 1897

Wyld's Hackney Carriage Pocket Directory, 1832

Books published after 1914

Adeney, Martin. *The Motor Makers*, 1988

Alderman, Geoffrey. *The Railway Interest*, Leicester, 1973

Armstrong, Anthony. *Taxi!*, 1930

Ascoli, David. *The Queen's Peace*, 1979

Bailey, Victor (ed.). *Policing and Punishment in Nineteenth-Century Britain*, 1981

Barker, T.C. (ed.). *The Economic and Social Effects of the Spread of Motor Vehicles*, 1987

——. 'Towards an historical classification of urban transport development since the late eighteenth century,' *Journal of Transport History*, Third Series, Vol. 1, September 1980

Barker, T.C. and Robbins, M. *A History of London Transport* (Vol. I, 1963; Vol. II, 1974)

Bouchet, Ghislaine. 'La traction hippomobile dans les transports publics parisiens (1855–1914)', *Revue Historique*, Vol. CCLXXI/1, January–March, 1984

Cardigan, Earl of. *The Wardens of Savernake Forest*, 1949

Chapman, J.W. *Philosopher John*, Cartmel, 1983

Cottrell, P.L. *Industrial Finance 1830–1914*, 1979

Country Life, *Old Euston*, 1938

Davis, Fred. 'The cabdriver and his fare: facets of a fleeting relationship', *American Journal of Sociology*, Vol. 65, 1959

Dutton, H.I. *The Patent System and Inventive Activity During the Industrial Revolution, 1750–1852*, Manchester, 1984

Dyos, H.J. and Wolff, Michael (eds). *The Victorian City*, 1973

Fitte, Ernesto. J. 'Crónica de un Cónsul Oficioso Británico', *Boletín de la Academia Nacinal de la Historia*, Buenos Aires, 1963

Georgano, G.N. *A History of the London Taxicab*, Newton Abbot, 1972

Harrison, A.E. 'Joint-stock company flotation in the cycle, motor-vehicle and related industries, 1882–1914', *Business History*, Vol. 23, 1981

Hoyle, Susan Ryley. 'The first battle for London: the Royal Commission on Metropolitan Termini, 1846', *London Journal*, Vol. 8, part 2, 1982

Hibbs, John (ed.). *The Omnibus*, Newton Abbot, 1971

Huch, Ronald and Ziegler, Paul. *Joseph Hume: the People's MP*, Philadelphia, 1985

Huggett, Frank E. *Carriages at Eight*, 1979

Jackman, W.T. *The Development of Transportation in Modern England*, 1916

Jones, Gareth Stedman. *Outcast London*, Harmondsworth, 1984

Kennett, David H. *Victorian and Edwardian Horses from Historic Photographs*, 1980

Laux, James M. *Into First Gear: the French Automobile Industry to 1914*, Liverpool, 1976

Lewchuk, W. 'The return to capital in the British motor vehicle industry, 1896–1939', *Business History*, Vol. 27, 1985

May, Trevor. 'Road passenger transport in Harrow in the nineteenth and early twentieth centuries', *Journal of Transport History*, February 1971

Morris, R.M. 'The Metropolitan Police Receiver in the nineteenth century', *Police Journal*, Vol. 47, 1974

Moylan, J.F. *Scotland Yard and the Metropolitan Police*, 1929

Munby, D.L. and Watson, A.H. *Inland Transport Statistics of Great Britain, 1900–1970*, 1978

Nockolds, Harold (ed.). *The Coachmakers*, 1977

Nicholson, T.R. *The Birth of the British Motor Car, 1769–1897*, 1982

Olsen, Donald J. *Town Planning in London: the Eighteenth and Nineteenth Centuries*, New Haven and London (2nd edn), 1982

Owen, David. *The Government of Victorian London, 1855–1889*, Cambridge, Massachusetts and London, 1991

Papayanis, Nicholas. 'The coachmen of Paris: a statistical profile', *Journal of Contemporary History*, Vol. 20, 1985

——. 'The development of the Paris cab trade, 1855–1914', *Journal of Transport History*, Vol. 8, March 1987

——. 'Un secteur des transports parisiens: le fiacre, de la libre entreprise au monopole, 1790–1855', *Histoire, Économie, et Société*, 1986

Pellew, Judith. *The Home Office, 1848–1914*, 1982

Plowden, William. *The Motor Car and Politics, 1896–1971*, 1971

Pool, Ithiel de Sola. *The Social Impact of the Telephone*, Cambridge, Massachusetts and London, 1977

Radzinowicz, Sir Leon. *A History of English Criminal Law and its Administration from 1750* (four vols), 1948–68

Reiner, Robert. *The Politics of the Police*, 1985

Reith, Charles. *A New Study of Police History*, 1956

——. *British Police and the Democratic Ideal*, 1943

Richardson, Kenneth. *The British Motor Industry, 1896–1939*, 1977

Roseveare, Henry. *The Treasury*, 1969

——. *The Treasury, 1660–1870*, 1973

Robertson, Cecil. *Coachbuilding: Past and Present*, n.d. (c. 1928)

Romer, Carrol. *The Metropolitan Traffic Manual*, 1922

Saul, S.B. 'The motor industry in Britain to 1914', *Business History*, Vol. 5, 1962

Sedgwick, Michael. ' "Intolerable Stigma" . . . or how Britain got her number plates', *Veteran and Vintage Magazine*, January 1974

Sekon, G.A. *Locomotion in Victorian London*, 1938

Smith, Charlotte Fell. ' Daniel Whittle Harvey, 1786–1863', *Essex Review*, Vol. XXIV, 1915

Sutherland, Douglas. *The Yellow Earl: the Life of Hugh Lowther, Fifth Earl of Lonsdale*, 1965

Thompson, F.M.L. *English Landed Society in the Nineteenth Century*, 1963

——. *Victorian England: the Horse-drawn Society*, 1970

——. 'Nineteenth-century horse sense', *Economic History Review*, February 1976

——. (ed.). *Horses in European History: a Preliminary Canter*, Reading, 1983

Thompson, John. *Horse-drawn Carriages*, Fleet, 1980

Turvey, Ralph. 'Some economic features of the London cab trade', *Economic Journal*, March 1961

Walrond, Sallie. *Looking at Carriages*, 1980

Warren, Philip and Linsky, Malcolm. *Taxicabs: a Photographic History*, 1966

Wilson, Charles and Reader, William. *Men and Machines: a History of D. Napier & Son, Engineers, Ltd, 1808–1958*, 1958

Young, Ken and Garside, Patricia. *Metropolitan London: Politics and Urban Change 1837–1981*, 1982

Young, W.A. and Gomme, A.A. 'The Chapman papers: a note on the hansom cab', *Transactions of the Newcomen Society*, Vol. 24, 1945

INDEX

Abbot, Christopher, 18, 21
Abbot, John, 64
Abbot, Vernon, 8, 18, 21
Adams, W. Bridges, 15
Alexandra Park Cab Show 1875, 55, 67
Armstrong, Sir George, 110
Asquith, Herbert, 62
Astley, Sir John Dugdale, 69, 70, 72
Attwood, Thomas, 39
Austin, Herbert, 143

bailee system, 10, 24, 57–8, 153
Baily, Capt., 3
Bardell, James, 46–7
Barham, Lady Caroline, 35
Baring, Alexander, 29
Bartholomew, Henry, 35
Bassom, Arthur, 87, 135–6, 146, 148
Bayley, E.H., 125–6, 161
Beasley, John, 58, 105
Beaumont, W. Worby, 130, 132, 146
Beavis, William, 87
Berliner Taxameter Gesellschaft, 134
bilking, 102–3
Bills of Mortality, 3, 29
Bird, Edward, 36
Birmingham, 36, 38, 39, 47, 67, 110, 143, 157, 158, 159, 160–2, Appendix 7
'bluchers', 119
Booth, Charles, 104, 106, 113
Boulnois cab, 38, 64
Boulnois, William, 8, 18, 21, 22, 23, 38
Bowring, Dr John, 39
Box, Richard, 24
Bradshaw, Joseph Hoare, 15–18
Brighton, 157, 159
Brind, Lt.-Col. William, 69
Bristol, 159, 160, 162, Appendix 7

British Motor Syndicate, 134, 143
Brougham, Henry, 34
Bruce, Alexander, 133
Bruce, Henry, 121
'bucks', 106–7
Burns, John, 114, 119, 125
Buxton, Sydney, 68

'cab and omnibus nuisance', 31, 33
cab companies
    ABC Cab Company, 146
    British Motor Cab Company, 139, 150, Appendix 6
    Chelsea Cab Company, 68–9
    City and Suburban Cab Company, 145
    Compagnie Française des Automobiles de Place, 136, 145
    Compagnie Générale des Hansom Cabs à Paris, 74
    Coupé and Dunlop Brougham Company, 143
    Coupé and Motor Cab Company of Great Britain, 143–4
    Dunlop Brougham Company, 143
    Eccleston Motor Cab Company, 141
    General Motor Cab Company, 136, 137, 144–5, 146, 149, 150, 162, Appendix 6
    Hansom's Patent Cabriolet Company, 46
    Landaulette Motor Cab Company, 146
    Leinster Cab Company, 68–9, 73
    London Electrical Cab Company, 130, 144–5
    London General Cab Co Ltd, 50

London General Cab Company, 68
London Improved Cab Company Ltd, 50, 51, 57, 62, 106, 117, 126, 152, Appendix 6
Motor Cab Company of Great Britain, 143–4
New London Cab Company, 161
New London Victoria Hansom Cab Company, 161
New Motor Cab Company, 150
Patent Safety Carriage Company, 46–7
Provincial Motor Cab Company, 162
Safety Cabriolet and Two-Wheel Carriage Company, 41–7 passim, 152
Shrewsbury and Talbot ST Cab and Noiseless Tyre Co, 73–5, 114
Six Days Cab Company, 66
Star Cab Company Ltd, 73
United Motor Cab Company, 136, 145, Appendix 6
Victoria Hansom Cab Company, 143
Victoria Motor Cab Company, 146
W. & G. Du Cros Cab Company, 131, 144
cab drivers
    badging, 28, 35, 98–9
    earnings, 104–6
    language, vii, 97, 103–4, 119
    licensing, 35, 38
    origins,
    motor cab drivers, 99, 100, 138–9
    tipping, 66, 103–4
Cab Drivers' Benevolent Association, 108–10

cab fares, 61, 80–1, 100
 back fare, 80–2, 83, 154–5
 extras, 146–50
 flexible, 65, 69
 and introduction of taximeter,
  136, 137, 156
cab shelters, 110–13
cab stands, 78, 85
cab strikes
 1853, 83, 121
 1868, 121
 1882, 61
 1891, 61, 114
 1894, 61–2, 114, 125
 1896, 114, 126
 1913, 150
Cabmen's Shelter Fund, 110–12
Cabriolet Union, 30–1
cabs,
 accidents, 35, 48, 70
 cost, 22, 51
 disappearance, v
 duty, 65, 80, 87
 hire-purchase, 21, 141–3
 hiring prices, 57–9, 61–2
 inspection, 48, 81, 84, 85, 86,
  131
 intensive working, 23
 introduction, 13–24 passim
 maintenance, 23, 52, 117–8
 municipal control, 92–4
 numbers, v, 48, Appendices 4
  and 5
 profitability, 11, 24
 season, 24, 58–9, 120
 see also electric cabs and
  motor cabs
Carpmael, William, 45
Cartwright, James Lock, 20
'chairmarking', 58
Challiner and Willoughby
  Carriage Tyre Company, 74
Chapman, John, 24, 36–47
  passim, 63, 162
Chapman, W., 59
chariots, see hackney chariots
Charley, W.T., 108–9
Chesham Automobile Supply
  Company, 141–3
Clement, Henry, 8, 9, 22
Cloud, George, 27
Colam, John, 118
Colquhoun, Patrick, 26
Congreve, William, 3
Cooper, W.E., 50

Crocker, I.S., 120
Cross, R.A., 124
Croydon, 93, 157
Cunynghame, Henry, 125

Dalziel, Davison Alexander,
  144–5, 162
Dawson, George, 20, 29
Defoe, Daniel, 2
Denman, Lord, 34
Dexter, J.T., v, 1, 51, 52, 107
Dickens, Charles, 32
Disraeli, Benjamin, v, 120
Doyle, Sir Arthur Conan, 36
driving test, 99, 139
Du Cros, Arthur, 143
Du Cros, George, 144
Du Cros, Harvey, 144
Dublin, 83, 162, Appendix 7
Dunlop Pneumatic Tyre
  Company, 143
Dunlop Rubber Company, 74, 143
Dupee, Revd John, 107–8
Dyke, Edwin, 52

Edge, S.F., 144
Edinburgh, 110, 158, 163,
  Appendix 7
electric cabs
 deficiencies, 130
 introduction, v, 130

Fairbairn, Henry, 115
Fearnhead, Peter, 46
Fellowes, Richard, 15–16
Fernie, Ebenezer, 41
Fitzgerald, Maurice, 18–20
Fitzgerald, Peter G., 20–1, 31
Fitzgerald, Robert, 20–2, 31
Fitzroy, Henry, 80, 83
Flower, G.R., 59
Forder cab, 48, 54, 66–73 passim
Forder, Frederick, 66–73 passim,
  160–1, 162
France, Joseph, 20
Fry, Herbert, 108
Fullylove, John, 38
funeral carriage proprietors, 8

Gardner, Lt.-Col. Alan, 69
Garwood, John, 51
Gerss, C.J., 18–20, 29
Gillett, W.S., 44–5
Gladstone, Herbert, 127, 128,
  137

Gladstone, W.E., 121
Glasgow, 157, 162, Appendix 7
Goode & Cooper, 50
Great Exhibition of 1851, 50, 59,
  80, 85
Great Horseless Carriage
  Company, 134, 143
Green, George, 10, 27
Greenwood, James, 95
Gunn, Thomas, 50
Gye, Frederick, 11

hackney carriage attendants, 82,
  84, 90
hackney chariots, 5, 11
hackney coach drivers
 agreements with proprietors,
  10–11
hackney coach proprietors,
 bankruptcy, 5
 capital requirements, 8–9
 conservatism, 8, 11, 15, 32
 criminal reputation, 26
Hackney Coach Commissioners,
  3, 4–7, 9, 11–12, 15–24
  passim, 25–30, 58, 76, 153
hackney coaches,
 cost, 8–9
 decline, 32
 earnings, 9–10
 inspection, 8
 introduction, 2–3
 numbers, 3–5, Appendix 1
 season, 7
Hamilton, Lord George, 108
Hansom, Joseph, 24, 36–47
  passim, 63, 110, 162
Harvey, Daniel Whittle, 76–8
Harvey's 'Tribus', 64
Harvey's Patent Curricle Tribus,
  64
Hawkers and Pedlars Office, 25,
  26
Head, Sir Francis Bond, 116
Heming, Dempster, 38, 40, 41
Henderson, Edmund, 87, 89, 90,
  92, 121, 123–4
Henson, W.S., 46
Hill, William, 11, 30
Hinckley, 38, 40, 47
Hollingshead, John, 95
Home Office, vi, 11, 21, 35, 65,
  76–94 passim, 99, 102, 110,
  123, 124–8 passim, 133,
  136–7, 139, 151–2, 155, 157

Hopwood, Francis, 125
Horse & Vehicle Insurance
    Company, 52
horses,
    cost, 9, 22, 52–4
    diseases, 52
    feeding costs,9, 56–7
    working life, 9, 54–5
Horses' and Drivers' Aid
    Committee, 140
Hume, Joseph, 7, 24, 26, 28

Improved Cabs Club, 54
Inland Revenue, Commissioners
    of, 51

James, William, 10
Jervis, John, 9, 22
Jesse, Edward, 5, 7, 22, 24, 27–8,
    30, 58
jobmasters, 65, 153

King, John, 5
Kirwan, Daniel Joseph, 96
'Knowledge', the, 99–100, 138,
    139, 154

Lambert, Henry, 117
Lawson, Harry J., 134, 143
Leaf, Edwin, 46
Leeds, 158, Appendix 7
Lewis, William Greathead, 39,
    40, 41, 44
licences, 6–8, 87, 89, 91, 99
    transfer of, 20–1
Liddell, Adolphus, 92
Liverpool, 110, 143, 157, 158,
    162, Appendix 7
livery stable keepers, 8
London Cabmen's Lord's Day
    Rest Association, 107
London Cabmen's Mission Hall
    Shelter, King's Cross, 107
London City Mission, 51, 107
London County Council, vi, 94,
    139, 155
London General Omnibus
    Company, 56
London hackney carriage, area
    defining, 3, 29, 92–4, 153
Lonsdale, Earl of, 68, 69, 70
Lough, Thomas, 125
Loughborough, 39
Louis, Major General Charles, 68

Lowe, Robert, 87, 121
Lowther, Honourable William, 68
Lyell, J.R., 102

Macnamara, Walter, 112
Manchester, 39, 67, 157, 158–9,
    162, Appendix 7
Manchester Cab Competition of
    1875, 67
Mandeville, Viscount, 69, 72
Mann & Overton Ltd, 141
Marrable, Thomas, 11, 28, 30
Marshall, James, 6
Marston, John, 67
Martineau, Harriet, 19
Mascart, Charles, 135, 136
Masterman, C.F.G., 149–50
Matthews, Henry, 100, 126
May, W.H., 20–1
Mayhew, Henry, 8, 51, 97–8
Mayne, Sir Richard, 78–9, 85,
    89, 92, 99, 121, 157
McCulloch, J.R, 19
Metropolitan Board of Works, 92
Metropolitan Fare Register
    Company, 135
Metropolitan Police, vi, 21, 25, 35,
    48, 63, 65, 76–94 passim,
    99, 102, 110, 112, 116, 117,
    128, 130, 133, 140, 148,
    155, 157, 158, see also
    Public Carriage Office
Michaels, Sam, 62
Middleton, Peter C., 141
Middleton, Walter E., 141
Mills, Alfred, 62
Milltown, Earl of, 68
Morley, Samuel, 108
motor cab types,
    Beardmore, 132
    Charron, 145, 162
    Darracq, 145, 162
    Renault, 137, 145, 148, 150
    Siddeley, 162
    Unic, 141, 145
motor cabs,
    depreciation, 146
    hire purchase, 141–3
    introduction, v, 128
    'type approval', 131
Mulliner, Henry, 143, 161
Mulliner, Herbert H., 143, 144
Musk, Robert, 106
Mutual Taxi-Cab Supply
    Company, 142

Napier, Montague, 144
Nasmith, David, 107
Needham, J.S., 38, 40, 41
Newcastle, 158, 162
Norman, Henry, 136
Nugent, Lord, 29

Oakley, Sir Henry, 125
omnibuses, v, 29, 31, 32, 33, 59,
    106, 116, 125
O'Neill, A.J,. 20
owner-drivers, 50–1, 74–5, 140,
    143

Paget, Col. Granville William, 69
Palmerston, Viscount, 85
Parlour, Joseph, 64
Paschal, Col., 85, 87
patronage, 5, 22, 29
pedestrians, 2
Pelican Club, 70
Pembroke, Earl of 68
Pennefather, A.R., 88–9, 91–2
Phillips and Brickland, 50
Phillips case, 1853, 82–3, 101
Pool, Charles, 26
Powell, William, 9, 30
'privilege', the, 50, 114, 115–28
    passim, 156
Prodgers, Mrs Giacometti, 102
proprietors' associations,
    Amalgamated Hackney
        Carriage Proprietors'
        Association, 120
    Hackney Carriage Mutual
        Benefit Society, 59, 135
    London Motor Cab
        Proprietors' Association,
        149, 150
    Owner Drivers' Association,
        143
    United Cab Proprietors'
        Protection Association, 62
Public Carriage Office, 85, 87,
    118, 133, 135, 137, 138,
    139, 146, 152, see also
    Metropolitan Police

Quaife sen., James, 30
Quaife, William, 30

'radius', the, 154–6
railway companies,
    Eastern Counties, 39
    Great Eastern, 117

Great Northern, 68, 125
Great Western, 116, 117, 126, 155
London and Birmingham, 116
London and North Western, 117, 121
London, Brighton and South Coast, 118
Metropolitan, 120
Midland, 50
South Eastern 124,
railway stations,
Cannon Street, 124
Charing Cross, 119, 124
Euston, 116–17
King's Cross, 125
London Bridge, 124
Paddington, 116, 155
St Pancras, 50
Victoria, 110, 118, 119–20
Rayner, J.H., 31
Registrar of Metropolitan Public Carriages, 35, 76–8
rent, 55, 65
Ridley, Sir Matthew White, 126
Robertson, Joseph Clinton, 39, 40
Roe Francis, 22–4, 31
Rotch, Benjamin, 15–18, 33
Rowe, Richard, 100
Rowland, H.W., 113, 124
Royal Society for the Prevention of Cruelty to Animals, 118
Rucker, Martin, 143
Russell, G.W.E., 125
Russell, Lord Arthur Wriotheslay, 108

Saggers, Charles, 27
Salomons, Sir David, 68
Savernake, Viscount, 71, 72
Scott, James, 51, 57, 117
Sewell, Anna, 96
Shaftesbury, Earl of, 108

Shaw, Major Ponsonby, 69
Sheather, William, 54
Sherman, George, 115
Shillibeer, George, 27, 29
Shrewsbury, Earl of, 72–5
Shrewsbury ST and Challiner Tyre Company Ltd, 74
Simmons, Fred, 135
Simms, Frederick, 133–4, 143
Sinclair, Sir John, 26
Société Française d'Etudes et d'Entreprises, 150
Société Générale des Compteurs de Voitures (Taximètres), 135, 136, 145
Society for Promoting Christian Knowledge, 107
Society of Motor Manufacturers and Traders, 132
Southern Development Ltd, 144
St Aldwyn, Viscount, 149
Staples, Richard Ponsonby, 18–21, 162
'stones', the, 1, 27, 28, 29
streets,
improvement, 26
obstruction, 1, 26, 33, 88, 106
Sturmey, James, 132

Tackley, William, 105
Taxameter Syndicate, 134–5
taximeter, 132–8, 156
Taylor, John, 2–3
Thatcher, Margaret, 94
Thompson, Captain Livingston, 68–9
Thorn, coachbuilder of Norwich, 66, 67
Thornton, Charles Wade, 28, 30
Tilling, Thomas, 49, 62, 154
Townshend, Marquis of, 108
trade unions,
Amalgamated Cab Drivers'

Society, 109, 113, 124, 157
Cab Drivers' Mutual Aid and Protection Society, 113–14
London Cab Drivers' Trade Union, 105, 124
Metropolitan Cab Drivers' Trade Union, 114, 124
Transport and General Workers' Union, 114
Traffic Syndicate, 144
trams, v, 59, 94
Treasury, 4, 5, 13, 16–24 passim, 25–31 passim, 79

United Cabdrivers' Gospel Temperance Association, 107
United Investment Corporation, 144, 162

Vauxhall Gardens, 7, 11
Villiers, T. Hyde, 20

Walker, Herbert, 117
Warburton, Henry, 34
Ware, Edward, 87, 133
watermen, hackney carriage, 26, 84–5
watermen, Thames, 2
Watermen's Company, 2
Wedgwood, Hensleigh, 77–8
Welch, Edward, 36
Wellington, Duke of, 11
West London Cabmen's Mission, 108
White, Fred, 105
Whitmore, C.A., 126
Wilkins, W.H., 98, 103, 104, 114
Williams. J.E., 18, 20–1
Wood, Sir Matthew, 33–5, 76
Wrottesley, Sir John, 26

yard money, 62, 106